STREET POLITICS

STREET POLITICS

Poor People's Movements in Iran

Asef Bayat

Columbia University Press

NEW YORK

Columbia University Press
Publishers Since 1893
New York   Chichester, West Sussex
Copyright © 1997 Columbia University Press
All rights reserved
Library of Congress Cataloging-in-Publication Data
Bayat, Asef.
    Street politics : poor people's movements in Iran / Asef Bayat.
    p.   cm.
    Includes bibliographical references and index.

    ISBN 978-0-231-10858-4 (cloth : alk. paper). ISBN 978-0-231-10859-1 (paper)

    1. Squatter settlements—Iran. 2. Squatters—Iran. 3. Vending
stands—Iran. 4. Poor—Iran—Political activity. 5. Iran—Politics and
government—1979– I. Title.
HV4132.56.A5B39 1997
322.4'4—DC21   97–18986
                                                    CIP

Casebound editions of Columbia University Press books are printed on
permanent and durable acid-free paper.
Printed in the United States of America

To my mother and father

Contents

An exhibit of *New York Times* photographs, "Pictures of the Times," documenting major world events in the past hundred years, was held in the New York Museum of Modern Art in July 1996. The exhibit devoted only one photograph to the Iranian Revolution of 1979: that of a "fanatical crowd" tearing the shroud off the dead Ayatollah's coffin during his spectacular funeral. And this was displayed next to two "related" photographs. The first showed a jubilant crowd of New Yorkers welcoming home the American hostages from Iran in a parade; the other, bodies strewn across an airport lounge after the bomb attack on Rome's airport by the Popular Front for the Liberation of Palestine (PFLP) in 1985. The exhibitors made sure that the necessary link—from Iranian Revolution to fanaticism and Islam to international terrorism—was established in the mind of the viewers.

This book is in part a reaction to such misrepresentations of a major social and political event of our time, the revolution of 1979. I attempt to show that the Iranian Revolution and its aftermath were much more profound and complex than these and many similar images suggest. As such this book is not a history of the Iranian Revolution; those unfamiliar with its events may consult the chronology of the revolution before they begin to read. Rather, the book is about the movements of ordinary people, the poor, during these turbulent years in Iranian history. The narratives aim at transcending the much-written-about public dimensions of elite politics, the clergy, and the "Great Satan." This study attempts to reveal instead what was happening under the surfaces of the revolution, in the back streets and alleyways of the cities, not only on the main boulevards.

At the same time, by narrating the poor peoples' movements in Iran in a comparative context, I will attempt to contribute to an examination of informal politics in Third World settings. I have analyzed this in terms of the "quiet encroachment of the ordinary." This book therefore explores the politics of the ordinary people, the individuals and families without institutional power of disruption, the "informal people"—squatters, street subsistent workers, the unemployed, and members of the underworld.

The analyses contained in this book are based upon multiple source materials ranging from published interviews and scholarly research conducted in Iran before and after the Islamic Revolution, newspaper reports, primary documents (such as tracts, posters, leaflets, pamphlets, and the like), personal interviews, and, finally, direct observation.

I have reviewed a massive number of dailies, weeklies, and monthlies, both official and opposition papers focusing on the period between 1977 to 1990; I have also included reports and analyses as recent as the early 1990s where they have been relevant. In addition, I have conducted more than a dozen in-depth interviews with key participants and observers in the movements under investigation in this book. The publication of my previous work on the Iranian Revolution (*Workers and Revolution in Iran*) encouraged some involved respondents—labor activists, organizers, reporters, and eyewitnesses—to voluntarily share their experiences with me. This work draws considerably on these narratives.

During 1980 and 1981 I conducted a survey of the housing conditions of the working class as part of the field work for a project on factory workers and the revolution. My visits to these poor residential areas have contributed to the analysis undertaken in the present study. During this same period and before 1979, I was witness to the activities of the unemployed and the street vendors, their organizations, mobilization, and confrontations with the authorities. I have used many of my memories of these and earlier relevant events, including visits to a number of sites in Tehran Pars (an area east of the capital city) during the waves of shantytown demolition in autumn 1977. Finally, during the summer of 1995 I returned to Tehran to update my data, collect further information, and fill the data gaps in the first draft of the manuscript. This resulted in further interviews with fifty squatters and street vendors.

These materials aside, I consider my own life experience to be the single most important source of my insights and data. By this, I mean my direct involvement, and intense interaction, in other words, my membership for a significant part of my childhood through early adulthood with the people who make up this study: the migrant poor. Although I now write as an academic, with all the requisite qualifications, I count the years I lived, struggled, and matured within this community in Tehran as among my richest resources.

I was born in the mid-1950s, in a small village located some sixty miles west of Tehran, which had no more than fifty mostly Azari-speaking households. I was one of six children born into a *khush-nishin*, a rural nonagricultural family. My grandfather, having lost two teenage sons to dehydration and a daughter to complications during childbirth, decided that my father, the only surviving son, should pursue a life more fruitful than that of a peasant. He thus became a shop-keeper in the village, selling goods that ranged from heating oil and sweets to Russian shoes. When, in the early 1960s, the Land Reform allocated plots of a dozen hectares each to our villagers, my father, being a *khushnishin*, remained a landless rural dweller, moving from one job to the next and remaining unemployed in between. At one point he was a petty-trader, then a bus driver, truck owner, mechanic, and driving instructor; he vacillated between the countryside and the city, bringing many modern things to our village life.

My father was one of the three men in the village who learned to read and write in my grandfather's Quranic sessions, succeeding, later, in completing primary school. My mother, however, like so many others in the village remained illiterate. By the time I was growing up, we were fortunate enough to have teaching classes in the village— first, in the warehouse of the absentee feudal lord, and then, with the arrival of the first Literacy Corps (*sepahi-ye danesh*), in a proper school. The village schools only went up to fifth grade; and my father, wanting us to get an education, found no choice but to take the entire family of nine to the city. We emigrated to Tehran in 1967.

I therefore left my village, venturing on a journey of which I had so often dreamed—dreams of bright lights and bus rides, morning-fresh bread, walking along the streets in the busy evenings, not to mention the Indian movies that our village school *farrash*'s son, who was from Tehran, used to relate to the village boys with commendable patience and in perfect Persian.

In Tehran we first settled in a lower-class neighborhood close to Ghazvin Street in south Tehran where the neighbors consisted mostly of rural migrants like ourselves. The area was surrounded by slums and the growing squatter areas that were filled with many colorful little shops and chanting street vendors, and in which I, like so many of my friends, learned to spend a good part of the daytime in the streets. Our one-story house was located in a narrow alleyway in the middle of which ran the sewage duct, a *jouy*. The house had a toilet, a small kitchen, and five separate rooms, two of which were rented to two separate families (a migrant worker and a *pasban*, a member of the low-status street police). Later we moved into a new house in the same vicinity but with more rooms; our migrant relatives, on the other hand, remained in the nearby slums of Javadieh and Mehrabad, to which we would pay regular visits. Our long-term trips, however, were to the village with which we maintained strong ties—ties we still retain even to this day.

My first experience of schooling in the city was with an Islamic institution. It taught the regular curriculum but placed special emphasis on extracurricular activities including daily collective prayers, Quran reciting, and Islamic entertainment. The teachers were mostly committed young Islamists, including clergymen. Indeed, at some point my grandfather, himself being a rural mulla, expressed delight at the possibility of seeing me one day a Qum-educated *akhund*. I later realized that my school represented an instance of Islamist civil activism during the late 1960s, a reaction to the secular education and the growing foreign schools that the children of the elites attended.

A few years later, in 1970, we moved to Cheezar, the remnant of an old urban village in the northern part of Tehran, where my father worked in a driving school. In the years that we resided in the first neighborhood, in South Tehran, a great deal happened. I became a true young Muslim, learning to recite Quran in public events, taking part in the local *hey'at*s and mosques, visiting the shrines of Qum, Mashad, and our local *imamzadeh*s, and being perhaps the only serious listener to my grandfather's religious *hikayat*—a grandfather who in this new setting seemed to have lost his village constituency and be unable to gain the respect of city dwellers, as the tide of modern education and secularization began to conquer even lower-class families. But, by the time we left that first neighborhood, I began to sense the pressure of the institutional indoctrination of my Islamic school.

The early 1970s, a period of an unprecedented oil boom, coincided with a period of relative prosperity for my family. We experienced some degree of upward mobility, acquiring a lower-middle-class lifestyle. My father's income rose, my brothers were accepted into college, my sister became a school teacher, and I obtained my diploma in a government high school that catered to students of lower-class and lower-middle class backgrounds. The school was located in Gholhak, close to the Husseinieh Ershad, where many of Ali Shariati's followers were gathered and where their study teams flourished later. In my last years of high school, I attended Shariati's popular lectures on radical Islam in the Husseinieh Ershad. However, by the time I began my university years, I had become an entirely secular teenager, moving into leftist campus politics that I maintained throughout my higher education in the United Kingdom. Despite these tremendous changes in my personal life, there was also some continuity. My family and I never suspended our strong ties with our village—with kin members, neighbors, and friends who remained in the village, as well as with those who left it and began to search for a better life in the city but mostly ended up in the "slums of hope." These pages have benefited much from the memories of these people—their struggle for survival, their values and mode of life, their hopes and despair.

The chapters of this book chronicle the struggles of similar ordinary men and women to survive and to secure a dignified life. They explore the dynamics of the poor's quiet encroachment and collective mobilization and discuss the intricate relationships of the poor with outside mobilizers, local leaders, and the state, as well as the dialectic of silent-individualistic and audible-collective struggles. I will examine in detail four instances of grassroots activities in revolutionary Iran, whose participants possibly overlap. These activities range from those relating to the occupation of homes and hotels—urban land squatting—to those of the unemployed and the street vendors. While each activity constitutes a distinct piece of social history, together they provide empirical narratives for my theoretical propositions on the "politics of the informals" and "street politics" that I present in the following introductory chapter.

In chapter 2 I offer a sociological background to the lives of the urban new poor in Iran, with a special focus on the city of Tehran. I trace the quiet encroachment of Iran's poor from the 1950s until the Islamic Revolution of 1979. In chapter 3 I argue that, despite many claims as to the active participation of the disenfranchised in the revolution, the urban poor largely remained on the margin of revolutionary events. The poor, although on the margin, were involved in their own quiet revolution in the back streets of their communities. They came under the banner of the Islamic Revolution only at its last stage, when the leadership adopted a strong pro-*mustaz'afin* (downtrodden) discourse, and continued under that banner through the first few months after the revolution when they were intensely wooed by both Islamic leaders and secular groups. Utilizing this favorable opportunity, the poor engaged in widespread collective mobilization. Chapter 4 tells the story of one of these mobilizations—the occupation of homes and apartments.

The convergence between the perspectives of the poor and the power-holders did not last long however. The disenfranchised were polarized. One segment was integrated into the new state structure, and the other, facing political constraints, returned to the strategy of individual and quiet encroachment. Chapter 4 explores the dynamics of this rupture by examining the squatters' movement in postrevolutionary Iran and tracing its history from the days of the Islamic Revolution to the squatters riots of the early 1990s.

In addition to discussing the actions of the poor in everyday life, in the communities (chapters 4 and 5), I attempt also to consider them in the domain of working life. Chapter 6, therefore, examines in detail the remarkable movement of the unemployed, a movement that is unique in the context of the developing countries. Chapter 7 analyzes the mobilization of the street vendors in large Iranian cities in an attempt to establish and maintain their subsistence-level activities in the street corners; this mobilization altered at the local level the power relations that ultimately emanated from the control of public space and business opportunity.

Finally, in the concluding chapter, I offer an overall evaluation of these types of grassroots activism. I discuss their merits and shortcomings, as well as exploring their implications both with reference to the specific case of Iran and, more generally, in relation to a number of theoretical issues.

Acknowledgments

No scholarly work is an entirely individual enterprise. And mine is certainly not an exception. Numerous scholars, activists, individuals, and institutions have assisted me in various ways during the preparation of the present volume.

I wish to thank the publishers of two of my articles—"Un-Civil Society: On the Politics of the 'Informal People,'" *Third World Quarterly* 18, no. 1 (1997) and "Workless Revolutionaries: The Movement of the Unemployed in Iran, 1979," *International Review of Social History* 24, no. 2 (August 1997)—for their kind permission to use materials from those articles in this book.

A grant from the Middle East Research Competition (MERC), Ford Foundation, Cairo, made a big portion of the project possible. My thanks especially to Dr. Najla Tchergui of MERC for her continuous encouragement. I conducted a good deal of research in the libraries of the University of Chicago; the School of Oriental and African Studies at the University of London; Columbia University; and Near Eastern Studies, Princeton University. At Princeton, the competent librarian, Ms. Ashraf, offered much support, while Shahab Ahmad hosted me in his campus residence. I thank them all for their aid.

My thanks are also due to the directors, employees, and colleagues in the Institute of Industrial Relations, University of California at Berkeley, and the Middle East Institute, Columbia University, where I was stationed during my sabbatical leave.

I received valuable assistance in Tehran, in the Markaz-i Motaleat va Tahghighat-i Shahrsazi va Me'mari-ye Iran, Ministry of Housing, and at the Research Institute of Tehran Municipality, and School of Social Sciences, Tehran University. I owe special thanks to those employees who kindly offered me data and guidance.

I have also benefited from the intellectual contributions of many scholars and friends, including Professor Ahmad Ashraf, Professor Ali Ashtiani, Professor Nicholas Hopkins, and Kuros Esmaili, who read and commented on sections of the early versions of the manuscript. Simon O'Rourke polished and Susan Heath scrupulously copyedited the final version of the manuscript. Clarisa Bencomo, Samir Shahata, Joe Storke, and professors Farhad Kazemi, Richard Bulliet, and Sami Zubaida read the various versions of the entire manuscript. I would like to express my appreciation for their invaluable comments and suggestions. I am particularly grateful to Professor Bulliet, of Columbia University, for his encouragement and special support. I also thank Manoocher Deghati, Reza Deghati, Emad Allam, and Ashraf Saloum who assisted me in the collection and preparation of the maps and photographs in this book.

Beyond scholarly contributions, there were many relatives and friends, as well as anonymous social activists, most of whom I have never met, who gave me priceless information and expertise. They did so with the sole aim of preserving our historical memory of poor peoples' struggles. Here I mention only Reza, Akbar, Roham, and Siamak. However, my greatest debt is due to Fateh and Tahereh, without whose assistance in arranging for interviews with various key respondents this book would certainly not be in its present shape.

Linda Herrera never ceases to be enthusiastic, encouraging, and supportive not only of the present project but of my entire intellectual enterprise. I cannot thank her enough.

Finally, perhaps here is the place where I can register my deepest tribute to my mother and my father who, like the subjects of this book, have endured tremendous hardship in their life in the hope of bringing up "worthy children." Without their love, trust, and daring, my journey from village to the West would never have taken place. I dedicate this book to them in appreciation of their limitless trust and tolerance.

of Pre- and Postrevolution Events

1796–1925:	Iran is ruled by the Qajar dynasty.
1905–1907:	Iran's constitutional revolution establishes rule of law; the first Parliament is set up.
1925:	Reza Shah, the father of the late Muhammad Reza Shah, ends the reign of Qajar dynasty; the Pahlavi dynasty is established. Reza Shah begins an ambitious program of economic, social, and educational modernization through a secular autocratic state.
1946:	Reza Shah is forced to abdicate by the Allied forces in favor of his son, Muhammad Reza.
1946–1953:	A period of democratic experience, when nationalist and Communist movements experience unprecedented growth.
March 1951:	The campaigns of the nationalist leader, Muhammad Mosaddeq, lead to the nationalization of oil industry; Britain threatens to invade Iran.
June 1953:	A CIA-engineered coup overthrows the secular nationalist government of Mosaddeq; the Shah, who had fled the country, returns to Iran. The democratic experience terminates. Iran becomes the most crucial ally of the West, notably the U.S., in the region.
1950s:	Independent political parties, associations, and movements are systematically suppressed. Programs of modernization, industrialization, and westernization assume new momentum.

January 1963:	The Shah inaugurates his White Revolution, composed of some significant reform measures, including land reform, the nationalization of forests, the enfranchisement of women, the literacy corps, and profit-sharing schemes.
June 1963:	A series of large-scale riots break out in Tehran and some other cities. Ayatollah Khomeini emerges as a religious opposition leader and is sent to exile in Iraq.
1960s–1970s:	Oil income increases, supporting economic development and social change. The new middle class and the industrial working class expand, together with the number of "modern" youths and women active in public. The old classes—feudal, traditional petty bourgeoisie, and the clergy—shrink or feel threatened. The regime remains autocratic.
May 1977:	The protest of the intelligentsia surfaces in the form of open letters to the Court.
January 1978:	A violent confrontation erupts between theology students and police in the holy city of Qum.
18 February 1978:	A mass demonstration and riot occurs in Tabriz, the capital of Azerbaijan.
March 1978:	Mass demonstrations spread to other urban areas.
7 September 1978:	Martial Law is declared in Tehran and eleven other major cities.
8 September 1978:	Hundreds of protesters are killed in Tehran on Black Friday.
September 1978 onward:	Industrial strikes spread nationwide.
6 November 1978:	The Shah appoints a military government; General Azhari's cabinet is formed.
10–11 December 1978:	Millions of people demonstrate against the regime. Soldiers in many places join the marchers.
31 December 1978:	General Azhari's cabinet collapses as Shahpour Bakhtiar, a leader of opposition National Front, agrees to form a new civilian government. This is followed by a general strike that brings the whole economy to a halt. Neighborhood councils emerge in the popular districts. Land takeovers are effected.
16 January 1979:	The Shah leaves the country.
1 February 1979:	Ayatollah Khomeini returns to Tehran from Paris.
5 February 1979:	Khomeini appoints Mehdi Bazargan as prime minister of his provisional government.
9 February 1979:	The Javidan Guard (Imperial Guard) attacks the

	barracks of the mutinous air force technicians in Tehran.
10–11 February 1979:	There are two days of insurrection.
11 February 1979:	The Monarchy is overthrown; Bakhtiar escapes; jubilant armed youths take over control of the streets. The radio declares the victory of the Islamic Revolution.
February–March 1979:	Mass demonstrations of military personnel, Kurdish people, Turkoman people, and women for democratic rights. The unemployed are mobilized. Outset of home and hotel squatting.
April 1979:	After a referendum Iran becomes an Islamic Republic.
August 1979:	There is an attack against the left, as well as against Kurdish and other ethnic minorities. Political vendors are assaulted.
4 November 1979:	The U.S. Embassy is seized; the hostage crisis brings down the Bazargan government. Meanwhile, following the embassy seizure, a new wave of labor unrest escalates.
2–3 December 1979:	Following a referendum, the Islamic Constitution is ratified.
25 January 1980:	Abul-Hassan Bani-Sadr is elected as Iran's first president.
April 1980:	A "cultural revolution" begins: the Islamization of education, cultural institutions, and industrial workplaces. Meanwhile a new crackdown on labor and unemployed movement is waged.
25 April 1980:	An American rescue mission to free the hostages fails.
25 July 1980:	The deposed Shah dies in exile in Egypt.
11 August 1980:	Muhammad Ali Rajaii, an Islamist prime minister, forms a cabinet.
22 September 1980:	Iraqi forces invade Iran. An eight-year war begins.
20 January 1981:	The American hostages are freed.
March 1981:	Conflicts between Bani-Sadr and the ruling Islamic Republican Party (IRP) surface violently when a rally organized by the president is attacked by supporters of the IRP.
10 June 1981:	Bani-Sadr is dismissed as commander-in-chief, and goes underground. Ayatollah Khomeini officially removes him from office on June 22.
20 June 1981:	Massive demonstrations in Tehran, organized by

	Mujahedin, against the ruling clergy turn into a bloody confrontation with Pasdaran. Twenty-four people are killed and more than two hundred injured in clashes. Widespread guerrilla warfare against the Islamic regime begins.
27 June 1981:	The headquarters of the Islamic Republican Party is blown up; seventy-four leaders of the Party are killed, including Ayatollah Beheshti. More than two hundred members or supporters of Mujahedin are reportedly executed during the following few months.
July 1981:	Bani-Sadr and the Mujahedin leader Masoud Rajavi escape to France, where they set up the National Council of Resistance.
2 August 1981:	Prime Minister Rajaii becomes president, and Education Minister Bahonar is named as his new prime minister the next day.
30 August 1981:	President Rajaii, Prime Minister Bahonar, and several others are killed in a bomb blast. Mahdavi-Kani is elected as prime minister on September 2.
September 1981:	The Iran-Iraq war intensifies. The liquidation of opposition, labor, and neighborhood councils escalates. Factional fighting between the "Imam line" and Hojjatiye begins.
13 October 1981:	Khameneii is sworn in as new president.
31 October 1981:	Hussein Mousavi is appointed as the new prime minister.
April 1982:	More than a thousand people are arrested in connection with the Sadeq Qutbzadeh (former foreign minister) group's plan to assassinate Ayatollah Khomeini. On April 20 Ayatollah Shariatmadari is ousted from the ranks of the religious leaders and placed under house arrest for his alleged link to the plot.
July 1982:	Heavy fighting continues at the war front.
4 January 1983:	Gasoline rationing ends.
11 January 1983:	Parliament decides to confiscate the property of Iranians who do not return from exile within two months.
4 May 1983:	The government dissolves the Tudeh party. Some one thousand Tudeh supporters are detained in the following days. Meanwhile the debate between

	free-marketers and etatists within the government comes to the surface.
10 July 1983:	The government clamps down on bazaar merchants.
11 February 1984:	Iraq begins the "war of the cities." In the meantime, opposition groups in exile continue their campaign against the Islamic government.
May 1985:	The "war of the cities" escalates; civilian targets are attacked.
16 August 1985:	President Khameneii is reelected. Candidates of Bazargan's Freedom Movement were excluded from the campaigns.
23 November 1985:	Ayatollah Montazeri is elected by the Assembly of Experts as Khomeini's successor.
3 April 1986:	Ayatollah Shariatmadari dies of cancer while under house arrest.
October 1986:	The "Irangate" scandal begins to surface.
17 January 1987:	In the "war of the cities," Tehran is bombed. Iran responds by attacking Baghdad.
2 June 1987:	A polarized IRP is dissolved on the order of Ayatollah Khomeini.
19 June 1987:	The leader of Mujahedin, in Baghdad, declares the formation of the Iranian National Liberation Army to fight against the Islamic Republic.
February and April 1988:	Another round of the "war of the cities" erupts.
12 April 1988:	The election of the third Majlis is held.
2 June 1988:	Rafsanjani, the speaker of the Majlis, is appointed commander-in-chief of the army by Khomeini. Mehdi Bazargan criticizes the war policy in an open letter.
18 July 1988:	Iran accepts UN Resolution 598 to end the war.
25 July 1988:	Mujahedin forces attack an Iranian city from Iraqi soil.
October 1988:	A postwar reconstruction plan is launched.
4 June 1989:	Ayatollah Khomeini dies.
Early 1990s:	Major debates, rethinking, and revision around the experience of the Islamic government emerge within the society. In the meantime, conflict between the "pragmatists" and "fundamentalists" continues.

STREET POLITICS

One

The Quiet Encroachment of the Ordinary

Between 1976 and the early 1990s a series of popular activities took place in Iran's large cities that did not receive sufficient attention from scholars, primarily because they were drowned out by the extraordinary big bang of the revolution. Their importance was dismissed in part because they seemed insignificant when compared with the revolution, that universal image of social change par excellence, and in part because they seemed to be ordinary practices of everyday life. Indeed, the origin of these activities goes back decades earlier, but it is only in the late 1980s and early 1990s that their political consequences began to surface.

This book is devoted to recovering such ordinary practices, prevalent in most developing countries, and making sense of their dynamics. By discussing these events, I attempt to construct a theory of informal politics.

A Few Minor Events?

Since the 1950s hundreds of thousands of poor families have been part of a long and steady migration from Iran's villages and small towns to its big cities, some seeking to improve their lives, some simply trying to survive. Many of them settled quietly, either individually or more often

with their kin members, on unused urban lands or/and cheap purchased plots largely on the margin of urban centers. To escape from
dealing with private landlords, unaffordable rents, and overcrowding,
they put up their shelters with their own hands or with the help of relatives in illegally established sites. Then they began to consolidate their
informal settlements by bribing bureaucrats and bringing in urban
amenities. By the eve of the Islamic Revolution the number of these
communities in Tehran alone had reached fifty. The actors had become
a counterforce, without intending to be so.

The advent of the Islamic Revolution offered the disenfranchised
the opportunity to make further advances. As the revolutionaries were
marching in the streets of big cities, the very poor were busy extending
their hold over their communities by bringing more urban land under
(mal-)development. And immediately after the revolution, many poor
families took advantage of the collapse of police control to take over
hundreds of vacant homes and half-finished apartment blocks, refur-
bishing them as their own properties.

As the option of home-squatting was limited, land takeover and illegal construction accelerated, despite the police crackdown. This contributed to a spectacular growth of both large and small cities in the
years following the revolution. What made these men and women a
collective force was a way of life that engendered common interests
and the need to defend them. The squatters got together and
demanded electricity and running water; when they were refused or
encountered delays, they resorted to do-it-yourself mechanisms of
acquiring them illegally. They established roads, opened clinics and
stores, constructed mosques and libraries, and organized refuse collection. They further set up associations and community networks, as
well as participating in local consumer cooperatives. A new and a
more autonomous way of living, functioning, and organizing the community was in the making.

The domain of work was subject to the same kind of silent
encroachment. The unemployed poor, alongside the middle-class jobless, resorted initially to an impressive collective action to demand
work, maintenance, and compensation. They were involved in a movement unique in the context of Third World politics. Although the
unemployed movement benefited a number of factory and office workers, a large majority remained jobless. Having exhausted collective
action, the unemployed poor turned to family, kin, and friends for sup-

port. But many more poured into the streets of the big cities to establish autonomous subsistance activities, engaging in street-vending, peddling, and street services and industries. They put up stalls, drove pushcarts, set up kiosks. Business sites were lit by connecting wires to the main electrical poles. Their collective operation converted the street sidewalks into vibrant and colorful shopping places. However, the authorities could hardly tolerate such a cheerful and secular counterculture, such an active use of urban space and thus waged a protracted war of attrition against the street vendors. Many shopkeepers whose favorable business environment had been appropriated by the sidewalk vendors joined the authorities in their clampdown. This confrontation between the vendors and the state/shopkeepers exemplifies a protracted instance of street politics in the Islamic Republic, which I will discuss in more detail later.

These kinds of practices are not extraordinary. They occur on a daily basis in many urban centers of the developing world. In the Middle East, for example, Cairo contains well over one hundred "spontaneous" communities, or *manatiq al-ashwa'yya*, housing over seven million people who have quietly claimed cemeteries, rooftops, and the state/public land on the outskirts of the city; these rural migrants and slum dwellers have also subdivided the formerly agricultural land surrounding the city and put up their shelters there unlawfully. By their sheer perseverance, millions of slum dwellers have forced the authorities to extend amenities to their neighborhoods[2] by otherwise tapping into them illegally. For instance, illegal use of running water alone in the Egyptian city of Alexandria costs the city an average of three million dollars each year.[3] The street vendors have taken over many public thoroughfares in order to conduct their business. Thousands of the city's poor subsist on tips from parking private cars in the streets, which they control and organize in such a way as to create maximum parking space. In the eyes of the authorities, such practices have caused major urban disorder in the country. The government policy of halting these practices has largely failed[4] as the poor have tended to respond by on-the-spot resistance, legal battles, or simply by quiet noncompliance. The accounts of Maidan El-'Ataba, Sayyeda Zeynab, Boulaq El-Dakrour, Suq El-Gom'a in Imbaba, and the forceful relocation of the El-Ezbakia book-sellers attest to only a few of the many instances of street politics in Cairo.[5]

The same phenomenon occurs in Asia as well. In South Korean

cities, for example, almost anyone can easily set up pushcart on a vacant street area, "but once a spot is taken and business established, it is virtually owned by the vendors." In these settings, "tax collections are nil, and regulating business practices is almost impossible. Louis Vuitton's Pusan Outlet could only stop a pushcart vendor from selling counterfeits of its bags in front of the shop by purchasing the spot. Nike International and Ralph Lauren have had similar problems."[6]

Latin American cases are quite well documented.[7] In the Chilean city of Santiago during the mid-1980s, for example, as many as 200,000 poor families were using "clandestine installations" of electricity and running water in the mid-1980s. Police and military vehicles drove through popular neighborhoods to catch the offenders. In response the residents had to "unhook at dawn and hook up again after the last patrol," as one settler put it.[8] Of those who had legal installations, some 200,000 had not paid for electricity and 270,000 had not paid for water.[9] "*Basismo*" is the term that signifies the recent upsurge of such grassroots activities in Latin America—with their emphasis on community and local democracy, and their distrust of formal and large-scale bureaucracies.[10] In a similar vein, more than 20 percent of South Africa's urban population lives in shacks and shantytowns. Many poor families have refused to pay for urban services. "*Masakhane*," or the "culture-of-paying" campaign organized by the government and business community after the first multiracial election in March 1994, represents an attempt to recover these massive public appropriations by the poor.[11]

Far from destructive behavior on the part of the "lumpen proletariat" or the "dangerous classes,"[12] these practices represent the natural and logical ways in which the disenfranchised survive hardships and improve their lives. What is significant about these activities, and thus interests us in this book, is precisely their seemingly mundane, ordinary, and daily nature. How can one account for such daily practices? What values can one attach to such exercises? How do we explain the politics of these everyday lives?

These are only some of the questions I hope to address in the course of this book by focusing on the case of Iran between 1977–1990. A discussion of these issues helps us arrive at some important conclusions with regard to the relationship between social movements and social change. First, adopting a relative distance from both James Scott and his critiques, my aim is to show how these ordinary and often quiet practices by very ordinary and often silent people engender significant social changes—the kinds of changes that are comparable to those that revolutions are said to achieve for them. Relying on the Iranian experience, I wish to deemphasize the totalizing notion of "the revolution" as the change par excellence, to discard the assumption that real change for all social groups comes necessarily and exclusively from a generalized political campaign. A totalizing discourse suppresses the variations in people's perceptions about change; diversity is screened, conflicts are belittled, and instead a grand/united language is emphasized. This suppression of difference by the dominant voice of the leadership has usually worked against the discourse of the ordinary, the powerless, the poor, minorities, women, and other subaltern elements. My aim, therefore, is to recover and give agency to one of those suppressed voices, that of the urban disenfranchised.[13]

Finally, I want to stress, in partial agreement with Gramsci, the significance of the local both as a crucial arena of social struggle and as a unit of analysis to examine social change. While a generalized/political/global (revolutionary?) campaign is essential for removing many obstacles for many real changes in favor of the poor, it is the local that serves as the essential criterion and locus of change. It is in the localities that oppression is felt and resisted, where the people actually experience the effect of national policies.

At first glance, the ordinary practices I have described above conjure up James Scott's "everyday forms of peasant resistance." Scott, Colburn, and others have highlighted the ability of poor people to resist the "oppressors" by such actions as foot dragging, dissimulation, false compliance, slander, arson, sabotage, and so forth. Peasants are said to act predominantly individually and discretely, but given repressive political conditions, their practices are functional to their needs.[14]

The "everyday forms of resistance" perspective has undoubtedly contributed to recovering the Third World poor from "passivity," "fatalism" and "hopelessness"—essentialist features of the "culture of poverty" with its emphasis on identifying the "marginal man" as a "cultural type."[15] Scott even transcends the survival strategies model, which limits the activities of the poor to mere survival within the daily context,[16] often at the cost of others or themselves. As Escobar suggests, the language of "survival strategies" may contribute to maintaining the image of the poor as victims.[17] Thus, to counter unemployment or price increases, they are often said to resort to theft, begging, prostitution, or the reorientation of their consumption patterns.

Scott's work is also important from a different angle. Until recently the prevailing concern of scholars, from both left and right, focused on the poor's political threat to the existing order; they were preoccupied with the question of whether the poor constituted a destabilizing force,[18] thus ignoring the dynamics of the the poor's microexistence and everyday politics. On the other hand, many of these authors still view the politics of the poor in terms of a revolutionary/passive dichotomy.[19] Such a paradigm surely limits the possibility of looking upon the matter in a different light—I do not mean by taking a centrist approach[20] but by adopting an entirely new perspective. The concept "everyday forms of resistance" certainly contributes to a shift in the terms of the debate.[21]

Yet Scott's "Brechtian mode of class struggle and resistance" is inadequate to account for the dynamics of the activities of the urban poor in the Third World. While it is undeniable that concerns of survival constitute the main preoccupations of the urban disenfranchised, they also strive to move forward and improve their lives, however calmly and quietly. Their struggles are not merely defensive, an everyday *resistance* against the encroachments of the "superordinate" groups; nor are they simply hidden, quiet, and mostly individualistic. In my understanding, the struggles of the urban poor are also surreptitiously *offensive*, that is, disenfranchised groups place a great deal of restraint upon the privileges of the dominant groups, allocating constituents of the life chances of those groups (including capital, social goods, opportunity, autonomy, and thus power) to themselves. This tends to involve the urban poor in a *collective*, open, and highly audible campaign. Moreover, in addition to seeking concessions from the state, their individual and quiet struggles, predominantly by direct action, also effect steady and significant changes in their own lives, thus going beyond "marginally affect[ing] the various forms of exploitations which peasants confront."[22] Scott's implicit subscription to rational choice theory would overlook the complexity of motives behind this type of struggle, where moral elements are mixed with rational calculations.

Can these undertakings then be analyzed in terms of urban social movements—understood as organized and territorially based movements of the Third World urban poor who strive for "social transformation" (according to Castells),[23] "emancipation" (according to Schuurman and van Naerssen),[24] or an alternative to the tyranny of modernity (in Friedmann's perception)?[25] The similarities appear to be quite striking: both movements are urban, struggling for analogous aims such as housing, community building, collective consumption, official recognition of their gains, and so forth. Yet they differ from one another in many respects. First, whereas social movements in general represent a long-lasting and more or less structured collective action aiming at social change, the activities I describe here carry, among other features, strong elements of spontaneity, individualism, and intergroup competition. They place special emphasis, moreover, on action over meaning, or, in Castells' terms, "urban meaning."

In addition, while these ordinary practices resemble both new and archaic social movements—in terms of being self-producing, possessing vague or nonexistent leadership, incoherent or diverse ideologies, and a loose or total lack of structured organization—they nevertheless differ significantly from both. The primitive social movements, explored by Eric Hobsbawm, were often generated or mobilized by distinct charismatic leaders,[26] whereas the type of activism I describe are mostly, but not entirely, self-generating. On the other hand, while the new social movements are said to focus largely on identity and meaning,[27] my protagonists concern themselves primarily with action. Therefore, in a metaphorical sense, these everyday encroachments may be seen as representing a movement in itself, becoming a social movement per se only if and when the actors become conscious of their doings by articulating their aims, methods, and justifications. However, should such public articulation occur, the characteristic of quiet encroachment is lost. In other words, these desperate everyday practices exhibit distinct undertakings with their own particular logic and dynamics.

The Quiet Encroachment of the Ordinary

The types of struggles I describe here may best be characterized as the "quiet encroachment of the ordinary"—a silent, patient, protracted, and pervasive advancement of ordinary people on the propertied and powerful in order to survive hardships and better their lives. They are marked by quiet, atomized, and prolonged mobilization with episodic collective action—an open and fleeting struggle without clear leadership, ideology, or structured organization, one that produces significant gains for the actors, eventually placing them in counterpoint to the state. By initiating gradual "molecular" changes, the poor in the long run "progressively modify the pre-existing composition of forces, and hence become the matrix of new changes."[28] But unlike Gramsci's "passive revolution[aries]," disenfranchised groups do not carry out their activities as a conscious political strategy; rather, they are driven by the force of necessity—the necessity to survive and live a dignified life. Thus, the notion of necessity and a quest for dignity justify their struggles as moral, natural, and logical ways to survive and advance their lives.[29] Gramsci's "passive revolution" ultimately targets state power. I wish to emphasize, however, that quiet encroachment, although it might indirectly follow generalized political implications, implies changes that the actors consider as significant in themselves without intending necessarily to undermine political authority. Yet these very simple and everyday practices are bound to shift into the realm of politics. The participants engage in collective action, seeing their doings and themselves as political only when confronted by those who threaten their gains. Hence one key attribute of these movements is that while advances are made quietly, individually, and gradually, the defense of these gains is always collective and audible.

Thousands of such men and women embark upon long and painful migratory journeys, scattering in remote and alien environs, acquiring work, shelter, land, and living amenities. Driven by the force of necessity (economic hardship, war, or natural disaster), they set out individually and without much clamor, often slowly and unnoticeably, as perseverant as the movements of turtles in a remote colony. They often deliberately avoid collective effort, large-scale operations, commotion and publicity. At times squatters, for instance, prevent others from joining them in specific areas; and vendors discourage their counterparts from settling in the same vicinity. Many even hesitate to share information about their strategies with similar groups. Yet, as these seemingly desperate individuals and families pursue similar paths, their sheer cumulative numbers transform them into a potential social force. This complex mixture of individual and collective action results from both the social position of the actors and, to use Tarrow's term, the "structure of opportunities" available for them.[30]

The most common agents involved in quiet encroachment movements encompass a variety of largely floating social clusters—migrants, refugees, the unemployed, squatters, street vendors, and other marginalized groups. Rural migrants encroach on cities and their amenities, refugees and international migrants on host states and their provisions, squatters on public and private lands or ready-made homes, and street vendors on the opportunity costs of business as well as on public space in both its physical and social facets—street sidewalks, intersections, public parks, and the like. What brings these groups into this form of struggle is, first, the initial urge for an alternative mode of life, requiring them to change jobs, places, and priorities, and second, the lack of an institutional mechanism through which they can collectively express their grievances and resolve their problems.

This latter point partially explains why the struggles of these subaltern groups often take the form of a silent repertoire of individual direct action rather than collective demand-making protests. Unlike groups of organized workers or students, the unemployed, emigrants, refugees, or street vendors are groups in flux; they are the structurally atomized individuals who operate outside the formal institutions of factories, schools, and associations. They therefore lack the institutional capacity to exert pressure, since they lack an organizational power of disruption—disruption, in the sense of "the withdrawal of crucial contribution on which others depend," one that is therefore "a natural resource for exerting power over others."[31] They may, of course, participate in street demonstrations or riots, but only when these methods enjoy a reasonable degree of legitimacy[32] and when they are mobilized by outside leaders. Under exceptional circumstances, land takeovers may be led by leftwing groups or the unemployed and street vendors may be invited to form unions. This happens mainly in relatively democratic periods, when political parties engaged in competition inevitably attempt to mobilize the poor in exchange for electoral support. That is how the unemployed were organized in postrevolution Iran, the self-employed women in Bombay, the housewives in postwar Britain, and the street vendors in Lima.[33] However, in the absence of electoral freedoms, the contenders tend to remain institutionally powerless since, more often than not, mobilization for collective demand-making is forcibly repressed in many developing countries where these struggles often take place.[34] This initial lack of institutional power is compensated, however, by the poor's perforce versatility in taking direct action, be it collective or individual, precipitous or piecemeal, which, in the long run, might evolve into a more self-regulating/autonomous local life.

Consequently, in place of *protest* or publicity, these groups move directly to fulfill their needs by themselves, albeit individually and discretely. In short, theirs is a politics *not* of protest but of redress, and is a struggle for immediate outcomes largely through individual direct action.

The Aims

What do these men and women aim for? They seem to pursue two major goals. The first is the *redistribution of social goods* and opportunities in the form of the (unlawful and direct) acquisition of collective consumption (land, shelter, piped water, electricity, roads), public space (street sidewalks, intersections, street parking places), opportunities (favorable business conditions, locations, and labels), and other life chances essential for survival and a minimal standard of living.

The other goal is attaining *autonomy*, both cultural and political, from the regulations, institutions, and discipline imposed by the state. The disenfranchised express a deep desire to live an informal life, to run their own affairs without involving the authorities or other modern formal institutions. This is not to suggest that tradition guides their lives, but rather to insist that modern institutions, in one sense, reproduce people's traditional relations as solutions to the problems that these institutions engender. In many informal communities in Third World cities, people rely on their own local and traditional norms during their daily activities, whether it be establishing contracts (e.g. marriage), organizing their locality, or resolving local disputes. In a way, they are compelled to exert control over their working lives, regulating their time and coordinating their space. They grow weary of the formal procedures governing their time, obligations, and commitments; they are reluctant to undertake the discipline imposed, for instance, by paying taxes and bills, appearing in public in particular ways, and most broadly in the practice of everyday life.[35]

This distrust of the modern state and of institutions has aroused two contrasting reactions. Some sociologists, notably followers of the Chicago school and politicians, dismiss the urban poor as marginals, outlaws, and criminals, and their communities as bastions of rural parochialism and traditionalism. This deviance, they suggest, can be corrected only by integrating these people back into the state and the society; in short, by modernizing them.[36] Others, notably Janice Perlman and Castells, have vehemently attacked the premise of marginality, arguing that far from being marginal, these people are all well-integrated.[37] Despite their differences, these rival perspectives share one important assumption. Both assume that the ideal man is the well-adjusted and well-integrated man—in short, modern man.

The fact is that these men and women are neither marginal (i.e. essentially traditional and isolated) nor fully integrated. Rather, their poverty and vulnerability drive them to seek autonomy from the state and from modern institutions. They tend to refrain from resorting to police and other government offices primarily because of the failure of bureaucracies and modern institutions to deliver for them. These institutions impose the kind of discipline (in terms of regulating their time, behavior, and appearance) that many simply cannot afford or with which they do not wish to comply. Only the the very poor may favor integration since, at least in immediate terms, it gives them more than it takes. Many slum-dwellers and those relocated from shantytowns, however, are inclined to live in squatter areas partly because they seem free from official surveillance and modern social control (for instance, in terms of the ability to communicate easily, appear in public, and practice their culture). While the poor tend to reject the constraining facet of modernity, they welcome its liberating dimension. Thus, while the squatters do want to light their homes with electricity, use piped water and watch color TV, they do not want to pay bills subject to strict bureaucratic regulations; they yearn for flexibility and negotiation. Similarly, street subsistence work, despite its low status, low security, and other costs, has the advantage of freeing people from the discipline and controlling relations of the modern working institutions.[38] Although somewhat romanticised, John Friedmann's characterization of the Brazilian barrios as a kind of postmodernist movement points to the alternative ways of life the poor tend to pursue. In his view, the barrios' emphasis on moral economy, trust, cooperation, production of use-values, local autonomy, and self-regulation in a sense challenges modern principles of exchange value, bureaucracy, and the state.[39]

Let me make two points clear. The first is that the notions of autonomy and integration in the view of both the poor and the state are far from straightforward. They are the subject of contradictory processes, constant redefinition, and intense negotiation. Informality is not an essential preference of the urban poor; it serves primarily as an alternative to the constraints of formal structures. Indeed, as the examples above illustrate, many poor people perhaps aspire and practice integrated life, only if they can afford its social and cultural—not to mention its economic—costs. Thus in the early 1990s the settlers of Islamshahr, an informal community in south Tehran, campaigned for the official integration of their community. Once that was achieved, however, new informal communities began to spring up around that township. In addition, just as do the poor, states also exhibit contradictory stands on autonomy and integration. Most governments tend in practice to promote autonomy as an effort to transfer their responsibilities to the citizens, hence encouraging individual initiative, self-help, nongovernmental organizations (NGOs), and so forth. Observers such as Gilbert and Ward consider these measures as a means of social control.[40] However, they fail to recognize the fact that at the same time governments display apprehension about losing political space. It is not uncommon to observe states simultaneously implementing conflicting policies of both promoting and restricting autonomous and informal institutions. Third World urban life, in short, is characterized by a combined and continuous process of informalization, integration and reinformalization.

The second point is that the rich and the powerful may also desire self-regulation and autonomy from the discipline of modern organizations. However in reality, unlike the poor, they mostly benefit from those arrangements; it is the powerful who institute them in the first place. Moreover, unlike the poor, the rich, by virtue of possessing resources (knowledge, skill, money, and connections) can *afford* to function within such institutions. They are able, for instance, to pay their bills or get to work on time.

The two chief goals of the disenfranchised—redistribution and autonomy—are quite interrelated. The former ensures survival and a better material life; the latter serves not only as an end in itself but also as a means to achieve the objective of the redistribution: acting autonomously from the state, poor individuals may be able to obtain public goods (illegal land, shelter, and so on) that they are unlikely to attain through legal and institutionalized mechanisms, unless they demand these goods through a powerful collective mobilization.

In the quiet encroachments, the struggles to achieve these unlawful goals are hardly planned or articulated. They are seen as natural and moral responses to the urgency of survival and the desire for a dignified life, however defined. In the Middle Eastern culture, the notion of necessity—the necessity of maintaining a dignified life—underlies poor peoples' sense of justice. The Persian phrase *chare-ii neest* (there is no other way) and its Arabic equivalent *na'mal eih?* (what else can we do?) articulate a moral language of urban politics, responses through which the poor often justify their acts of transgression.[41] And this idea of dignity is very closely associated with the *public judgment*, with the community or friends and foes determining its meaning. To maintain a dignified life, a family needs to possess certain cultural/material abilities. Preserving *abirou* or *'ard* (honor) through generosity, bravery, and more important, through securing the *haya* (sexual modesty) of the women in the family mark a few such resources. But the essential components more relevant to our discussion include the ability to provide, the ability to protect the *harim* of the household from public intrusion, and finally the ability to conceal possible failures (*abirourizi*, or *fadiha*). For a poor head of a household, not only would the failure to provide for his family jeopardize their survival, it would also inflict a blow to his honor. Homelessness, for instance, signifies an ultimate loss in all these accounts. A dwelling, beyond its function of protecting the household from physical dangers (cold, heat, and the like), serves also as a cultural location. By preserving the *harim*, safeguarding people from moral dangers, a dwelling conceals shortcomings and preserves *abirou* before the public gaze. The rich may also share similar values, but the poor have a lower capacity to conceal failures, thus making their dignified life more vulnerable.

In this perception of justice informed by necessity, one who has a basic need may and should fulfill it, even if illegally, so long as he does not harm others like himself. The rich can probably afford to lose some of their wealth. When the state begins to challenge these notions, thus violating codes of justice of the poor, the morally outraged poor tend to rebel.[42] Yet I have to stress that this moral politics does not preclude the poor from the *rational* use of any political space in which they can maximize their gains. Bribing officials, forming alliances with political parties, utilizing political rivalries, and exploiting governmental or nongovernmental associations are all part of the rules of the game.

Becoming Political

If these movements begin without political meaning, and if illegal encroachments are often justified on moral grounds (as a way to survive), then how do they turn into collective/political struggles? So long as the actors carry on with their everyday advances without being confronted seriously by any authority, they treat their doings as ordinary everyday practice. Once their gains are threatened, they become conscious of their actions and the value of their gains, and they defend them collectively and audibly. I describe the logic of transformation from individual to collective action later. Suffice it to state here that the numerous antigovernment riots by squatters, street vendors, and other marginalized groups point to the centrality of collective resistance among these atomized poor. The struggle of the actors is not about winning a gain but primarily about defending and furthering gains already won. In such conjunctures, the contenders may go as far as to give some structure to their activities, by networking, cooperating, or initiating more structured organizations. Such organizing is aimed at maintaining, consolidating, and extending those earlier achievements.

When does the state enter the arena? State opposition usually occurs when the cumulative growth of the encroachers and their doings pass beyond a tolerable point. Depending on the efficiency of the particular state, the availability of alternative solutions, and the resistance of these quiet rebels, states normally tolerate scattered offensives, especially when they have still not become a critical force. The trick for the actors, therefore, is to *appear* limited and tolerable while expanding so much that resistance against them becomes difficult. Indeed, many (squatters, vendors, and car-parkers) try deliberately to halt their spread in certain areas by not allowing their counterparts to join them. Others resort to bribing minor officials, or minimizing visibility (for instance, squatting in remote areas or vending in less provocative areas). Almost all take advantage of undermined state power at times of crises (following a revolution, war, or economic breakdown) to spread further and entrench their position. In brief, the protagonists exploit these three opportunities—crisis, bribing, and invisibility—that allow them to remain apparently tolerable while they are in fact multiplying.

Once the extent of their expansion and impact is revealed, however, state reaction and crackdown often becomes inevitable. In most cases, crackdowns fail: they are usually launched too late, when the encroachers have already spread, become visible, and achieved a critical mass. Indeed, the description by most officials of the process as "cancerous" captures the dynamics of such a movement.[43]

The sources of the conflict between the state and the disenfranchised have to do with the economic and political costs that quiet encroachment imposes on both the authorities and the rich. The informal and free-of-charge redistribution of public goods exerts a heavy burden on a state's resources. The rich—real estate owners, merchants, and shopkeepers—also lose properties, brands, and business opportunities. The alliance of the rich and the state adds a class dimension to the existing political conflict.

Beyond the economic dimension, the poor peoples' drive for autonomy in everyday life creates a big crack in the domination of the modern state. A fully autonomous life renders states irrelevant. Popular control over contracts, regulation of time, space, cultural activities, working life—in short, self-regulation—reclaims significant political space from the state. Herein lies the inevitability of conflict. Street politics[44] exemplifies the most salient aspect of this conflict, accounting for a key feature in the social life of the disenfranchised.

Street Politics

By street politics, I mean a set of conflicts and the attendant implications between a collective populace and the authorities, shaped and expressed episodically in the physical and social space of the streets— from the alleyways to the more visible sidewalks, public parks, or sport places. The street in this sense serves as the only locus of collective expression for, but by no means limited to, those who structurally lack any institutional setting to express discontent. This group includes squatters, the unemployed, street subsistence workers (e.g., vendors), members of the underworld (e.g., beggars, prostitutes), petty thieves, and housewives. The term signifies an articulation of discontent by clusters of different social agents without institutions, coherent ideology, or evident leadership. Two key factors transform the streets into an arena of politics. The first follows Foucault's general observation about space as power.[45] It results from the use of public space as a sight of contestation between the populace and the Authority. At one level, what makes street activity political is the active or participative (as opposed to passive) use of public space; thus, the use of street sidewalks, crossroads, urban land, the space for assembly, and public practices of culture all become the sites of contestation. These sites increasingly become the domain of the state power that regulates their usage, making them orderly. It expects their users to operate passively according to rules set by the state. Any active and participative use challenges the control of both the Authority and those social groups that benefit from such order.

This kind of street life and these types of activities are by no means a novelty. They could be seen in sixteenth- to eighteenth-century Europe[46] and, until very recently, in the urban Middle East.[47] They did not entail street politics, however. What makes them political are novel features: in contrast with the past when local communities enjoyed a great deal of autonomy and self-regulation, they are now under centralized governments that regulate and control the street and local life.[48]

The second element in shaping street politics is the operation of what I have called the *passive network* among the people who use public space. Any collective political act—mobilization—requires some degree of organization, communication, and networking among its actors. For the most part this is constituted deliberately, either formally or informally. Thus squatters, the unemployed, or immigrants from the same place of origin may establish formal associations with constant communication and regular meetings. Or they may instead develop informal contacts among themselves. Vendors on the same street, for example, may get together on an ad hoc basis to discuss their problems or simply to chat and socialize. In both formal and informal cases, the participants would have an *active* network among themselves in that they become known to each other, talk, meet, and consciously interact with one another. However, contrary to Tilly's perception of organization—one with high "catness" and "netness" or strong cohesion and interpersonal communication[49]—networks need not be active. The street as a public place possesses this intrinsic feature, making it possible for people to mobilize without having an active network. Such a mobilization is carried out through passive networks—the instantaneous communication among atomized individuals, which is established by the tacit recognition of their common identity and is mediated through space. A woman who enters a male-dominated party instantly notices another female among the men; vendors in a street notice each other even though they may never speak to each other. Unlike, say, dispersed tax strikers, a passive network exists among both the women in the party and vendors in a given locality.

The tenants of a council housing unit, illegal immigrants to a country, tax strikers, the women in a male-dominated party, vendors in a street, or spectators at a football match all represent atomized individuals who, at a certain level, have a similar status and an identity of interests among themselves (see figures 1.1 and 1.2). For Bourdieu, each of the above groups signifies a "theoretical group," becoming "real" only when they are "represented."[50] Bourdieu does not explore how such representation takes place, however. In his formulation, a fundamental element of groupness—the network—is either ignored or taken for granted.

The fact is that these juxtaposed individuals can potentially act together. But acting together requires a medium or network for establishing communication. Illegal immigrants or tax-strikers cannot resist state action unless they begin to deliberately organize themselves, since no medium like space brings them together (see figure 1.3). Tenants, spectators, vendors, squatters, and the women described above, even though they do not know each other, may act collectively because common space makes it possible for them to recognize their common interests and identity (see figure 1.4)—that is, to develop a passive network.

What mediates between a passive network and action is a common threat. Once these atomized individuals are confronted by a threat to their gains, their passive network spontaneously turns into an active network and collective action. Thus the threat of eviction brings many squatters together immediately, even if they do not know each other. Likewise the supporters of rival teams in a football match often cooperate to confront police in the streets. This is due not simply to psychologically induced or irrational crowd action but to a more sociological fact of interest recognition and *latent communication*.

Already organized individuals also may attempt to *extend* their (passive or active) network to those other than their immediate members. Students, factory workers, or women's associations, for instance, who demonstrate in the streets do so in order to publicize their cause and gain solidarity. The very act of demonstration in public means, in a sense, attempting to establish communication with those who are *unknown* to the demonstrators but who might be subject to similar conditions as themselves; the demonstrators hope to activate this passive communication in order to extend collective action.

It has to be stressed that the movement from passive into active networking and collective action is never a given. It is subject to the same complexity and contingent upon similar factors as the movement from a consciously organized network into mobilization.[51] Factors such as a legitimacy crisis of the state, division within the ruling elites, break-a   h   m

o   d   x

n   p   b

FIGURE 1.1

No network: Atomized individuals without a common position

a   a   a

a   a   a

a   a   a

FIGURE 1.2

No network: Atomized individuals with a common position

FIGURE 1.3

Active network: Individuals with similar positions brought together
deliberately—association with an active network

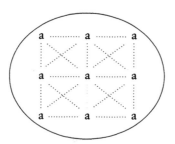

FIGURE 1.4

Passive network: Atomized individuals with similar positions
brought together through space

down in social control, and access to resources may all facilitate collective action; and, in turn, the threat of "repression,"[52] intergroup division, and the usefulness of temporary compliance are likely to hinder mobilization. The point here is not that a threat to evict a group of squatters may not necessarily lead to their collective resistance; trade unions may also acquiesce before a threat of layoff. The point rather is to show how groups of *atomized individuals* without active networks and organization can and *do* engage, often instantly, in collective action;this is due to the operation of passive networks among them.

This unplanned, unstructured, and instantaneous possibility of group action renders the street a highly volatile locus of conflict and thus of politics. It is the operation of passive networks that lies behind the political danger of the streets: the streets represent public space par excellence. No wonder every unpopular government pays such close attention to controlling them. While states may be able to restrict deliberately organized demonstrations or rallies, they are often incapable of prohibiting street populations from working, driving, or walking—in short, from street life. The more open and visible the public place, the broader the operation of passive networks and therefore the possibility of collective action becomes. Passive networks, in short, represent an inherent element of street and backstreet life; they ensure the instant cooperation of the individual actors once those actors feel a threat to their well-being. In the absence of the concept of passive networks, many find it difficult to make sense of the surprising, unexpected, and spontaneous mass eruptions that take place in urban settings.[53] This dialectic of individual and collective action—the possibility of collective resistance together with their moral justification for individual encroachment—perhaps explains the resiliency of the disenfranchised in carrying on their struggle for survival and the betterment of their predicaments.

The Making of the Quiet Encroachment

How universal is the quiet encroachment of the ordinary? And under what conditions is such activism likely to emerge? Quiet encroachment in developing countries seems to evolve from a combination of structural and cultural factors that render it a historically specific phenomenon.

To begin with, the raw material of the movement, the actors, originates largely from the desperate clusters of the urban unemployed and underemployed, as well as from other marginalized groups.[54] It seems that natural population increases (primarily resulting from poverty) and especially the classical model of rural-urban migration (resulting from the maldistribution of land, rural unemployment, natural or man-made disasters, urban bias, and limited industrial expansion) have been the primary reasons for urban unemployment. Evidence shows that for the most part the urban economy is unable to absorb fully the amount of labor created by natural population growth.[55] Thus a large number of relatively educated and first-time job-seekers remain out of work. Overall, urban migration serves as the primary factor. On average, nearly half of the increase in urban population in the Third World has resulted from migration. This rate for both Ghana and Tanzania was 60 percent, and for the Ivory Coast 70 percent.[56]

Beside this classic scenario, some new developments have in recent years multiplied the size of these groups. A global crisis of populist modernization in a number of Third World countries since the 1980s, and the collapse of socialist economies since the 1990s, have led to massive de-institutionalization, proletarianization, and marginalization. Alternative strategies—structural adjustment and stabilization programs—tend to make a sizable segment of already employed people redundant, without a clear prospect of boosting the economy and creating viable jobs. In the early 1990s, during the transition to market economies in post-Socialist, adjusting Latin American and Middle Eastern countries, formal employment fell by 5 to 15 percent.[57] In Africa the number of unemployed grew by 10 percent or more every year throughout the 1980s, while labor absorption in the formal wage sector kept declining.[58] By the early 1990s open unemployment in Third World countries increased dramatically.[59] Thus a large number of the once well-to-do and educated middle classes (government employees and students)and public sector workers, as well as segments of the peasantry are pushed into the ranks of the urban poor in labor and housing markets.

The state's unwillingness and inability to offer adequate work, protection, and urban amenities puts these new urban poor in a similar collective position, if not a collective identity, as the unemployed, squatters, slum dwellers or street subsistence workers—in short, they become potential street rebels. The lack of an institutional setting leaves these men and women to struggle in their atomized formations. Many developing countries seem to have experienced similar processes. What distinguishes the form of mobilization within these nations has to do with local political cultures and institutions.

The repressive policy of the state renders individual, quiet, and hidden mobilization a more viable strategy than open, collective protest. Under such conditions, collective and open direct action takes place only at exceptional conjunctures—in particular, when states experience crises of legitimacy such as the revolutionary crisis in Iran during 1979; Egypt after the 1967 defeat; and South Africa after the fall of apartheid in the early 1990s.

However, where some degree of political openness prevails, competition between political parties provides a breathing ground for the collective action of ordinary people. The rival political groupings and patrons, in order to win electoral and mass support, inevitably mobilize the poor (as in India, Mexico, Peru, Brazil, and Chile in the early 1970s).[60] This is unlikely to happen under autocratic systems where winning votes is not a concern of the political leadership. In short, quiet encroachment is largely the feature of undemocratic political systems, as well as of cultures where primordial institutions serve as an alternative to civic associations and social movements. This may partially explain why in most Middle Eastern countries, where authoritarian rule dominates and where family and kinship are pivotal for individuals' support and security, it is largely the strategy of quiet encroachment that seems to prevail.[61] In many Latin American nations, on the other hand, where some tradition and practice of political competition and political patronage operate, mobilization tends to assume a collective, audible, and associational character; urban land invasions, urban poor associations, and street trade unionism appear to mark a major feature of urban politics in this region of the world.[62]

States may also contribute to quiet encroachment in another way. This type of movement is likely to grow where both the inefficient state bureaucracy and rigid formal organizations, notably the "mercantilist" state described by De Soto (1989), predominate; such institutions tend to encourage people to seek more informal and autonomous living and working conditions. The situation in more efficient and democratic settings is, however, quite different. The more democratic and efficient the state, the less ground for the expansion of highly autonomous movements; under such circumstances, the poor tend to become integrated into the state structure and are inclined to play the prevailing games, utilizing the existing means and institutions, however limited, to improve their lives.[63]

Two

Mapping Out the "New Poor"

By the late 1970s the quiet encroachment of the disenfranchised had clearly marked Iranian cities. Rural-urban migration, the housing problem, spontaneous communities, demands for collective consumption, and the spread of street subsistence work had all been discussed and presented as major developmental failures. The urban poor were seen as both villains (by policy makers) and victims (by the opposition)—they were the villains of development and modernization and the victims of the "maldevelopment" and "pseudomodernization" that Iranian society had been going through since the 1940s.

This chapter describes the main features of the "new poor" by focusing on the city of Tehran. It spells out their origin, size, and economic, communal, and housing conditions. It argues that by the eve of the Islamic Revolution the poor constituted a fairly distinct social group identified chiefly by the place of their residence.

The New Poor

The category "poor" is not simply an economic one. It points primarily to social and cultural identity. Seen as a social category, the prerevolution urban poor in Iran were a modern entity, a quite distinct social group. The members of this group, called interchangeably the urban poor or the disenfranchised, were distinguished chiefly by their low-income, low-skill, low-status, and insecure position.[1]

At times the much criticized term "marginality" is employed to describe this group. It so happens that this term is an exact equivalent of the Persian term *hashiyenishini*, which has been widely used in official language in Iran. Understandably, the problem with this terminology is that those in the tradition of Chicago School sociologists tend to essentialize the concept by giving the poor certain cultural essentials that separate them from mainstream urban life.[2] However, I think that the concept can be taken as an empirical category—as a structural and historical process in the developing world that tends to exclude segments of urban populations from developmental achievements and modern institutions.[3] In this sense the urban poor in Iran, somehow overlapped with the industrial working class, were distinguished from other social groups primarily by their social exclusion and their residential status as squatters and slum dwellers.[4]

In Iran the new urban disenfranchised developed as a consequence of policies that both Reza Shah and Muhammad Reza Shah pursued from the 1930s onward.[5] Modernization resulted in rapid urban growth, urban migration, the creation of new social classes (some of which were highly prosperous), and a general rise in income. At the same time it led to the economic and social marginalization of an important segment of the urban population. It is by and large this process of marginalization that characterized the marginal or new poor, the disenfranchised.

Poor people, of course, existed long before modernization in Iran, as well as in the other parts of the Middle East.[6] Beggars, porters, vendors, hawkers, and various menials filled the quarters of Iran's nineteenth-century and earlier cities. However, the context in which they operated differed. Up until the early twentieth century, in the major urban centers such as Tehran, Isfahan, Tabriz, and Shiraz, marked social cleavage was based less on class than on communal differentiation. People granted their loyalties first and foremost to their *mahalles*, or quarters.[7] The rich, the poor, the middle classes, ulama, merchants, and shopkeepers lived largely side by side, intermingled socially, communicated on a daily basis, and shared cultural traits and religious beliefs.[8] They all participated in the same religious rituals—*takiyeh*, *ta'ziyeh*, and *muharram* processions[9]—which cemented more or less homogeneous cultural and behavioral patterns, despite the persistence of patronage linking rich and poor.

The new poor are the product of a modern stratification system. From the early twentieth century on, the traditional stratification pattern began to give way to a "dual class structure."[10] The integration of Iran in the world economy, along with the eventual establishment of a manufacturing industry, resulted in the creation of new social groupings, notably a modern bourgeoisie, a working class, and modern bureaucrats, all residing exclusively in urban areas. These social changes were accompanied by the modernization of urban form, residential pattern, and social structure.[11] The traditional pattern of community changed into what Khosrowkhavar has characterized as a "neo-community," and is marked by ethnic and origin heterogeneity, a tendency to modernize tradition and care about public space, community participation, and the state control of public order.[12]

Tehran, a walled city of nineteen square kilometers with 160,000 inhabitants in 1905, grew to house over 300,000 in the early 1930s, with segments settling in new *mahalle*s that sprang up outside the city wall. In 1930 this wall was destroyed and modern straight streets were constructed. This marked a new phase in urban structure. With the establishment since the 1940s of city planning, the old *mahalleh* system gave way to a planned zonal pattern based largely upon class segregation. The low-income groups were invariably ignored by the various urban comprehensive plans. The free market on land and its high price, and unaffordable construction standards set by the plans—such as size of plots, the form of construction, problems of gradual building, and cost of preparation—all pushed the poor to put up their shelters informally just outside the city limits. This process was speeded up particularly after 1966 when the notorious Provision 100 of the Municipality Law was approved. The law authorized demolition of unlawful constructions both within the city limits as well as in the buffer zones, *harim*, created around the cities.[13] Subsequently, informal and marginalized settlements began to grow, leading to the formation of distinct poor communities.

In Slums and Squatter Settlements

By the eve of the 1979 revolution, Tehran, with a population of some five million, exhibited a remarkable and perhaps unique class (economic, social, and cultural) hierarchy. Located on a north-to-south sloping landscape, the geophysical pyramid of the city reflected its social and economic hierarchy. To the far north, the highest district was the site of the most affluent populations. The lowest lands of the city were allocated to the poor, new migrants, and other strata of the working class. The middle areas, from east to west, housed the middle classes.[14]

A number of squatter settlements and lower-class neighborhoods located in the old Tehran "villages" had spread into northern and central areas of the city. Their scale, however, was insignificant in comparison to those in South Tehran. The poor were thus pushed to settle in the vast southern plain, encompassing a variety of slums and squatter settlements, beginning roughly from Mawlavi Avenue. Many of the slums, especially those located in old Tehran (such as Munirieh, Mawlavi, Park-i Shahr, Maidan-i Soush, Railway Station) were formerly the neighborhoods of the relatively well-off traditional middle class who gradually moved into the modern northern areas, leaving the poor behind to be joined by the new rural migrants. These quarters then turned into overcrowded slums[15]—urban services deteriorated, illegal additions were made, and homes were redesigned or partitioned to accommodate the needs of the poor. Yet other settlements, such as Naziabad and Kouy-i Nuhum-i Aban, were deliberately created through a strategy of spatial segregation. By the mid-1970s Tehran had some fifty slums and squatter communities. Similar settlements spread also in other Iranian cities, such as Tabriz, Kermanshah, Hamadan, Bandar Abbas, Ahwaz, Bousher, Shiraz and Mashad. Among these, Tabriz (with 7.6 percent) and Ahwaz (4 percent) had the highest ratio of squatters to total population.[16] Even so, the overall scale of those settlements was smaller than their counterparts in such Third World countries as Egypt, Pakistan, Turkey, the Philippines, or the Latin American nations.

Like many of their equivalents in the Third World, the slums in Tehran were overcrowded, muddy, dirty environs, with narrow alleys in the middle of which ran *jouys*, open waste-water/sewer ducts, playgrounds for barefoot children. But Tehran's poor neighborhoods had their own peculiar features. Small, dense, and hurriedly built one- or two-story houses lined the edges of narrow alleyways. Despite the inadequacy of space, homes were characterized by little ponds in the middle of their courtyards. Small identical mud or brick rooms faced into the courtyard on three sides. Each room was usually occupied by a tenant household (with three or more children), which might live and share the bathroom and kitchen with the landlord. The entrance door and window (when they existed) of each room looked out beyond the courtyard onto the neighbors. Thick curtains on the doors were the only shield against the curious. The square front yard was the central gathering place for almost all daily activities and important events: it could be a washing area for women, a space to spread the laundry, a playground for children, a secret rendezvous for young adults, a battleground for squabbling tenants (or quarelling tenants and landlords), a joyous wedding hall, or a grieving funeral home. In slum dwellings there was no room for privacy. Within each individual household, the extreme limits of space exposed the most private affairs. The physical density led poor residents to incorporate the alleyways into their own private spheres. In these poor communities the line between private and public could hardly be drawn. While young females spent much of their time indoors or in the courtyards, male youngsters hung out mostly in the *sar-i koucheh* (intersections of the alleyways and the streets). The *sar-i koucheh* functioned as perhaps the most important space where youth street culture took shape. It was here that the youth formed gangs and group solidarity, articulated their local identity, smoked, checked out the passersby—notably the adult girls—and were recruited for cultural and religious events.

In the southern landscape of Tehran, meanwhile, lay the estates of the traditional brick-making industry whose enormous chimneys resembled the "satanic mills" of the industrial revolution. Around these mills sprang up the main squatter communities of the metropolis—including caves, tents, hovels, shacks, shanties, and urban villages—which lacked almost all city amenities. Although many spontaneous settlements mushroomed also in the north, east, and western margins of the city, the southern plain maintained its lead well through the postrevolution years.

The squatters usually called their communities by the terms that described the mode of their construction. Thus *Muftabad* meant the community built free of charge; *Zoorabad*, by force; *Halabiabad*, those made of tin containers; and *Hasirabad*, of bamboo leaves. The settlements exhibited a great diversity in terms of infrastructure, as well as in socioeconomic and property relations.[17] But most shelters were located in tiny spaces—over 63 percent of squatter households occupied 2.5 square meter single rooms, when the average standard

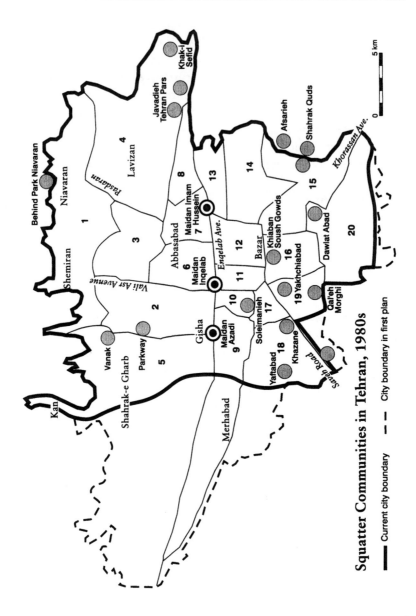

Squatter Communities in Tehran, 1980s

━━━ Current city boundary   – – – City boundary in first plan

Behind Park Niavaran

Niavaran

Shemiran

Kan

Shahrak-e Gharb

Vanak

Parkway

Gisha

Merhabad

Pasdaran

Lavizan

Javadieh
Tehran Pars

Khak-i
Sefid

Afsarieh

Shahrak Quds

Khorassan Ave.

Maidan Imam
7 Hussein

Abbasabad

Maidan
6 Inqelab

Enqelab Ave.

Vali Asr Avenue

Khiaban
Soush Gowds

Bazar

Dawlat Abad

16 Yakhchiabad

19 Yakhchiabad

Qal'eh
Morghi

Saveh Road

Soleimanieh

Maidan
9 Azadi

Yaftabad

Khazane

5 km

0

1
2
3
4
5
8
10
11
12
13
14
15
16
17
18
20

size was to be 18.5 square meters.[18] This contrasts sharply with informal communities developed mainly after the revolution in the villages around Tehran—such as Islamshahr, Akbarabad, and Sultanabad—wherein per capita space was 10.6 square meters, well above those in Nairubi, Rabat, or Tunis, which ranged from 5 to 6.7 square meters.[19] Most of the squatters owned their shacks or tents but had no legal title to land.[20] The size of the communities also varied, ranging from sites with less than 10 units to ones with over 600 households.[21] The gowd residential community, a virtually underground settlement created by the brick-making industry in South Tehran, sheltered 1,040 households and over 46,000 inhabitants;[22] in 1976 Halabiabad housed some 12,000 households and 60,000 residents.[23] And by the late 1970s about 56,000 residents were concentrated in Zoorabad, a hillsite squatter community in Karadj.[24]

By 1980 at least one million poor lived in the slums[25] of Tehran and an estimated 400,000 resided in the squatter communities. This figure excluded spontaneous settlements that lay outside the city limits, such as those around Varamin, Qarchak, and Shahriar. If these were included, the total squatter population of Tehran would probably reach some 500,000, or over 15 percent of the city's population;[26] slum dwellers and squatters together accounted for 35 percent.

Informal settlements in Iran have, in many respects, been different from those in other developing nations. Their total size is smaller, and the quality of housing better. Nondurable shelters—such as shacks, tents, boats, or rooftops homes—constituted only about 1 percent of total housing units; most squatters, particularly those in urban villages, lived in relatively spacious red-brick homes. And finally, although land invasion and forceful seizure did take place, illegal constructions were erected mainly on purchased land.[27]

The vast majority of the urban underclass—squatters, slum dwellers, and unskilled migrant workers—originated from among the impoverished rural masses of various ethnic and linguistic backgrounds who emigrated both before and after the land reform program of 1962. Apart from such "pull factors" as the availability of jobs, higher income, and better living conditions in the cities, especially in Tehran, important "push factors" were also involved. A decline in agriculture, forceful expulsion from land, sale of land, reduced income, and bad living conditions were among the most important of these.[28]

The poor in Tehran came primarily from the Turkish-speaking regions (Azarbaijan, Zanjan, and Hamadan in the northwest and west), the central provinces, and the villages around the capital.[29] After the Second World War Tehran experienced large-scale emigration from Azarbaijan where the insecurity of war and struggles over regional autonomy pushed many rural people out of the area. The immigrants settled in poor districts of South Tehran, notably Javadieh.[30] A survey of Zoorabad (in Karadj) in 1981 showed that some 55 percent of 56,000 residents of this squatter community were Azari speakers from Azarbaijan, Zanjan and Hamadan.[31] The mostly rural origin and ethnic backgrounds among the migrant poor marked their cultural/social segregation from the Westernized urban rich, who stigmatized the poor as *dihaati* (rural/backward). For the disenfranchised, the multiethnic migration created ethnically based neighborhoods that later influenced the cultural evolution and community mobilization of the inhabitants before and after the revolutionary upheaval of 1978–79. Although these ethnically based communities commanded a high degree of internal cohesion and solidarity, they also caused intercommunity conflicts and disunity at times.

Beyond ethnic variation, squatter settlements were also differentiated along the occupational quality and income level of their occupants. By 1979 some communities, such as Zoorabad in Karadj and those urban villages in Ray and Shahriar, were mostly industrial working-class communities: many (about 50 percent in Ray and over 30 percent in Zoorabad) worked in the nearby modern industries, while others were skilled laborers with fairly high job security. In fact, no more than 10 percent of the inhabitants were earning a street subsistence.[32]

These settlements, however, were not typical. Their industrial character was due, principally, to their proximity to the largest industrial sites in the country, located in the south and south east of the capital city, stretching up to Karadj. Both in Tehran and even more in other cities, the squatter poor subsisted chiefly (between 60 and 80 percent of heads of households) by engaging in unskilled construction jobs and various types of insecure casual work. They mostly worked in sweatshops or as street vendors, shoe polishers, car cleaners, lottery-ticket sellers, doormen, waiters, shop assistants, servants, and porters— across the vast underground economy (see table 2.1). Nevertheless, contrary to popular image, "fake, black and unhealthy occupations"

TABLE 2.1

Occupational Structure of Squatters in Selected Settlements
in Iran, based on Case Studies in Various Years

	Bandar Abbas (1972)	Ahwaz (1973)	Naqadeh (1974)	Tabriz (1975)	Zahedan (1978)	Zoorabad* (Karadj) 1979
Unclassified	5.2	8.0	—	6.6	8.0	6.1
Unskilled worker	56.2	43.0	33.1	41.1	43.0	?
Semiskilled worker	7.4	19.0	14.4	20.0	19.0	?
Skilled worker	3.0	11.0	5.8	18.9	11.0	30.0
Street vendors	19.3	9.0	16.1	7.8	9.0	7.9
Low-status employee	6.7	—	11.6	—	—	?
Farmer	—	10.0	—	—	—	?
Craftsmen	2.2	—	19.0	5.5	6.0	?
Total	100.0	100.0	100.0	100.0	100.0	100.0

Source: The Iranian Center for Urban and Architectural Studies, *Hashiyenishini dar Iran*, Report on phase 4, vol. 2, p. 26.
*Deduced from scattered data from the same report.

such as begging, drug-dealing, and prostitution constituted no more than a small fraction of their activities.[33] For instance, a 1971 study of Tehran's several squatter settlements showed that over 80 percent of squatters were involved in unskilled or semiskilled jobs, including construction, street vending, and low-paid government employment. They remained jobless on average between three to five months of the year, while working hours brought to each household (with an average number of 4.6 members) only Rls 4460 (about sixty dollars) a month.[34] Other surveys in the 1970s confirmed the very high job insecurity among the squatter poor. Slum dwellers seemed to have higher incomes and job security.[35] They were also less distant, geographically and socially, from mainstream urban life and were descended from older migrant generations. Many of them had been born in the cities.

These variations notwithstanding, by the late 1970s one could observe a sizable *marginalized* urban underclass, identified by their geographical, social, and to a large extent economic exclusion from the formal mainstream urban life. While the bulk of the new poor preferred the existing conditions of their life to their past,[36] vulnerability in everyday life remained the salient feature of their collective existence—in securing a place to live and a subsistence job, in debt payment and in maintaining their dignity (*abirou*). The identity of this underclass was very much tied to their place of residence. They evolved into a fairly distinct social entity—an identity articulated both by themselves and others.

Slum dwellers carried their identities in the public discourse, not as much with reference to their poverty or work conditions as to their communities, which in the meantime connoted their particular social and economic conditions. Thus *Naziabadi* or *Mardum-i Javadiyeh* described the social identity of the slum dwellers in Naziabad and Javadieh. On the other hand, squatters saw themselves and were chiefly viewed as *zaghehnishinan* or *alounaknishinan* (literally settlers of shacks and shanties) with some regarding them as belonging to a "fourth class."[37] The official language, however, generally referred to them as the *mardum-i hashiyenishin*, residents of city margins. Others looked at the new poor through the eyes of denigration, pity, and poetry. The middle-class use of demeaning words—*amaleh* and *hammal*—stressed the urban poor's degraded status. *Amaleh* generally means "unskilled construction laborer"—incidentally the major occupation among the underclass. Yet its derogatory use presented the poor as a caste, making them conscious of their particular position in relation to others: "My daughter tells me" stated a squatter,

> When I go to school through this long and muddy road, my cloths get all dirty, and I really get embarrassed among my classmates. And the women of this neighborhood are now singled out (*ma'rouf*). When they go shopping in other areas, people look at them with disdain. Their appearance shows that they are poor (*faqir*).[38]

In addition, the image of the new poor has entered the movies, TV programs, and critical literature. Khosrow Golesorkhi's moving recitation, during his court trial, of his poem "Under the Javadiyeh Bridge" expressed a sense of both pity and piety.[39] Short stories by Samad Behrangui[40] and Gholam Hussein Sa'edi[41] focused chiefly on the misery of the underclass and their wretched life. Anomie and rootlessness among urban migrants was a principal theme in Jalal Ale-ahmad's social criticisms.[42] And Sa'edi's "Garbage Place" (*Ashghaldouni*), which became the movie *Dayere-ye Mina*, dealt with the social psychology of the lumpen proletariat whose life, according to Ali Akbar Akbari, did not differ much from that of the "poor petty-bourgeoisie" or the urban underclass.[43] So in this period, although the new poor became a part of the public imagination, the image remained one of powerlessness. It was not until after the Islamic Revolution that the poor were granted an element of agency, when the term *mustaz'afin* began to dominate the public language. The following chapter discusses in detail the complexity of this agency over the course of the Iranian Revolution.

Three

The Disfranchised and the Islamic Revolution:
"Our Revolution and Theirs"

This momentous Islamic Revolution is indebted to the efforts of this class—the class of the deprived, the class of the *gowdnishin*, the shanty dwellers, the class that brought about the victory of the revolution, and yet did not expect any reward.

—Ayatollah Khomeini, in a speech to a group of gowd settlers of South Tehran[1]

Swear to God, this is unfair; we were told: "a revolution has occurred." Then we came to believe that our situation would change and that we would not suffer that much anymore. But the only thing we saw of the revolution was this: one day we heard from the TV that the Shah had gone and Mr. Khomenini had returned! And nothing else.

—A settler of the South Tehran squatter community[2]

The Revolution

On February 11, 1979, Tehran radio announced the victory of the Iranian Revolution with feverish jubilation. A mood of ecstasy overtook the populace, who rushed into the streets en masse. Women milled through the crowd, handing out candies and *sharbat*, sweet drinks. Vehicles sounded their horns in unison, beaming their lights as they drove down the main streets that only days before had witnessed bloody clashes between the protesters and the army. These same streets were now being patrolled by the revolutionary militias, the Pasdaran. For those present, it was a day of incomparable victory.

This victory day was the culmination of more than eighteen months of mass demonstrations, bloody confrontations, massive industrial actions, a general strike, and much political maneuvering.[3] The genesis of the revolution can be traced to the structural changes that had been underway since the 1930s, when the country began to undergo a process of modernization. This process accelerated after the 1953 coup, engineered by the CIA, which toppled nationalist prime minister Muhammad Mosaddeq and reinstated the Shah.

The modernization policy and the economic changes initiated by the state under both Reza Shah (1925–1946) and his son, the late

Shah, resulted in the growth of new social forces—much to the dismay of the traditional social groups. By the 1970s a large and well-to-do modern middle class, a modern youth, women engaged in public activism, an industrial working class, and the new poor—slum-dwellers and squatters—dominated the social scene. With the exception of the latter group, these groups were the beneficiaries of the new economic development; they enjoyed high status and high economic rewards. However, the persistence of the Shah's age-old autocracy prevented their participation in the political process. This angered them. At the same time the old social groups—represented by the traditional bazaaris or merchants, the old urban middle strata, the declining clergy, and those who adhered to Islamic institutions—were also frustrated by the strategy of modernization since it undermined their economic interests and their power bases.

With all the institutional channels closed through repression for the expression of discontent, the populace was increasingly alienated from the state. In the meantime, corruption, inefficiency, a sense of injustice, and a feeling of cultural outrage marked the social psychology of many Iranians. During the tense years of the 1970s, therefore, at the height of the Shah's authoritarian rule and during a period of remarkable economic growth, many people (except perhaps the upper class and the landed peasantry) seemed dissatisfied, albeit for different reasons. But all were united in blaming the Shah and his western allies, especially the U.S., for that state of affairs. It is therefore not surprising that the language of dissent and protest was largely antimonarchy, antiimperialist, Third Worldist, and even nationalist, turning in the end into a religious discourse.

The opportunity for popular mobilization arrived with what we used to call the "Carterite breeze" (*nasseem-e Carteri*). President Carter's human rights policy in the late 1970s force the Shah to offer a political space for a limited degree of expression. This expression built up cumulatively and in the course of less than two years swept aside the monarchy. It all began with a limited relaxation of censorship, which allowed some literary/intellectual activities (in the Goethe Institute and the universities in Tehran) and public gatherings of Islamists (in Oqba Mosque). It continued with distribution by the intellectuals and liberal politicians of openly critical letters to high-level officials. While this was all going on, an insulting article against Ayatollah Khomeini in a daily paper, *Ettilaat*, triggered a demonstration in the shrine city of Qum that left some demonstrators killed. To commemorate this, a large-scale demonstration took place in the Azeri city of Tabriz in the north. This marked the beginning of a chain of events that formed a nationwide revolutionary movement in which diverse segments of the population—modern and traditional, religious and secular, men and women—participated in massive numbers, and in which the ulama, the Shi'i clergy, assumed its leadership.

Over twenty-five years of the Shah's autocracy since the 1953 coup had removed or destroyed almost all the effective secular political and civil organizations. The coup crushed both the nationalist and communist movements; trade unions were infiltrated by the secret police (SAVAK); publications were strictly censored; and hardly any effective NGOs remained.[4] The main organized political dissent came from the underground guerrilla organizations, the Marxist Fedaian and the radical Islamic Mujahedin, whose activities were limited to isolated armed operations.[5] Student activism also remained restricted either to campus politics inside the country or to actions carried out by Iranian students abroad. In short, the secular groups, while badly dissatisfied, were organizationally decapitated.

Unlike the secular forces, however, the clergy had the comparative advantage of possessing invaluable institutional capacity; this included its own hierarchical order—over ten thousand mosques, *husseiniyeh*s, *huwzeh*s, and associations, which acted as a vital means of communication among the revolutionary contenders. Young Islamists, both boys and girls as well as young clergymen, linked the institution of the ulama to the people. A hierarchical order facilitated unified decision-making and a systematic flow of order and information; in the mosques higher-level decisions were disseminated to both the activists and the general public. In short, this institutional capacity, in addition the remarkable ambiguity of the clergy's message, ensured the ulama's leadership.

Given the insecurity, poverty, inequality, and high inflation characteristic of the poor communities, the availability of a mobilizing force of revolutionary agitators was sufficient for many observers to assume the active participation of the disenfranchised in the Islamic Revolution. The portrayal of the revolution by new Islamic leaders as the *inqilab-i mustaz'afin*, the revolution of the downtrodden, signified the supposed centrality of the underclass to the revolutionary process. The Islamic leaders derived their own legitimacy and that of the revolution by propounding this image of participation by the *mustaz'afin* and the *koukhnishinan*.

Politicians apart, many scholars have also come to similar conclusions. Some have pointed to dislocated rural migrants as the fundamental social basis of the Islamic Revolution.[6] Others have written that the miserable living conditions, violent behavior, and the déclassé character of the lumpen proletariat made them fit to support the Khomeini-type revolution.[7] Many writers have stressed the institution of *hey'at*, ethnically based and ad hoc Islamic sermons, as the mechanism through which the poor were mobilized by the clergy.[8]

What all these conclusions imply is a functional, structural, and even essential affinity between the poor and political Islam. Lacking adequate empirical backing, they are largely theoretical constructs based upon either an ideology or a deduction whereby the economic and social position of a group a priori determines its political behavior. These authors also share an assumption that privileges generalized/global or political struggles over local mobilization.

By focusing on the city of Tehran, I argue here that the urban poor were not revolutionary in the conventional sense of wanting to transform the existing macro power structure. Indeed the disfranchised remained on the margins of the revolutionary campaign nearly until the end. Yet, I will suggest, they were not passive. Rather, the poor were involved in a parallel struggle to bring about change in their own lives and communities. They were engaged in the kind of struggles— quiet encroachment at the localities—that, unlike that of the revolution, seemed to them both meaningful and manageable.

The Poor and the Revolution

Reviewing the major daily paper reports (*Kayhan, Ettilaat,* and *Ayandegan*) during 1977 and 1978, one encounters detailed accounts of daily demonstrations, strikes, and riots in various cities and provinces, sometimes with unusually detailed descriptions of the number of participants, slogans voiced, leaders, speeches delivered, resolutions read, as well as the nature and outcome of the events. They report the procession of various members of the population: teachers, students, workers, lawyers, nurses, the clergy, women, guilds, and unions, with each group and institution carrying its own symbols. Among these participants one hardly comes across squatter groups or, for instance, men of Khak-i Sefid. My interviews with a number of young middle-class participants in the street demonstrations and riots confirm this observation. Janet Bauer, an American anthropologist who carried out fieldwork among the poor communities of South Tehran and a number of rural communities for the eighteen months just before the revolution (June 1977 through late 1978), also observed that "up through the end of 1978, relatively few women (or men) from the lowest income neighborhoods of Tehran were actively participating in street events."[9] In addition, out of a sample of 646 people killed in Tehran in the street events during the revolution (from August 23, 1977 to February 19, 1978) only 9 or just over 1 percent came from the shantytowns.[10] The largest proportions were among artisans and shopkeepers(189), students (149), factory and workshop workers (96), and state employees (70).

Why were the poor, especially the squatter settlers, generally aloof from the revolutionary struggles?

Poverty, inequality, and oppression do not by themselves induce antistate political action. The crucial questions are: how do the poor perceive their poverty, oppression, and day-to-day troubles? Who do they blame? What mechanisms and strategies, if any, do they devise or resort to to tackle those problems? Finally, to what extent are external political forces interested and able to "activate" the poor by offering a different analysis and treatment of their problems?

The members of the underclass in Tehran clearly viewed themselves as poor, unfortunate, afflicted, and even wretched—the terms used were "*faqir va bichareha*"(the destitute), "*badbakhtha*" (the unfortunate), and "*tabaqeh-ye se'iiha*" (third-class people). They were aware of the differences between their lives and those of the rich.[11] Yet it is not clear whom they blamed for their misfortune. At times they attributed their problems to "their fate, destiny, and God's will." Nevertheless, in general they expected the "government," perhaps as a great patron, to ameliorate their difficulties.[12] As for the Shah, if anything they seemed to view the monarch as outside the circle of their day-to-day troubles.

In some ways the migrant poor of the 1970s in Iran (especially those in Tehran) are reminiscent of eighteenth-century mobs in the preindustrial cities of southern Europe such as Rome, Palermo, or Istanbul.[13] Like them, the migrant poor seemed to regard the ruler, in their case the Shah, as the great patron, the provider of livelihood, and the source of justice: they both admired him and feared his power. It was to this ultimate arbitrator that the poor turned in times of acute crises. "To his excellency, the crowned father of the nation, Shahanshah Aryamehr!" pleaded a squatter who had lost his home to demolition agents in 1977: "I have borrowed 100,000 tumans to build my home. Now, the agents have demolished it. Who should I go for compensation? I am hungry and wretched. I always pray and will pray for your well-being. I beg Your Excellency to consider my case.[14]

There were some who, even after the downfall of the Shah, believed that "the country needs a *taaj-o-takht*"[15] and that without its monarch it could not continue to function.[16] Although in the perception of the poor it was clear that the local officials, the municipality agents, the bureaucrats, and the other rich sucked the blood of the poor, they thought the Shah probably did not know what was done in his name. "The Shah himself does not mind, and he does not know about this problem [of the municipality demolishing their homes]. It is these bullies and bureaucrats who destroy our homes." "The one who is sitting at the top [the Shah] does not want to see people's homes get ruined. He doesn't know. It is the [Municipality] agents who destroy homes."[17]

Far from tactical statements to gain "political insurance," these appeals reflected the urban underclass's mythology about their monarch.[18] This mythology may perhaps be traced back to their rural communities, where the tradition of patronage was so widely practiced among the peasants and the rural poor. I can recall how we, the residents of a village in the Central Province, constructed a transcendental image of the Shah. We always wondered, for instance, up to what grade the Shah had studied if the maximum were twelve. Our answers varied from twenty to one hundred! We also imagined what he ate: always roast turkey? With what? About this, we were quite sure: it must have been with golden forks. When transistor radios came to the village, they brought his mythical qualities much closer to home. Folk tales about the power and the generosity of kings abounded. Even the shaikh of the village advanced stories of this nature. He had large portraits of the royal family on his wall. The deeds and discourse in the village conveyed a sense of sympathy, admiration, and yet apprehension.

As these personal stories illustrate, the poor's image of themselves and the Shah contrasted sharply with those of the revolutionaries (the participants and the agitators alike) who seemed to charge the state and its head with all the country's social, economic, and political shortcomings. From these groups the disenfranchised were largely marginalized. They were located on the periphery of the city's political economy in many respects.

Among the squatters, the number of the employees working in large-scale formal enterprises was minimal (see chapter 2). In this sense the composition of the squatters in Iran was quite different from that of Turkey, Egypt, or most of Latin America, where large numbers of the middle and working classes have been forced to reside in informal settlements and have brought outside experiences with them into the shantytowns.[19] In Tehran the poor communities were located on the fringes of the city or in the enclosed spots within it, inhibiting inhabitants' contact with the city's mainstream life. For instance, only about 40 percent of the men (and just 4.5 percent of women) of a poor district in South Tehran traveled more than sixty minutes from their homes daily.[20] Although a few settlements spread in wealthier areas (like Shahabad community near Niavaran Palace) their number was very insignificant.[21] Their access to the print media was also limited, as most of the heads of households in these communities were illiterate.[22]

The urban poor also lacked meaningful formal associations of their own that could act as political intermediaries between them and the national elites. There was no equivalent to the Latin American popular organizations in the Iranian shantytowns. Although a kind of neighborhood association (*anjuman-i mahalli*) did exist, they were state-sponsored and their leaders were in alliance more with the local bureaucracy than with their "constituencies." There is no evidence to suggest that these state-sponsored associations were used by the poor to serve their own interests as, for example, many state-run unions were converted to serve the factory workers.[23]

This is not to suggest that the poor in Iran were uninterested in collective activities. Rather, important political factors were involved in their nonorganization. Formal associations between the poor and national movements develop normally in conditions where (as, for instance, in India, Turkey and some Latin American countries) the existence of representative democracy allows a relatively genuine rivalry between political parties. To secure the votes of the large popular sector, parties inevitably attempt to mobilize the poor, which in the end makes the poor conscious of their power and their political leverage at the national level.[24] Even illegal movements, such as Sendero Luminoso movement in Peru, mobilize the poor in the shantytowns in exchange for securing the latter's political support.[25] In addition, organized industrial workers, who make up a large segment of the squatters in Latin America, often play a significant mobilizing role by bringing their experience of collective action from the factories into the shantytowns.

In the Iran of the 1970s these conditions were largely absent. The political dictatorship of the Shah had made genuine party rivalries impossible, let alone the possibility of bargaining for the electoral support of the poor. Industrial workers did not constitute a significant portion of the squatter population, although they do seem to have had a significant presence in the inner-city slums.[26] Moreover, the industrial workers themselves were largely deprived of independent labor organizations. The independent trade union movement had been suppressed since the coup of 1953[27] and the official factory unions had been infiltrated by the secret police, leaving little room for genuine union activity and collective action.[28] These circumstances prevented the poor—living in the slums or the squatter settlements— from setting up voluntary and formal associations in their neighborhoods.

In practice, traditional networks in the form of kinship, ethnic relations, and self-help relations took the place of formal community organizations. To tackle their daily problems, the poor relied on their relatives, friends, and fellow villagers. They assisted each other in providing loans, labor, and advice, and in taking care of children, the unemployed, and the elderly. This is not to say that conflict was not endemic to life in poor communities. Daily disputes over children, gang-like groups (laats), ethnic differences, competition over scarce resources such as land, water, or other resources characterized the life of the poor.[29] Nevertheless, the poor did exhibit a strong sense of unity and coordination when their common channels of survival, especially their dwellings, were put in danger.[30]

Community rituals were crucial in bringing the poor together. Weddings, funerals, Nowrooz (the Iranian new year), and religious commemorations provided fertile grounds for cooperation and networking. Islamic institutions were particularly significant. The months of Ramadan and Muharram[31] were the time of intensive religious activities. All members of the communities—men, women and children—would attend the mosques, husseiniyehs or hey'ats.[32] These establishments, places of religious practice, also served as sites of cultural activities, friendly association, leisure, and deliberation over matters of common interest.

It is commonly assumed that these institutions were utilized by the clergy to mobilize the poor in the anti-Shah campaign during the Iranian revolution of 1979.[33] There is, however, no solid evidence of this. Indeed, both secular (left or liberal) and Islamic agitators (the antiregime clergy) largely ignored the underclass, concentrating instead on the politico-intellectual training of young educated groups, chiefly students. In eighty-eight sermons, messages, and letters, in the fifteen years prior to the revolution, Ayatollah Khomeini made only eight passing references to lower-class people, compared with fifty references to educated youths, students, and universities.[34] In turn, Ayatollah Mutahhari's elitist approach is clear through his warnings about *avaam-zadegui* or populism;[35] and for Ali Shariati, it was intellectuals, not the popular masses, that constituted the revolutionary force.[36] Interestingly the term "*mustaz'afin*" entered Khomeini's discourse only during the height of the revolution (Aban 1357), when he used it merely to repudiate the Communists[37] and attempted to offer an alternative (Islamic) conceptualization of the poor. Indeed, the clergy directed its attention to the *mustaz'afin*, or the lower classes, predominantly *after* the revolution. They did so, first, because the lower classes were seen as a solid social basis for the new regime; second, because lower-class radicalism in the postrevolution forced the clergy to adopt a radical language; and third, because the clergy's emphasis on *mustaz'afin* could disarm the left's proletarian discourse after the revolution.

But during and before the revolution the activities of both leftist and religious militants were limited to casual agitation among the squatters during the government crackdown on illegal settlements, such as the Fedaian Guerrilla Organization's bombing of the municipality building of Rey in 1977 to exhibit its solidarity with poor squatters.[38]

Religious sermons (*rowze-khani*), preaching, and prayers certainly did exist in underclass neighborhoods. I myself was an active participant in these activities throughout my adolescent years. But they focused almost exclusively on religious injunctions and stories, Islamic behavior, purity, and the like. It was perhaps true that "nothing brings us together more than the love for Imam Hussein," as a young squatter proudly stated. These "*hey'at*s have a positive role in uniting us and keeping us informed about each other." But the occasions did not go, as he attested, beyond "socializing" and simply "sacrificing Imam Hussein and weeping [for his dead body]."[39]

For the marginal poor, the revolution remained by and large a practice whose slogans, aims, and ideals appeared distant and detached from their daily concerns and comprehension. They were concerned primarily with those matters that were essential to maintaining their daily survival. They needed concrete and immediate solutions to their problems. These were bound to be limited to their localities.

Until the last phase of the revolution, the poor in general seemed for the most part silent, on the fringe of events. They were not, however, passive. Indeed, they were involved in a parallel struggle to bring about change in their own lives and communities. The disenfranchised were engaged in the kind of struggles that, unlike the revolution, seemed both meaningful and manageable, as well as in bringing about a kind of change no less significant than the one the Islamic Revolution was to bring about.

The Parallel Struggles

> We have been here for a long time now, since everything in the village was destroyed, and our house was demolished. Even in those days we hardly had a decent house in the village. But whatever happened, we managed somehow. That village, called Nowrouz, had a little orchard in it. One day my husband, who was forty then, came home and said: "Pack up! we are going to Tehran." And we came. In those days, no one was living in the Halabiabad. There was not even such a place as Halabiabad at all. But when we came, we searched all over the garbage and mud to look for tins and tin plates. [We collected them] then we put them on the top of each other, added some mud in between. And began to live in them. That was the first day. But my husband was jobless. So he looked for a job, for anything to live by. One day he worked as an *amaleh* [unskilled construction laborer], another day *hammali* [working as a porter], then garbage collecting, and selling *labou* [cooked sugar beets]. But he almost always remained unemployed. We managed somehow until our children grew up.[40]

Fundamentally, it is the will to survive and a strong resilience in the face of hardship that motivates the poor to change the pattern of their lives. By doing so, they also change the social environment in which they live and hence the nature of politics. It is true that often, though not always, they proceed individually and quietly, but these individual and quiet actions entail collective and noisy consequences, involving issues of power and politics.

Khaleh Fatimeh, one of the founders of the Halabiabad squatter settlement in South Tehran, is one such actor. The exigency of her (and her husband's) life and their desire to survive the hardship caused them to venture on a long journey. They packed up, taking a chance and settling in a remote and mysterious land where they hoped to begin a new and better life. To escape from the agony of high rent, bills, formal institutions, and the insecurity of dealing with urbanites, they "naturally" set up their own dwelling in the cheap, common, state land outside the city boundaries. They began a new life, raising chickens, goats, and children.

As protagonists, however, they were not alone. Others gradually joined them as the years passed. Many came directly from villages or small towns; some emerged from the nearby overcrowded slums, escaping the hardships associated with life there. By 1976, 12,000 households were living with Khaleh Fatimeh in the settlement they named Halabiabad. The settlers gradually began to demand security of tenure, improvement of dwelling units, and services ranging from electricity, running water, and sewer systems to social needs such as health centers and transportation.[41] When their demands fell on deaf ears, they resorted to quiet direct action. They stole electricity from the nearby power poles and obtained water illegally and ingeniously from the main water pipes in the streets; they extended their private domain into the public space of the alleyways. They made their living by engaging in diverse activities, chiefly in the unauthorized and underground economy. This kind of work was carried out by and large in the social and physical space of the street corner, the kiosk, *basaat*, or behind wagons and hand trucks. For security, they began to establish community networks, informal associations, and cultural/religious groupings to compensate for their anomie and uprootedness. With the incremental agglomeration of people organized along similar lines, the sector of spontaneous habitation was complete.

This quiet encroachment process represents the kind of significant sociospatial change engendered by people such as Khaleh Fatimeh. But they hardly considered this change and the activities associated with it as political; they saw them simply as natural ways to survive and improve. Nevertheless, the political outcome of this change followed before long. It was manifested in the contestation between the poor, whose strategies for survival required a good degree of autonomy in the practice of everyday life, and the modern state, which took for granted its power to maintain order and regulate space, time, work, community life, and leisure. This active or participative use of public space, embodied in the poor's initiative in spontaneously taking over and constructing land/space, came into sharp conflict with state control of order. The state's solution was to attempt to eradicate these informal communities. On the other hand, the tendency of the poor to practice a cultural autonomy (with respect to dwellings, community, and work) flew in the face of the state's intervention in people's ways of life.

By the summer and autumn of 1977 the squatter areas had emerged as battle grounds. The municipality's demolition squads, escorted by hundreds of paramilitary soldiers, as well as dozens of bulldozers, trucks, and military jeeps, raided the settlements to destroy illegal dwellings and to stop their further expansion.

The policy of violent eradication was not new. Much earlier, in 1953, the state had resorted to violent action in evicting the migrant poor from the cavelike settlements in South Tehran. The new wave of action against illegal housing started in 1974 and culminated in 1977. The major targets included those communities located in east Tehran (Javadiyeh in Tehranpars, Majidiyeh, and Shemiran-nou in Narmak), and in the southern and southeastern peripheries (in Afsariyeh, Mushiriyeh, Kavousiyeh, Soleimaniyeh, Mesgarabad, Dowlatabad, Aliabad, Cheshmeh-ali, and many more). Similar operations, although on a smaller scale, were also undertaken in other cities including Shiraz, Zanjan, Ghazvin, and Karadj.

The assaults were normally carried out at night, when collective resistance against demolition was very difficult—when the residents were either in bed or away from their shelters. The municipal agents would ask people to come out of their dwellings and the bulldozers would wreck the shacks and shanties, leaving behind the rubble of tin plates, car tires, and mud bricks. "Well, yes," observed a resident of Javadieh in Tehran Pars,

when we got out of the house that night, I saw something that I hope nobody will ever see again. The whole neighborhood had been surrounded by the soldiers who had sneaked in quietly and stopped anyone from turning a light on. . . . Yes, they had brought four bulldozers. They forced everybody out of their homes, and then started to demolish them. In one house, a whole family including children went up on the roof top, and said "we won't come out." But the agents destroyed the house. The man fell and the house collapsed on him. And the woman, as soon as she saw this, fainted and dropped her child from her hands.[42]

According to a series of reports based upon over one hundred observations and interviews with squatters, hundreds of homes were demolished in Tehran in the autumn of 1977 alone. This involved at least thirteen bloody clashes between the squatters and the government forces, leaving a dozen dead.[43]

At times the crowd, bewildered and outraged, remained shocked and helpless. At other times, confronted with the demolition agents, they resorted to every method possible to protect their homes. The squatters attempted to talk the agents out of their plans, pleaded with them, and argued about the immorality of their destructive acts. Women sought sanctuary in their homes with their children and a copy of Quran, making their shelter a kind of a sacred place, a shrine that could not be demolished. A few, probably *bisaz-o-befroush* (land developers) offered bribes. Many hoisted the Iranian flags and hung portraits of the monarch on their walls, chanting "Long Live the Shah, Long Live the Shah!"

Few of these scattered efforts managed to save homes. The pervasiveness and frequency of the attacks did not leave much doubt among the squatters that "tomorrow might be our turn." The necessity of collective resistance was genuinely felt. "We are not united; we ourselves are responsible for whatever ills happening to us, because we don't stick together"[44] echoed the mood of the crowd. Yet in the end they did demonstrate group solidarity. Collective resistance included both spontaneous and planned crowd action.

During or following many attacks, the indignant crowd responded with rage and fury, resorting to clubs, stones, shovels, and whatever was at hand. On many occasions they ransacked municipality offices, set government cars on fire, and beat up and, on a few occasions, even killed the demolition squad agents. During the autumn of 1977 at least thirteen major confrontations were reported. These crowd actions did succeed in repelling a number of raids.

You see they [the demolition squad] wouldn't dare come during the day. They did come once, but on that occasion people got together and beat them all up. They all ran away, but the head of the *shahrdari* [the district municipality] could not. The crowd got him and beat him with stones and clubs so much that he was torn apart. Then we put him into a cemetery. The crowd smashed their cars. They also set a couple of them [the cars] on fire. And now they [the squatters] have prepared themselves with knives, clubs, shovels and pickaxes. They are on guard every night in case the agents come to raid again.[45]

While some vigilante groups were formed to defend the settlements, diplomatic activities were also initiated to negotiate with the authorities to legally halt the demolition. On several occasions clusters of locals, among them women and children, assembled in the streets to discuss strategies. Most deliberations seemed rather disorderly, with the participants seldom coming to an agreement. A few concrete initiatives, nevertheless, were taken. Small crowds (of two hundred or so people) were organized and dispatched with women in the forefront to negotiate or appeal with the authorities in the local municipality, local council, Rastakhiz Party, and the royal palace. But each time they were driven away, often with false promises. The squatters were thus forced to rely primarily on their own defense initiatives and on a war of attrition.

Following each demolition and the departure of the government agents, the squatters would reappear on the ruins of their wrecked shelters and try once again to put together the rubble to resurrect their homes. "If they demolish even for 50 times, we will rebuild again," said a shantytown dweller.[46] The lack of an alternative solution, together with a sense of justice and a vague dream of victory in the long run, allowed the poor to carry on their resistance. "Of course not, they can't simply kill all of us!," a squatter stated assuringly, "They [the government] have lifted restriction [on home building] in other areas, they will eventually do the same in here too."[47] And eventually they did.

Facing a crisis of such proportion—daily clashes in the shantytowns followed by revolutionary riots in the streets of central Tehran—successive cabinets acted with desperation and confusion, moving from one decision to the next. Their response to the crisis varied according to the political mood of the day, ranging from tenancy reform to the construction of low-income housing and, finally, tolerance of spontaneous settlements. But each and every policy offered the poor new opportunities and leverage to keep their pressure mounting.

The Poor, the State, and the Revolution

Aware of the acute problems of high rent, the high cost of land, and the shortage of housing, the government of Jamshid Amuzgar, in the midst of shantytown clashes in October 1977, began to force owners of vacant apartments to rent out some 24,000 units in Tehran. About 70,000 tenants sent applications, 55,000 of them came from poor families, migrant workers and university students; all of these applicants had requested single rooms. The monthly rent was set between 8 percent to 12 percent of the price of the homes.

By summer 1978 it had become clear that practical difficulties doomed the policy to failure. For instance, while the municipality was authorized to rent out an entire home to a tenant, it could not rent individual rooms within a given house. So the hopes of low-income families who could afford to rent single or double rooms were dashed. The project did not bring many tangible results for middle-class home-seekers either. In almost all cases, the landlords refused to comply with the new regulations. Only seventy-two such homes were rented out in the course of one year[48]. Some landlords proceeded to place a few pieces of furniture in the vacant flats, pretending their apartments were already occupied. In the end both landlords and tenants remained dissatisfied.

Following the fall of the Amuzgar government on August 27, 1978, Manucher Azmoun, a cabinet minister under Prime Minister Ja'far Sharif-Imami, unveiled a new plan to build "inexpensive housing units" for "the masses of the people." Some of these were to be located in the low-income vicinities of industrial plants near Tehran.[49] This hardly seemed a practical policy, given the bureaucratic bottlenecks and the urgency of the situation. Thus, on September 11, 1978 (Shahrivar 20, 1357), three days after the "black Friday" massacre, when scores of demonstrators were killed in lower-class neighborhoods in defiance of martial law, the government submitted to the strategy that the poor themselves were already pursuing.[50] For the first time, the state recognized the legalization and consolidation of squatter communities.

The policy began gradually, each step determined by the political exigency of the day. During September and October 1978, for example, it was decided that squatter settlements would receive electricity. Some 35,000 squatter families submitted applications to the municipality in response to the government's decision.[51] The mayor of Tehran, Shahrestani, sought for the first time the "participation of the people in the planning of the city."[52] In a dramatic policy reversal, Azmoun announced that the concept of *kharej-i mahdudeh* (literally outside city boundary)[53] had "caused inflation in housing and rent, a serious hardship for the people." The government thus officially endorsed home construction beyond the municipality limits. An important condition attached to the plan, however, was that these areas were not to be entitled to basic urban services.[54] Even this condition was dropped within a few days. Thus, on September 26, 1978, the government authorized construction of homes within the new and enlarged (by 500 hectares) city limits of 250 kilometers, along with a pledge to provide the squatters with piped water and electricity.[55]

The policy in itself was a radical concession. Thanks to their resistance and to the broader revolutionary protests, the underclass had won a long battle. However, these concessions did not tame the mobilization of the underclass. Far from it, they further legitimized their street politics. Land occupation continued, independent from both government initiatives and the leadership of the revolution.

Earlier troubles in the shantytowns in the summer of 1977 had produced the Shah's decree that the demolition of shantytowns and illegally built homes be discontinued; this in turn led the government, in October 1977, to lift restrictions on squatting in sixteen districts in the south, southeast, and Shahr-e Rey, although it continued to stop squatting in the remaining restricted zones. Squatters in such southern and southeastern areas as Hashimabad, Nazarabad, Kouy-i Deylaman, Zahirabad, Afsariyeh, Homayounshahr, Qal'eh Morghi, Yakhchiabad, and others were legally allowed to maintain or further construct dwellings.[56] However, red tape delayed the process of obtaining building permits for which the squatters were hardly inclined to wait. The mere fact of legal authorization legitimized further land takeovers. Illegal housing mushroomed not only in the newly permitted zones but also beyond them. Some squatters could not distinguish between the authorized and restricted zones and hence went ahead, taking over plots; others, among them many affluent opportunist developers (*bisaz-o-befroush*), simply ignored the new rules. When confronted with the demolition squads, almost all referred to the royal decree to justify their claims.[57]

With the escalation of riots and demonstrations, the attention of the security forces was diverted from the shantytowns. Thus even when the politicians were enacting legislation to end intervention on building, the underclass poor were busy reclaiming hundreds of acres of land in the vicinity of the city. In South Tehran, during October and

November 1978 (Aban 1357), scores of slum dwellers from Darvazehghar, Khazane-ye Farahabad, Khaniabad, Naziabad and elsewhere took over a plot of roughly one hundred acres. The news spread, bringing more people onto the scene. "Everybody was looking for a piece of land."[58] They divided the plots by drawing lines with white chalk powder, leaving no room for streets or alleyways. When allocation was complete, each remained responsible for his own plot. They made sure to leave someone on guard on the land, except at night when martial law forced them to stay indoors. A large number installed national flags on the lots to discourage attacks by government forces. To offset the common threat, they made sure to act collectively in order to maintain their hold over the land.[59] Similar actions continued in other parts of the capital city and in various other towns until the collapse of the Shah's regime, which triggered yet a new squatters' movement with a larger scale and novel features.

Mobilization in the Popular Neighborhoods

It was not until toward the end of the Shah's regime in December 1978 that youths brought the concrete experience of the revolution home into the underclass neighborhoods. The community-based organizations of the Islamic Consumer Cooperatives and Neighborhood Councils served as the most effective link between the revolutionaries and the underclass communities.

The condition of dual power during the last phase of the revolution, December 1978 to January 1979, characterized the eroding power of the ancien régime and the mounting authority of the opposition. Demonstrations of millions of people during the holy month of Muharram, on December 10 and 11, in the midst of the military rule, underscored the regime's vulnerability to the revolutionary movement. The collapse of the military cabinet of Azhaari, the coming to office of Bakhtiar, and the return of Ayatollah Khomeini from exile in Paris created favorable conditions for the transfer of power.

At this stage, the old administrative and decision-making centers in the cities were relinquishing their power, and new organs of authority were emerging. In most urban areas, police authority collapsed, the old city councils gave up authority, and the municipalities ceased functioning. As a consequence, various revolutionary committees sprang up to fill the vacuum. Militant youths took control of various provincial towns and cities in Rezaieh, Shahpour, Ardabil, Maragheh, and

Ajabshir in Azarbaijan Province, as they did in the cities of Ramsar and Langroud in Gilan Province.

Setting up committees in different districts and neighborhoods, bands of militant youth mobilized to foil counterrevolutionary attacks on properties and public amenities by regime thugs. The committees were, in the meantime, involved in certain police functions: maintaining order, administering traffic, welfare activities, food distribution, petroleum rationing, and street sanitation.[60] "In Langroud [a Caspian Sea town]," a daily paper in Tehran reported, "the police have withdrawn. They no longer show up in the streets. The town is now controlled by the people. Every night some two thousand volunteers are guarding the city. [To coordinate their activities], youths have devised secret codes in each district."[61] This situation lasted until the aftermath of the insurrection on February 10 and 11, 1979.

Islamic Consumer Cooperatives

From December through January, the distribution of food was disrupted in the midst of the cold Tehran winter. The disruption was caused partially by the general disorder in the national distribution system that had resulted from the general strikes and governmental dysfunction. It was also due to the profiteering activities of some businessmen who indulged in hoarding. Similar practices by well-off but nervous families contributed to the problem. As the leader of the Revolution, Ayatollah Khomeini had called upon the business community to be fair, but his appeal fell on deaf ears.

The urban poor were immediately affected by the maldistribution. In order to relieve hardship and to possibly neutralize the poor at this late stage, Islamic Consumer Cooperatives were set up. They aimed, in effect, at forcing down price rises by a policy of dumping, providing the needy with basic materials including food, warm clothing, and the like.[62] Initially some twenty-five cooperatives started operating in the poor southern neighborhoods of Tehran, such as Bab-i Homayoun, Naziabad, Khazaneh, Maidan-i Khorasan, and Shadshahr in early January 1978.[63] At the beginning the cooperatives were mobile stores on the back of trucks driving through the poor settlements; later they developed into more stationary shops and large outlets.

The founders of the cooperatives, encouraged by the clergy, were philanthropists from diverse urban backgrounds, ranging from mechanics, shoe-makers, and drivers to fruit sellers, government employees, and students.[64] A manager of a bookstore, for instance, filled his bookcases with basic food supplies for sale at low prices. Bazaar merchants contributed to the cooperatives by extending credit or providing certain scarce commodities, such as fuel. While the initial capital for the cooperatives came mainly from the affluent middle classes, the labor power and executive elements were drawn largely from the popular neighborhoods themselves, predominantly from enthusiastic youth groups. These youths volunteered to sell merchandise, supplying their fellow customers with plastic bags and carton boxes. They were also responsible for transporting commodities from wholesale markets to cooperative stores.[65] Often the volunteers provided the coops with "shelves, scales and weighing devices, and even refrigerators. They constantly keep in touch with their relatives and acquaintances asking them to offer the cooperatives with short-supplied food stuff."[66]

A Coordinating Committee of the Consumer Cooperatives was set up in order to monitor the activities of the local coops throughout the city. It attempted to organize the supply of scarce commodities to individual coops. Cooperatives of this sort subsequently expanded into provincial towns throughout the country.

The ancien régime's reaction to the alternative supply systems was first apprehension and then defeat. The regime was witnessing the birth of a new civil order over which it had no control. Far from being able to appropriate or incorporate it, the regime simply resorted to the tactic of disruption. Security forces ransacked scores of cooperatives in Tehran and other cities; they set many coops on fire and detained volunteers[67]. Immediately following each attack, however, the cooperatives reorganized their operations and began work. They continued to function until the fall of the Shah. Following a brief halt after the revolution, they resumed work, albeit with a different form and structure (see chapter 5).

The Neighborhood Councils (*Shuraha-ye Mahallat*)

The Neighborhood Councils (NCs) represented neighborhood-based groups informally organized to alleviate the daily needs of the local people by mobilizing them. They were established to respond to the economic and civic exigencies brought about by this phase of the revolution. NCs differed from the *Komitehs*. The latter were initiated by local youths primarily to maintain public order and withstand counterrevolutionary sabotage. After the revolution they were incorporated into the state as part of the urban security forces functioning alongside the old police institution.

In early January 1979 NCs were set up in a number of popular districts in Tehran and in provincial cities. They also emerged in order to contain the counterrevolutionary activities of agents of the incumbent government. The regime's thugs began to attack not only institutions such as the Islamic Consumer Cooperatives but also public properties, in order to falsely represent the revolutionaries as violent. In response, groups of militant youth, often under the direction of a local leader or clergyman, were organized in the neighborhoods to deal with such sabotage. In the popular districts, however, the most pressing issue was the shortage of fuel caused by strikes, maldistribution, and possibly by sabotage. Beyond the issue of fuel, the NCs concerned themselves also with a number of other areas of civil life, including the supply and distribution of daily necessities, medical care, defense, and political work.

The NCs mobilized young people in each locality to supply and distribute the basic and daily needs of each neighborhood. They delivered fuel, fresh bread, and foodstuffs to the doorsteps of the inhabitants who otherwise had to line up in front of the stores for hours. A large amount of these supplies was offered free of charge to the very poor, the elderly, and the sick.[68] The initiative began in Yakhchiabad, a popular neighborhood in South Tehran, where over 3,240 liters of heating and cooking fuel were distributed. The NCs also monitored local stores to prevent maldistribution (hoarding or favoritism) and overpricing. In some settlements, women in particular were in charge of inspecting the price tags of the merchandise and reporting any misconduct, for which the culprit was punished by public denunciation and boycott.

Some NCs supervised areas as large as Narmak, in east Tehran. The council divided the area into several administrative districts. In every district the council issued households with special coupons for fuel, petroleum, and chalk coal, to make sure the locals obtained their fair share.[69] Maintenance and development of the neighborhoods also came under the supervision of the NCs. They repaired local water pipes, remedied power outages, and dug deep wells to supply water to the local bakeries, public baths, and households in communities such as Afsariyeh in South Tehran where running water was lacking.

Although the Iranian Revolution was comparatively short and peaceful, violence did occur in certain instances. To alleviate the conditions of the injured, a number of *shura*s attempted to organize medical teams with the cooperation of physicians and nurses within these urban communities. The teams were to train local volunteers in first aid and assist the inhabitants with their regular medical needs. Women were particularly instrumental in these efforts. The NCs mobilized the youth sending them door to door to collect sheets, blankets, and medicine to be used in the hospitals to care for the injured. They also made special efforts to ensure that medical doctors' automobiles as well as garbage trucks received adequate petrol.[70]

Defense seemed to be on the agenda of most of the Neighborhood Councils. The NCs needed to encourage the volunteers in each locality to form vigilante groups to maintain order where the police system had virtually collapsed. At the same time they organized political discussion meetings, disseminated news (particularly the number of the "martyrs"), distributed leaflets, and circulated the tapes of the revolutionary leaders.

It was concrete local measures of this nature, generated by these popular organizations and administered in a decentralized and comprehensible manner, and not simply the *hey'at*s (ad hoc religious sermons), which brought the experience of the *inqilab* (revolution) into the communities of the underclass.

Structurally, the NCs represented loose and informal associations with limited division of labor, where leaders were recognized and respected rather than formally elected. Attempts were underway, however, to establish a more solid structure in the councils, by forming executive committees which had decision-making power. The executive committees were to identify the daily needs of the locality, mobilize resources, and assign tasks to volunteers from among the local people and youth from other areas. The institutionalization of the civic and community organizations would most likely have continued had the revolutionary crisis lasted longer. The victory of the revolution brought these activities to an end, giving rise to new grassroots movements with different structures, scales, and constituencies.

Despite their civic functions, the activists of the Popular Organizations (the ICCs, LCs, and Security Organizations), did possess political biases that at times contradicted their presumed principles. Their repudiation of ideologically rival elements as "saboteurs" was in conflict with the principle of community "solidarity and cooperation."[71] This, however, did not reduce the vital role of the Popular Organizations in responding to an immediate need, creating the nucleus of civil associations, and finally linking the experience of the revolution to the immediate concerns of the underclass. Youth played a decisive part in this process. The young revolutionaries from better-off areas went into the popular neighborhoods where they found the underclass youth ready for mobilization.

Certain sociological traits distinguished underclass male youth sharply from their parents and sisters. A good number of them had attended high schools and were more mobile. Many were second-generation migrants, with more contacts with other social groups.[72] They had witnessed the modern middle-class lifestyle and desired to be a part of it. They longed to pursue the leisure, fashions, and dating games of the rich boys.[73] But these required money, social skills, and a suitable cultural environment—all of which they lacked. Even going to the uptown parks "gives us new complexes . . . when we rarely have the opportunity to even talk to a girl."[74] Their shabby and tacky imitation of Westernized youth became a matter of ridicule and denigration, forcing them to rehearse within their own *sar-i kouchehs* (intersections of alleyways and streets). The north Tehranis used the derogatory terminology of *uzgal* and *dihaati* to refer to this group of youths who knew that they were poor but were fascinated by the lifestyles and values of the rich. Frustrated by the impossibility of attaining such life-styles and by the ensuing confusion in terms of identity, they turned against what they could not be or have. Hence the underclass youth joined the revolution in its moment of breakthrough, becoming the indignant postrevolutionary critical "mass on the stage" (*mardum-i dar sahneh*). They were the street warriors, the thugs, of the clerical figures who in return offered them regular income, power, and a divinely sanctioned social role, setting the scene for a novel stage in street politics in Iran.[75]

Until the very end, the disenfranchised, the squatter poor in particular, remained on the fringes of revolutionary events. Only at the end were they drawn into the discourse and the practice of the Islamic Revolution, primarily through the activities of popular organizations, the Islamic Consumer Cooperatives, and the Neighborhood Councils. Although on the periphery of the large events, the underclass were not passive in their daily lives. They were involved in the process of gradual but significant change that their struggle for survival had engendered. Their diverse struggles for subsistence came into being years before the revolutionaries set out in 1978 to demonstrate in the streets of Tehran and other big cities. Lacking an institutional mechanism to advance their demands collectively and coherently, they resorted to quiet direct action in acquiring shelter, setting up collective consumption, acquiring jobs, and consolidating their communities.

This process represented a crucial change in the lives of millions of poor who pursued similar actions. Indeed many of these developments occurred outside state regulations, with the poor living an informal life. They made their advances gradually, albeit with great hardship. Once the state began to exert its authority, they resisted. The resistance of the poor squatters did not represent deliberate political struggle against the state as such, nor even opposition to private landowners or the system of private property. Rather, their campaign originated primarily from the violation of their sense of justice and was reflected in the struggle over the use of public space, community development, and cultural autonomy.

What the poor saw as a natural, rational, and just way of sustaining their livelihood was, according to the state, a breach of law. Unauthorized land takeovers, illegal siphoning of electricity and running water, demanding basic amenities, extending private domain into the public space, squatting on public thoroughfares, using streets as markets, assembling in the communities—to the state all these activities meant chaos, loss of control, and political instability. For the poor, however, these unlawful activities were seen as just acts, necessary to sustain dignified lives. The response of the squatters to the municipality's demand for ownership titles to the land was: "we do not need a *sanad* [ownership titles], our *sanad*s are our wives and children [who need a dwelling]."[76] As a squatter during the 1977 riots stated:

> They [the municipality] say that we are in the *kharej-i mahdudeh* and that the city cannot afford to give water, paved-roads and so on to these areas. But still people cannot simply sleep in the streets! They must have a shelter to live in. Besides, these people cannot afford to get a place in the city. So they come here to make a dwelling. . . . The municipality must not destroy these homes. You know how much money, energy and effort we have put on these?" [77]

In retrospect, the local/community struggles of the Iranian poor to improve their lives were not necessarily less significant than those of the revolutionaries targeting state power. After all, many poor people continued waging similar campaigns as before. They continued to migrate massively, squat vacant apartments and lands, march in the streets to demand jobs, and make a living in the underground economy. The occurrence of the revolution did not alter their needs substantially, although it established a new structure of opportunity for mobilization. It implanted in the poor a new spirit and new experiences, offering a broader ground for their usual claims, albeit more militantly and daringly. The quiet encroachment of the ordinary surpassed in continuity the revolutionary struggle. The following chapters explore the manifestation of this form of politics, as well as the story of these mobilizations in the spheres of both living space and working life.

Four

The Housing Rebels: The Occupation
of Homes and Hotels, 1979-1981

Khaleh Sakineh and Hassan[1] were among the many hundreds who had joined the crowd, carrying their entire belongings in a tremendous rush. Utensils, bed, boxes, and babies hung down from their shoulders; and chickens and children followed the multitude. Mobilized by young activists, the crowd had emerged from a South Tehran slum. Young men directed the crowd toward an empty building. Upon their arrival the group flooded into the house taking over the empty rooms. The activist leaders began putting up banners and billboards around the structure, informing the public that the homeless poor were squatting this vacant home.[2] Thus was a large home in Mirdamad, an upper-middle-class neighborhood in Tehran, taken over.

This was one way in which the poor secured their dwellings. Others, like Hassan's brother, Mahmoud, had been involved, days earlier, in taking over a piece of land in Dowlat Abad where he hired his wife's cousin to put up a shelter into which he and his family moved the following day. In the same way as the inhabitants of many neighborhoods who had scattered around like blots of dropped ink, Khaleh Sakineh and Hassan became homeowners literally overnight. Unlike Hassan's group, Mahmoud's operation was rather discreet and without much clatter. Thus they began a new life in the new community. The revolution had paid off for both families, as well as many thousands more.

This and the following chapters show that the silent revolution, or quiet encroachment, which the urban poor had inaugurated decades prior to the Islamic Revolution continued ceaselessly after the insurrection of February 1979, albeit in a different context. The new squatters' movement represented a break from the past; the Islamic Revolution altered the form and structure of the squatters' activities. Between 1979 and 1981, under political uncertainty, various political groupings emerged, striving to gain popularity and support by mobilizing the disenfranchised groups. The resultant political competition within the oppositional groups, and between the opposition and the government, offered an opportunity for squatters to mobilize radically. Thus the squatter poor experienced, through kinship and individual initiatives, not only creeping direct action but also some kind of a social movement—one characterized by collective effort, some degree of organization and network, and a perception of social change.

Taking over Homes and Hotels

The new squatters' movement emerged against the background of the insurrection of February 10 and 11, 1979, when the Islamic Revolution had reached its climax. An enormous energy had been released and a tremendous void had emerged. In this "moment of madness," the body politic tingled with every little move in any segment within the society. It was a time of great dualities—of enormous hope and despair, of exhaustion and rejuvenation, of relaxation and energy, of a sense of job-done and work-to-begin.

The central authority had collapsed. There was no secret police, no municipality guards, not even a traffic police. Following the insurrection, the power vacuum began to be filled by various grassroots organizations, as well as by opportunistic, self-declared power heirs in various sectors of the society. Many business people deserted companies; managers left factories; the rich abandoned homes, hurriedly leaving behind million-dollar properties. In the end, some 150,000 housing units—palaces, hotels, villas, and unfinished apartment blocks remained; their original owners had either rushed to the West, or were in hiding somewhere in the country. The properties would later fall under the control of the *Bonyad-i Mustaz'afin* (the Foundation of the Dispossessed).[3]

Landless peasants confiscated large agribusiness estates; hundreds of factories were taken over by workers; and the state offices began to be run by their employees. The revolutionary youth took the charge of the city police. Even the unemployed, who intrinsically lacked any institutions in which to function, took control of the streets by regulating the traffic. It was the time of role-playing, of making a difference, of being counted, of taking revenge, of seizing the moment. It was at this moment of madness, of the new social order, that the new squatters' movement came into life.

Only days after the insurrection, a group of tent-settlers at the southern margin of the capital warned that if the new regime did not provide them with decent housing, "we will occupy vacant apartments." Two days later, some three hundred families, most of them armed, took over apartment blocks in Dowlatabad in South Tehran.[4] In the days and weeks that followed thousands of homeless families, poor tenants, and students joined the protagonists in Tehran and other urban centers, occupying empty apartment blocks, luxury homes, villas, and deserted hotels.

Tehran witnessed the largest incidence of squatting, mainly in the southern plain of the city, but homes, hotels, and apartments were occupied in other areas as well. Mirdamad, Maidan-i Azadi, Maidan-i Inqilab, Tajrish, Park-i Laleh, and Khiaban Hashemi, plus the townships of Tehran Pars, Kianshahr, Islamabad, Nizamabad, Dowlatabad, Shahrak-i Najafabad, and Gilanshahr account for only a few of the reported cases. In the latter three communities alone, according to a report, over 4,500 villas had been taken over by the "poor" in the first months of the revolution.[5]

Home invasions took place collectively, with kin folk, village mates, and neighbors acting together, often mobilized by the leftist and Islamic activists, and at times with sophisticated planning. On December 21, 1979, some thirty families from the poor neighborhoods of Maidan-i Soush and Gowdnishinan, in South Tehran, took over half-finished apartments near Islamabad in the southeastern plain. The group was led by a thirty-year-old, left-wing factory worker. The news spread among neighbors and acquaintances, and hundreds of families from the vicinity invaded the area. About 400 households occupied 308 homes.[6] In another early operation, at the beginning of 1980, some forty-one squatter families who occupied homes located in South Tehran gowds, forced the Municipality to supply them ready-made apartments in the Shahrak-i Soush. The Municipality purchased the occupied homes from the settlers in order to level them for development.[7] A few communities grew even larger as the occupation of newly built apartments continued. About five hundred families had settled in the township of Kianshahr by 1985.[8]

Young activists played a crucial part in organizing the homeless. "We were a group of left-wing workers who had known each other for years. . . . We began planning to expropriate so many vacant homes and apartments."[9] The core group had some twenty members, each relating to a dozen contacts who were active in popular areas such as Shadshahr, Darvazehghar, and Halabiabad. The core group would identify vacant properties, and the contact teams mobilized the homeless and brought them to the target buildings. "We would begin our invasion in a specific time. Then men, women, and children carrying their utensils, rugs, heaters, beds, and whatever would join in the occupation."[10] In this manner, they occupied buildings in the Shadshahr, Mirdamad, a neighborhood near Maidan-i Azadi, Maidan-i Inqilab, and Khiaban Hashemi.

Provincial cities also experienced home invasions. They included Qasr-i Shirin, Sanandaj, and Kirmanshah in the west, Abadan (in South Iran), Arak and Tonkabon (in Central Province), and Mashad (a holy city in East Iran).[11] In Abadan, in addition, some one hundred oil industry workers' families moved in to the apartments previously occupied by "the military personnel, SAVAK [the Shah's secret police] employees, policemen, and loyal workers."[12] These units were believed to belong to the *Sazman-i Kargaran* (Workers Organization) of the company, but had been allocated illegitimately to the above-mentioned people. In Kirmanshah, during the first week after the insurrection, one hundred and fifty families of flood victims were mobilized in a carefully planned campaign by left-wing youths who led them to occupy the government-built apartment blocks in the Shahrak-i Valiye'ahd. The apartments were originally to be allocated among these flood victims, but only for an unaffordable sum of Rls 500,000 (more than U.S.$6,500).[13]

Beyond homes and apartments, many luxury hotels also became the target of highly organized occupations in which university students typically took the lead. The students participated not only as mobilizers of the poor but also as beneficiaries in their own right. During October 1979, over one thousand students, complaining that the government failed to provide them with suitable dormitories, took over the International Hotel and the Royal Garden Hotel on Takht-i Jamshid Avenue.[14] Around the same time, mostly left-wing students occupied the Hotel Imperial, the Hotel Sina, and many more in Tehran. Both male and female students thwarted the resistance of the hotel employees, who were afraid of losing their jobs. The squatters guarded the buildings, resisting the *hizbullahi*s, informal groups organized by some clergy, who attempted to oust the original occupiers.[15]

The major impetus for hotel occupations came from the radical Islamic groups, which mushroomed in those days under the leadership of such figures as Ayatollah Beheshti, Sheikh Muhammad Karrubi, and Hojjatal-Islam Hadi Khosrowshahi who sanctioned and guided the activities of the militant Muslim students in taking over hotels and luxury villas. These clerical leaders were not only constructing mass support for themselves; they were also undermining the weak Provisional Government. Sheikh Muhammad Karrubi (brother of Mehdi Karrubi) began his agitation activities (in September 1979) by seizing a two-story house in north Tehran (Serah-i Zarrabkhaneh) as the headquarter for his Committee for Housing for the Downtrodden (Komite-ye Khaneh Baraye Mustaz'afin). Around him gathered young men from different walks of life—leftists, *mujahed*s, *laat*s or street bullies, and opportunists. Many of them came from South Tehran, acting as Karrubi's executive soldiers. Bands of young males grouped in the streets identifying homes, hotels, and land for the sheikh, who would "officially" assign these dwelling-places to the needy as well as to his own associates.[16] "I also received a few assignment orders," stated a participant in the operations, "and consequently I managed to transfer about ten families from Naziabad into these homes."[17]

Immediately following an occupation, the squatters would appoint a committee, a *shura*, to take care of the internal order within the buildings and organize against external threats of eviction. In the occupied hotels the *shura*s assigned rooms to "needy students" who came largely from the provincial towns. Normally each room was given to two or more students. "For instance, I used to live with my parents in Tehran," described a student squatter, "but I shared a room with a friend in the hotel."[18] In line with their ideological commitment, the students often took organizational work very seriously. They held largely free and competitive elections for the *shura*s, and formed various executive committees to operate the daily lives of the residents. In

the Hotel Royal Garden they formed Committees to deal with residence, transportation, cooperation with the employees, and defense.[19]
"The students, both boys and girls, maintained order and discipline,
protecting the Hotel by a twenty-four-hour petrol of the building."[20]

Most squatters came from poor migrant families who either could
not afford to pay rent or were living in tents and shacks in other parts
of the cities. In Dowlatabad the newcomers came from various poor
communities of South Tehran, including the *alounak*s (shacks) of
Tehranpars, Tehranvila, Darvazehghar, Naziabad, and Maidan-i
Soush. "We used to live in a damp basement," said a women squatter
in Dowlat Abad, "I get terrified thinking that we might still be forced
to return to that place."[21] Residents in the squatters' settlements of
Halabshahr in District 2 in Tehran seized the opportunity to upgrade
their position, moving in to empty apartments and houses located in
Mahalle-ye Seraj.[22]

Not all the squatters came from poor backgrounds; nor were all
desperately striving for a place to live. Some relatively affluent developers and local bullies (*laat*) also furthered their own interests. A revolutionary committee member claimed that some of the squatters had
already "owned a home." They simply sold these to others to make
money.[23] Some of them, he reported, had escaped from prisons during
the revolutionary chaos; they were now involved in gambling and drug
dealing.[24] Corruption at the level of the officials themselves also played
a role. The Pasdaran Committees, who were in charge of controlling
the neighborhoods and were later to assign expropriated apartments
to the homeless, actually gave a number of homes away to their own
relatives, friends, and "ideologically correct" families.[25]

The mass of student squatters was mostly from the provincial
towns; their complaints about their accommodation problems in the
rent-notorious capital city dated back to many years before the revolution. Yet the logic behind their mobilization had less to do with an
immediate need for housing and more with a desire to negate the opu-
lence that they admired in private but turned against because they
could hardly afford to be part of it. For leftists, as one leader put it,
"the occupation of the hotels which belonged to the large capitalists
was in accordance with our political and ideological lines."[26] These
radical measures also fit well with the strategy of the hardline Islamic
leaders of putting pressure on the moderate Provisional Government
of Mehdi Bazargan. The largely political motive (as opposed to sheer

need) of the students in taking over properties was later reflected in their early eviction by the authorities.

Life in the Occupied Dwellings

Unlike the students, the poor began to consolidate their positions in the occupied residential blocks. Squatting for them represented a long-awaited objective they could not afford to lose. Once they moved in, they began completing the unfinished apartments, putting up windows, glasses, and tiles. In Dowlatabad, each household spent some Rls 20,000 (U.S.$280 at 1979 exchange rate) to install doors and windows. The squatters divided the apartments, each family occupying a single room, and brought their chickens, goats and even their cows into the settlements.[27]

Within the occupied buildings, the left-wing activists organized literary and language classes, held political and ideological meetings, and taught social skills to the youngsters.[28]

Upon squatting, some men began opening their businesses in the same neighborhoods, whether in the apartments, by the door, or in the street. Street butcher shops were opened, poor grocery shops started to operate, and the unemployed looked for jobs on construction sites. Yet most men maintained their previous occupations, which required them to commute longer hours. Like their fathers, children, too, had to commute long hours to attend their previous schools. The problems of the squatters who had resided in the affluent parts of north Tehran seemed even greater. They had to shop in the stores of the affluent. Class tension remained another problem. In their gestures, jokes, and day-to-day interactions, the rich expressed their distaste over being neighbors with the dispossessed migrant poor.[29]

None of these shortcomings, however, reduced the attraction of being the master of one's own dwelling. Thus the biggest challenge remained to protect these homes from the forces of eviction. To this end, some families made sure that a member of family stayed at home during the day. Some men who stayed behind to protect their dwellings from the eviction forces lost their jobs, so it was mainly women who undertook the task of dealing with the authorities and defending the dwellings. Maintaining the dwellings, however, required an organized resistance.

Like the students, the poor squatters in a number of communities went as far as to constitute more structured organizations: the *shura*s, elected or appointed councils, represented and organized inhabitants of a building, or many occupied blocks within a neighborhood. The *shura*s bore the responsibility of tackling problems that might jeopardize the inhabitants security of tenure. They were to upgrade the community, deal with day-to-day problems, maintain cleanliness, resolve disputes, and administer cultural events. More immediately, they were to coordinate the relations of the communities with the outside world, including hostile neighbors and especially the original owners of the properties.[30] Several local power centers had emerged, each claiming sole authority over the affairs of the neighborhoods, and all, by implication, were hostile to the organization of the *shura*s. They ranged from the local Pasdaran Kommitte, the clergymen, and the local mosques to the office of the Construction Crusade and the local municipality. To counter the threats and intrigues coming from these bodies, the organization of councils seemed vital.

In a southwestern outskirt of Tehran, according to Bassri and Hourcade, the four hundred families that had taken over three hundred and eight apartments elected a left-wing council in which women played an active role. The households of each street (*koucheh*) elected three representatives all together, making a twenty-one-person general assembly. The general assembly, in turn, elected a five-member central council, which was to meet once a week and was responsible for the decisions concerning the entire neighborhood. Once consolidated, the council went so far as to create a coordinating council to organize all squatters at the level of the city of Tehran. It organized rallies and called for a rent strike by poor tenants.[31]

In a sense, the *shura* associations attested to the "spatial solidarity" among the inhabitants who came from different social, ethnic, and linguistic backgrounds but shared one important goal: protecting and upgrading the already occupied homes.[32] Out of this common interest and mechanical solidarity, based upon what John E. Davis termed domestic property (land and buildings that are used [or usable] for shelter),[33] grew friendship and kinship ties that further cemented the local bond. Young adults within the communities married; neighbors looked after each other's children and watched one another's belongings; and children played with their new mates.

Despite this rejuvenated mood and the highly energetic local atmosphere, the specter of the bearded Pasdaran and the nightmare of eviction kept haunting these housing rebels. Knowingly or unknowingly, they had violated a fundamental property right that all the governments in the postrevolution period were committed to protect. The confrontation between the squatters and the authorities thus seemed unavoidable.

Being Evicted

The occupation of residential buildings, homes, and hotels constituted one of the first challenges to the new authorities in the revolutionary period. There had been other incidents that defied the Islamic regime, such as nationalist rebellions in Kurdistan and Azarbaijan, the activities of the left-wing organizations, seizure of farming land in the north, and the takeover of factories by the workers in most parts of the country.

Housing seizures, however, proved to be a more acute crisis. In direct actions such as factory takeovers, the government was confident that it could eventually secure the ownership of the enterprises.[34] These enterprises would eventually belong either to the state or to the original owners; the most workers could do would be to maintain some degree of control over the operation of the workplaces through the organizations of the factory *shura*s. The situation with regard to the buildings was quite different. With a simple hint of governmental recognition, the squatters would virtually usurp the occupied properties. There was no easy, short-term, and middle-of-the-road solution, especially since many unfinished apartments, unlike the luxury villas and hotels, belonged legally to individuals such as school teachers and the government employees for whom the previous regime had built homes as part of their benefits. The new authorities were consequently caught up between threats of disorder and chaos, of losing their legitimacy as the "servants of the dispossessed," and of being irrelevant.

On the other hand, the instability of the Islamic regime, with the intense power struggle at the top and the constant turnover of politicians, meant there was hardly a consistent policy to deal with the problem. The Housing Foundation along with a number of radical clerical leaders such as Khosrowshahi, Karrubi, and Beheshti, encouraged takeovers; the provisional government of Mehdi Bazargan opposed the action vehemently; the subsequent Rajaaii's cabinet tolerated it without, however, giving it official recognition. Indeed, the authorities' response to the squatting crisis during the first two years remained largely decentralized; it was handled mainly by the local power centers, especially the local committees or Pasdaran, and the local mullas and their armed men centered in the local mosques. The committees' position on the issue depended on which authorities they were following—sympathetic or critical. The radical clergy's sympathy for the squatters had in general the political aim of undermining the Provisional Government. Yet, since the squatters were mobilized generally by the radical left groups, the Pasdaran were quick to oppose the squatters on the ground that they were acting as the agents of the "communist counterrevolution."

The success of the local Pasdaran in ending the occupation, and the extent of the squatters' hold over the occupied properties depended on a balance of forces at both national *and* local levels. The power struggle at the top (between the liberals and the radical clergy) offered breathing space to the ordinary citizens in their mobilizational efforts. This macro schism reflected itself at the localities, with groups allying with this or that governmental tendency or personality. But there were other players on the local level as well: the squatters, their leftist allies, the local Pasdaran, local mosques and mullas, and the owners of the occupied homes. In short, the degree of the squatters' hold over the occupied properties varied a great deal. It depended on how organized they were, how forceful the original owners were, who the owners were (either the old elites or ordinary people), and which officials the squatters resorted to (sympathizers or opponents). This may explain why some squatters managed to stay on; others lasted over six years; and some, like those in the occupied hotels, were evicted after a few weeks.

The ways in which the government and the Pasdaran confronted the housing rebels varied considerably. They adopted different tactics that ranged from issuing strongly worded warnings, using religious verdicts publicly denouncing the "un-Islamic" nature of their actions, to divide-and-rule tactics, cutting water and electricity, arrests, and armed raids. Some, mainly students, left without much resistance; others did so after obtaining compensation or a promise of alternative housing; many resisted and stayed on, though some agreed to pay some compensation to the government.

Students were among the first to vacate the hotels, largely of their own free will. Immediately after the seizure of the U.S. embassy by the militant muslim students (on November 4, 1979) many hotels were evacuated. Even prior to that event, ideological division within the organizing student bodies in the hotels had already undermined the viability of long-term occupation. The students sympathizing with the Mujahedin argued for peaceful evacuation; they thought these kinds of direct actions would undermine the nascent revolutionary regime's position with the West. The Marxist students, in contrast, wanted to stay unless the government did something for their housing conditions. In many hotels this division paralyzed the protective function of the shuras.[35] With the seizure of the U.S. embassy, as a left-wing participant in one operation put it, "the justification behind the occupations lost its validity." In this situation, the "excuse of student housing [for the occupation of the hotels] also shed its legitimacy."[36] Although a number of the students retained some hotels (for instance, those in Takht-i Tawous and Karim Khan in Tehran) because the owners were tawghouties (opulent royalists), the political/ideological logic of student squatting made their occupation far less viable.

The situation with the poor squatters was quite different. For them, squatting was not a political or ideological battle but simply a way to survive. Defending their gains was vital. And this alone would make their eviction difficult. As a squatter stated:

> From the beginning, I have sacrificed all of my things on this revolution.
> . . . I have sold my carpet and TV [to pay for my costs]. Now I won't leave this home. You see, we too have the right to live a life. [I want to say to] those who want us to leave this place: first give us a place of our own.[37]

The squatters were invariably denounced in public by some religious authorities as "counterrevolutionaries." "They are opportunists who have taken advantage of the good will of the revolutionary leadership and the Provisional Government," declared Hojjat al-Islam Khansari, the leader of the committee located in Nizamabad. "They have illegally seized these apartments, in the days when our combatant people were engaged in armed struggle [during the revolution]."[38]

For the most part, the religious authorities condemned the squatters and justified their eviction on religious grounds. Upper echelon clergy, such as Ayatollahs Qomi and Mar'ashi, issued fitwas ruling that occupying homes was haram, unIslamic. In one specific case in Mashad, they ruled that the "prayer of the Muslims in such homes are not acceptable."[39] In response, squatters referred to earlier proclamations by Khomeini on free housing and urban services. "Does the government not plan to provide housing for the mustaz'afin?" asked a squatter of the authorities who demanded his eviction, "We have behaved exactly according to the government policy."[40] Their resistance thus grew not simply from the moral economy of the poor, nor purely from their rational conviction. Rather, it represented a moral politics on the part of the rational poor.

Ignoring such verdicts or interventions, the squatters left the authorities with no other option but to take action that at times had far-reaching political consequences. In Dowlatabad, in Tehran, the Pasdaran cut off running water in the public taps on the grounds that, according to a resident, "its use was announced to be *haram* [religiously prohibited]."[41] Such pressures, however, failed to yield results. Following several warnings to the squatters to vacate, the Pasdaran in one case raided a squatters' community at night. The settlers expressed their outrage at the assault by organizing a five-hundred-person angry demonstration in front of the Pasdaran headquarters, demanding the release of five women who were arrested. Scuffles broke out and shootings followed, leading to the withdrawal of the Pasdaran.[42] Five years passed, during which time the Pasdaran patrolled, off and on, around the settlement, reminding the squatters of their insecure position. On February 10, 1985, the Pasdaran returned in full force to finish the evictions. In response, thousands of the inhabitants of Dowlatabad staged a demonstration. "The demonstrators blocked the Be'sat highway, and the streets around the township, bringing the traffic to a halt." In the confrontations that followed, a large number of the squatters and Pasdaran were injured. The security forces withdrew once again, only to return two days later with the aid of the paramilitary (gendarme). They were confronted with fierce resistance again, and left.[43] This was the end of the affair for a time.

Squatters made special efforts to organize themselves more systematically at the local level, often with the aid of left-wing groups. They designed strategies to confront the security forces, to outline alternative solutions, and to negotiate with the authorities. In the township of Kianshahr, in South Tehran, after four years of unsuccessful eviction attempts, the settlers elected a number of local leaders to appeal to a populist clergyman, Ayatollah Montazari. He referred them to the municipal authorities. Not being prepared to accept any responsibility, the latter in turn suggested the squatters present their case at the Friday prayer sermons where most officials, including the prime minister, would be in attendance.

In the meantime, an already-established Council of the Apartment (*shura-ye apartimaan*) invited people into the local mosque to discuss the plan. They agreed that they would not leave the apartments and would take their case to the Friday prayer session. One of the proposals pointed out that "If these houses belong to police personnel, we are prepared to purchase them. The government may begin building new apartments for the personnel with our monthly payments. Otherwise, we demand the government to build suitable houses for us." The day of Friday prayer arrived. The settlers presented their petition to the prime minister, who assured them that they could stay in the apartments until an appropriate law was enacted with regards to these properties. One year later, however, the Pasdaran raided the community to force them out. The dwellers remained steadfast and the security forces were once again repelled.

While evictions continued in many spots in Tehran, due to its political sensitivity, things appeared easier in provincial urban areas. In the holy city of Mashad, the government was able to end, albeit after several unsuccessful attempts, the occupation of the apartments of Aabkouh, which had been taken over few days after the revolution. On December 12, 1980, some four hundred armed security men raided the buildings, and in one surprise move forced out some five hundred squatters.[44]

The prevailing tactic of the authorities consisted of divide-and-rule. They would offer a segment of the squatters the promise of alternative housing or the consolidation of their tenure, in exchange for repudiating more uncompromising, especially leftist, factions.[45] Once the *shura* members were divided, the situation would be ripe for the security forces, backed by the lawsuit of the original owners, to exert pressure. Alternatively, through enforcing new elections or creating alternative *shura*s, the government would eventually eliminate the dissenting groups.[46] This tactic was reinforced especially after 1982 when, following the suppression of the liberals, the Mujahedin, and the left, the regime began to consolidate itself. Although apartment seizure stopped, evictions lingered on for some years to come.

Most apartment squatting lasted between two and six years. Only a fraction of the squatters were allowed to stay on. For the rest, forced evictions eventually occurred. The major problem was that the squatters had aimed at the wrong targets. Unlike their counterparts in Portugal in 1974 or in Britain in 1968–70, who aimed at forcing property owners (in Portugal) or local governments to provide homes with reasonable rent, the Iranian squatters had seized the properties of other citizens.[47] Although some properties belonged to the previous government, foreigners, or very rich landlords, many belonged to the citizens—government employees, teachers, or police personnel who were not considered particularly opulent. Some had not even completed their payments to the contractors. These citizens were adamant to resecure their properties.

On the other hand, the government's promise of housing for the poor through the Fund 100 program initially created some hope among the poor. The activities of the *Jihad-i Sazandegui* (the Construction Crusade) seemed initially a viable grassroots solution. But these measures were both limited and far off.[48] These shortcomings, together with the soaring price of land and rent, a new wave of urban migration, and the release of war refugees, therefore encouraged the poor to focus on the alternative strategy of spontaneous settlements through the occupation of urban land.

Taking over empty apartments and land around the cities represented a key means by the poor to survive homelessness and the hardship of urban housing. The actors also aimed at mastering their own physical space and practicing their autonomy by liberating themselves from the whims of landlords and government regulations. In this sense, the squatter activities of the poor represent an extension of their daily practice involving the constant struggles for the redistribution of resources and the expansion of their autonomy.

But what facilitated such practices at this particular juncture was, apart from the urge for survival, a political space created by the revolution. This political space opened up a new opportunity and granted a new character to the squatters' practice, making it an exceptional measure. The experiment of widespread home takeover was the first its kind in Iran, and was not repeated in the postrevolutionary period.[49]

Unlike the occupation of hotels by students, home squatting by the poor was not intended as an ideological challenge against private property. While the students attempted to create a bigger squatter movement by involving more participants, poor squatters were wary of such measures. They preferred more silent, limited, small-scale operations. They knew that at times of encroachment, visibility, solidarity and clamor, would be counterproductive. Some even attempted to curtail the extent of their activities. Yet when the challenging moment of eviction and thus defense of their gains arrived, the poor did their best to extend their movement by advocating involvement, participation, and solidarity.

Also, unlike the student takeovers, the squatter activities of the poor were not meant as a deliberate protest action to force the state to solve the housing problem. Their measure was the solution to that problem. Whereas squatting for the students largely meant a deliberate political action, for the poor it meant simply a living practice, a form of daily resistance and struggle to survive and improve life, to redistribute collective goods and win autonomy. Both groups, the students and the urban poor, were involved in illegal acts. Whereas ideological bias justified the students' action, the notion of necessity warranted that of the poor. As a squatter of the Nizamabad apartment blocks in South Tehran firmly stated:

> We are *mustaz'af— mustaz'af* in a real sense; otherwise we wouldn't invade the apartments in such a manner . . . We have been tenants for a long time; have had enormous hardships; a miserable life. All of our concern has been to feed our children, and pay rent, which in most cases, we simply could not manage. Our children have never tasted any kind of fruit throughout the year. After the strikes that broke the Shah's back—and ours as well!—our situation got worse; so that we could hardly pay our rent, and make ends meet. So we had no choice but to resort to squatting these apartments.[50]

Indeed, the motives behind each group's actions influenced their outcome a great deal. Many students relinquished the occupied hotels, especially after the seizure of the U.S. embassy in Tehran, when they reexamined their political motives and found their action politically unsound. But the motive of the poor, the necessity to survive, made them more determined to defend their gains. Their eviction proved to be not so easy.

A squatter movement of this sort, if it occurred under nonrevolutionary conditions and/or especially under a liberal democratic state, might be seen as one which questions bourgeois legality and private property.[51] The Iranian case was, however, quite different, since the emergent political space created by the revolution and the initial support of the populist clergy justified to a considerable degree the squatters' cause. The radicalism of the poor and that of the populist clergy had a reinforcing effect upon each other.

Maldistribution and the sheer shortage of urban housing were problems upon which the squatters had reflected, problems the government strove to address. However, with the government's inability to resolve the housing problem (discussed later), together with an almost total collapse in private investment in housing, the flooding of war refugees, and the new waves of rural migrants, basic dwelling continued to remain a chief issue that galvanized the social activism of disenfranchised groups.

Although the squatter movement made important gains by allocating homes among some poor families and by affecting public housing policy, it faced its limitations before long. The time for organized and radical direct actions had come to an end. Activist support for the movement was curtailed by the advent of political repression. In addition, the short supply of usurpable homes and the subsequent legal complications of takeovers made the option nonviable. In short, the extraordinary conditions that had given rise to the birth of the movement soon came to an end. The poor needed to adopt a sustainable strategy to suit the subsequent period of political normalcy and stability. They did so by returning to a strategy of individual and silent encroachment. Quiet squatting and illegal construction of thousands of plots of land in the back streets of the urban centers and beyond was seen as the most viable solution. The following chapter spells out the dynamics of this movement.

Five

Back-Street Politics: Squatters and the State

I have talked to many residents of these shahraks [settlements]. Apart from many who have come from other towns and villages, there are also those who come from different [Tehran] neighborhoods. I myself was a tenant in a home [in Tehran]. . . . But realized that I could not afford to pay the rent. Negotiations with the landlord went nowhere . . . So one day a colleague of mine said to me "Why don't you take a look at the areas around Saveh Road." Well, I came here and settled. Now, I am happy that at least my family lives under a roof.

—A squatter in Saveh Road in South Tehran[1]

Is is common among scholars to examine the politics of the poor in terms of a set of simple dichotomies—conservative/radical, orientation to individual resistance/collective action, and adherence to primordial loyalties/civil associations.[2] The narratives of this chapter demonstrate the inadequacy of such dichotomies in uncovering the complex nature of the poor's politics. The disenfranchised, indeed, combine and experience all of these seemingly contradictory positions. Change in the political climate, the efficacy of tactics used, and their own ability to mobilize account for major factors determining the variation in their methods. Concern for the concrete and the immediate compels the poor to adopt pragmatism; unlike the intellectual class, the disenfranchised cannot afford to be ideological.

In postrevolutionary Iran, the poor realized that radical, direct, collective action (e.g., squatting in hotels and homes) belonged to an exceptional conjuncture, and that the phase of political normality and regime-stability required a movement with a new strategy—low-key, nonprovocative, often individualistic, requiring patience, precision, and perseverance.

Because squatting homes and hotels proved to be a nonviable solution, many poor turned to the alternative strategy of colonizing silently the territories outside the big cities, away from the watchful eyes of the police, putting up shelters and setting up communities without much regard to regulations or legality. This largely discreet direct action allowed the disenfranchised to evade the burden of high rent and state control by constructing communities at the margins of government influence, where family, kinship, and local norms governed their daily lives. To secure their status in the face of the state, economic hardship, and social anomie, both traditional networks and modern associations became an inseparable part of their communal life. While kinship and ethnic identities cemented their collective existence with the informal norms governing their daily lives, the modern associations (Neighborhood Councils and Consumer Cooperatives) even in their restricted forms strove to articulate spatial solidarity overriding ethnic and kinship divisions.

Here I examine the dynamics of this alternative community construction, spelling out conflicts of interest and perceptions between these settlers and the authorities. The elements of conflict revolved around three major areas: First, over the meaning of migration from one place to another; second, over the distribution of social goods (e.g., public land, drinking water, electricity, roads, schools, clinics, clean air, etc.); and third, the struggle over the extension of autonomy, of cultural and political space free of state control.

Usual Business

Even at the height of the occupations of hotels and homes, the process of illegal squatter settlement had never entirely stopped. Earlier chapters have described how during the revolution the needy (as well as greedy developers) continued squatting on many plots of urban land, erecting dwellings overnight. The process continued immediately after the revolution, despite parallel home and hotel occupation. But both the limited supply of vacant apartments suitable for occupation and the attendant legal complications rendered squatter settlement as the most viable immediate alternative to the housing crisis and excessive state control. Thus *hashiyenishini* and *zaghehnishini*, the construction of illegal communities, continued to increase, affecting even the smaller towns.

Many large cities experienced gradual but extensive land invasions and illegal construction. In Tehran the increase was more rapid. The number of shanty dwellers, or *zaghehnishinan*, began to climb quickly from the very first year of the revolution. The shanty settlements (*zagheh*) of Zanjan-i Jonoubi Street increased by 140 percent; and those of Soleimanieh, Resalat Highway, Zanjan-i Shomali Street, and Tajrish almost doubled. In the meantime, new spontaneous communities emerged in Maidan-i Azadi, and in South Tehran.[3] Thus, the total population of the gowdnishinan (inhabitants of gowds) and shanty dwellers within the capital city reached some 100,000 households by early 1980.

In 1980 the municipality formally enlarged the city limit from 225 square kilometers to 520 square kilometers, recognizing many informal communities on the margins of the city by extending urban services. Despite this, figures show a sharp drop in Tehran's annual growth rate from 5.2 percent in 1976 to 2.9 percent in 1986.[4] The decline was at the cost of extensive growth just outside the formal city limits, on agricultural lands, nearby villages, in planned townships, and informal communities. Thousands of urban poor acquired land, legally or illegally, and constructed more durable homes with reasonable materials such as mud or baked bricks. A large number created permanent settlements. Large areas experienced spontaneous construction around Shahr-i Rey, Varamin, Nizamabad, Shahrak-i Mamazan, Shahrak-i Qiam, Kianshahr, Shadshahr, and Qarchak in the southern plain of the capital city, and Khak-i Sefid in Tehran Pars. From the west the city stretched as far as Karadj and its satellite towns Rajaiishahr and Mehrshahr, encompassing numerous enlarged communities such as Shahrak-i Quds (see maps 1 and 2). In 1990 the population of these townships reached some 1.2 million.[5] As early as 1986, 23 of the settlements that had mushroomed around the capital qualified for integration into the city bus service. These settlements had a population of well over 460,000, six times their size in 1976.[6]

Perhaps for the first time, rural communities at the margin of the city began extensively to house the urban poor. These new urbanized villages provided cheaper land for home construction, lower density, cheaper goods and services, and more autonomy from typical urban regulations. Agriculture was only a minor activity; the inhabitants, mostly immigrants from other rural areas as well as from the inner city areas of Tehran, were dependent on the economy of the urban center. Population of these spontaneous communities grew nearly 17 percent per year between 1976 and 1986, and 10 percent between 1986–1991 (from 904,000 to 1,284,000);[7] at the same time Tehran's overall

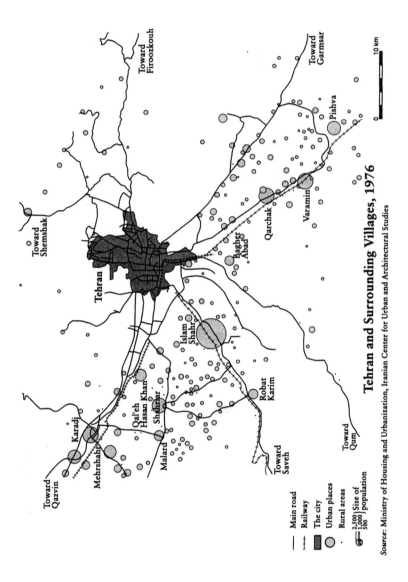

Tehran and Surrounding Villages, 1976

Toward Firoozkouh

Toward Garmsar

10 km

Pishva

Qarchak

Varamin

Toward Shemshak

Bagher Abad

Tehran

Islam Shahr

Qal'eh Hassan Khan

Shahriar

Robat Karim

Malard

Karadj

Mehrshahr

Toward Qazvin

Toward Saveh

Toward Qum

Main road

Railway

The city

Urban places

Rural areas

2,500 Size of
1,000 population
500

Source: Ministry of Housing and Urbanization, Iranian Center for Urban and Architectural Studies

growth rate declined from 2.9 percent to 1.4 percent as many poor and
middle-class Tehranies, as well as low-income families from other
cities, moved into marginal settlements and urbanized villages.[8]

Islamshahr and Bagherabad are two such communities. Islamshahr,
Tehran's largest satellite community, where the capital's largest popular protest took place in April 1995, is located 18 kilometers southeast
of the city. Originally known as Shadshahr, it grew out of ten neigh-
boring villages with a population of 1,000 in 1966; by 1976 its population had reached 50,000. Since the revolution it has grown an average of 18 to 23 percent annually, housing an estimated 300,000 to
500,000 people by 1990.[9] Over 70 percent of them came from the capital city.[10] Most of the inhabitants worked in the streets, workshops,
and factories in the vicinity.

Bagherabad with 15,000 inhabitants is located near Varamin, 10
kilometers south west of Tehran. The population of this shahrak con-
sists of poor migrants of various ethnicities including Kurds, Lours,
Azaris, Baluchis, Arabs, and Afghans, and some who came from the
slums of the capital.[11] They spread out in a village that once housed
only eighty-seven peasant households. "Beginning in the early seven-
ties," remembered an elderly inhabitant of the old village,

> the landlords sold their lands and deserted the village. With them gone,
> the agriculture deteriorated, leading to the out-migration of peasant
> families. Then, the newcomers appeared little by little. As soon as any-
> one arrived in the village, he bought a plot of land, which at the time was
> very cheap . . . put up a shelter, placed his wife and children in it, and
> left for work in the city. Many worked as laborers in Tehran. They
> spread the news around [about the village]; and their friends came and
> joined them. And in this way, the village got larger. But these people
> hardly did any agricultural work . . . Now if you move around Tehran
> these days, you will find a new shahrak every few miles.[12]

Indeed, by the early 1990s new shahrak communities, including the
shantytowns and urban villages, numbered well over one hundred
within and around the Greater Tehran.[13] In 1992 the mayor of Tehran
admitted bitterly that, "The land area of Tehran has rapidly expanded
from 200 square kilometers in the first year of the revolution to 600
square kilometers at present." He went on, "This rapid expansion has,
for the most part, been devoid of any order and legal procedures.
Much of the construction has been *qachaqui* [illegal], carried out in the
middle of the night. Homes have been turned into shops and many

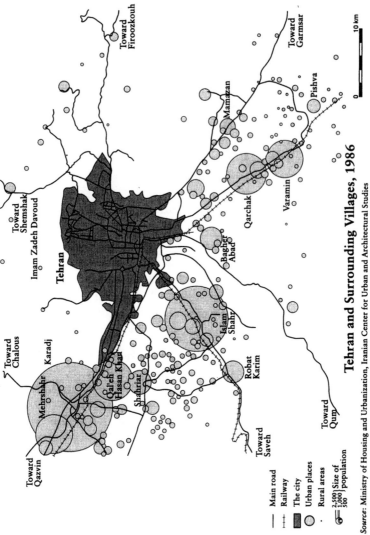

Toward
Firoozkouh

Toward
Garmsar

10 km

Mamazan

Pishva

Toward
Shemshak

Imam Zadeh Davoud

Tehran

Qarchak

Varamin

Bagher
Abad

Toward
Chalous

Karadj

Islam
Shahr

Mehrshahr

Qaleh
Hasan Khan

Shahriar

Robat
Karim

Toward
Qazvin

Toward
Saveh

Toward
Qum

Main road

Railway

The city

Urban places

Rural areas

2,500 Size of
1,000 population
500

Tehran and Surrounding Villages, 1986

Source: Ministry of Housing and Urbanization, Iranian Center for Urban and Architectural Studies

buildings·have been built on public thoroughfares and public spaces."[14] In 1994 some 674,000 low-income people were living in the informal settlements around Tehran.[15]

The capital was not alone in experiencing squatter colonization. *Hashiyenishini* mushroomed also in the provincial cities and towns, including Mashad, Tabriz, Bakhtaran, Arak, Hamadan, Isfahan, Shiraz, Bandar Abbas, Maragheh, and Ahwaz to name only a few.[16] By the end of the 1980s, in the holy city of Mashad in the far east, the size of the *hashiyenishinan* had reached some 500,000 residing in squatter settlements such as Kouy-e Aab-o-Bargh, Seyedi, Najafi, Al-Mehdi, Hemmatabad, and Kouy-e Tollab. This last was the site of three days of riots in 1992, the country's biggest political event of that year. These settlements outside the capital developed mainly after the revolution. The squatters consisted of the rural migrants, Iran-Iraq war refugees, Iranians expelled from Iraq, and Afghanis. Kouy-e Aab-o-Bargh was built by the gradual colonization of the hillsides overlooking the city by migrants fleeing from the nearby rural areas of Ghouchan, Dargaz, and Torbat-i Haydariyeh. Altogether they managed to build some 2,000 homes under the high pressure electricity poles supplying Mashah, not neglecting to take a share of that electricity.[17]

Between 1980 and 1983 the land area of the city of Bakhtaran grew from a mere 6 square kilometers to about 80 square kilometers.[18] In 1984 the mayors in the northern cities of Tabriz and Urumiyeh warned about the threat of *hashiyenishini* and illegal nighttime constructions, calling for measures to halt the trend.[19] In short, as experts confirmed, by the end of the 1980s, "against our expectations, the *hashiyenishini* spread even to the small and medium-sized towns in the country."[20]

Why So Much Expansion?

Undoubtedly the Islamic government inherited a good portion of the problem from the previous regime, but in the early years after the revolution the situation deteriorated further. It was estimated that during the 1970s, 200,000 new homes a year were needed to keep up with demand.[21] This number jumped to 300,000 during the postrevolution years.[22] Yet the relative supply of housing declined sharply. In the first years following the revolution, private investment in housing almost totally collapsed. The total number of homes with permits built in 1982 (just over 11,600 units) was only one-tenth of that in 1979 (some 160,000 homes).[23] To ameliorate the situation, the government aimed both to ensure renting vacant accommodations and to build low-cost dwellings. Rent enforcement failed due to the landlords' non-cooperation, even though the measure was supported by draconian state control over land and housing transactions. On the other hand, despite the much publicised policy of home construction for the poor, and large sums of money at the disposal of the Housing Foundation the results were less than impressive.[24] By 1982 the Foundation had distributed not more than 12,000 plots of land to low-income families in Tehran at a time when, according to the Chief Justice, Ayatollah Moussavi-Ardabili, some 200,000 "homeless families" were living in the capital.[25]

Rapid increase in the urban population played a key role in the urban housing crisis. Between 1976 and 1986 the urban population grew by about 72 percent, with an annual growth rate of 5.5 percent (from 15,715,000 to 26,991,000). Three main factors contributed to this. First, the influx of 2.5 million Iran-Iraq war refugees, many of whom were forced to live in makeshift housing and temporary tents in the major urban areas. Second, by the mid-1980s an estimated 2 million Afghan refugees had entered the country, many of them relocating in big cities such as Mashad, Zahedan, and an estimated 120,000 to 300,000 in Tehran. Finally, rural-urban migration played the biggest role. During the decade 1976 to 1986, over 2,225,000 rural people left their homes to live and work in the cities—about 1.5 million to Greater Tehran.[26] The population of some cities, such as Bakhtaran, more than doubled.

The early migrants rushed to the big cities expecting to harvest the fruit of the revolution—free housing, jobs, or high income. Many opportunist developers also joined the bandwagon of the *mustaz'afin* taking over urban land for rent or sale;[27] these seemed insignificant, however, compared to the needy. Thousands of villagers camped in the big squares and thoroughfares of Tehran to get their share of the free homes that radical clergy like Ayatollah Khosrowshahi had promised to the *mustaz'afin*. Later migrants were pushed out of the rural areas largely by economic necessity. The rhetoric of the new leaders with regard to the high value of agriculture and rural development in an Islamic Iran was rarely translated into practice. While the *Jihad-i Sazandegui* (Construction Crusade) carried out many development projects (in particular road construction and electricity supply),[28] the poor farmers' income from agriculture remained sluggish. In 1982 a rural household earned less than half—44 percent—of an urban family.[29] A survey by the *Jihad-i Sazandegui* in 1984 on migration in the provinces of Hamadan and Isfahan showed that over 85 percent of the poor migrants had left their villages because of low income, and inadequate water and land.[30]

Hence scores of poor villagers, war refugees and displaced people, against the wishes of their political leaders, chose to live in the cities to utilize the available services and opportunities. However, just as before the revolution, the high price of land and costly legal procedures—stipulated in the city plans—continued to exclude not only these emigrants but also many low-income urbanites from the formal housing market. Even the formalized squatter communities, such as Islamshahr, began to create their own informal settlements once city planning was put into effect.[31] Thus some poor families managed to purchase plots of land outside the city limits where they built their shelters illegally; some settled in nearby villages with secure land holdings and buildings but lacking urban services. Many simply took over pieces of public and legally obscure land, as far as possible out of public sight—behind a hill, in a river bed, under big bridges, or out of town. Certainly the poor utilized the existing political opportunity; yet they justified their unlawful actions by the moral principle of necessity. While some resorted to "land belongs to God," most reasoned forcefully that "*chare-ii neest*," "there is no other way out."[32] In the end they shaped new communities that in some ways differed from their prerevolution counterparts. The massive and rapid dislocation of migrant families with diverse origins marked the hybrid character of these communities: they contained more residents of urban origin, they were less communal and traditional in their social relations and institutions and contained a wider range of occupations.

Shaping the Communities

Having secured a dwelling, the most urgent need for the settlers was to obtain water and electricity. Later on came sewerage systems, refuse collection, clinics, schools, roads, and cultural activities. To ensure these essentials, the poor utilized self-help initiatives to organize collective campaigns, but when these efforts did not yield results, they resorted to silent but direct action. Once the gains were assured in this discreet fashion, the poor did everything they could collectively to defend them. As the disenfranchised laid further claims, they consolidated their position and captured wider arenas of power.

In 1980 some 48,000 households remained without running water and 18,800 were without electricity in Tehran alone. By 1986 the number of families without running water in the urban areas of Tehran Province was twice that of six years earlier. In the same year 538,000 families in other cities lacked piped water.[33]

In the new squatter communities, electricity was either nonexistent or had to be purchased from the small power generators that richer dwellers installed in certain squatter communities to earn an income.[34] Drinking water had to be supplied either from outdoor fountains or from ad hoc elevated reservoirs that residents had connected to their homes through plastic hoses. Purchasing tanker water was also common; every day water tankers would drive into the heart of the slums, where they were surrounded by women and children with buckets. Both the inadequacy as well as the cost of water and electricity, however, became a heavy burden. In 1983, 17,000 inhabitants of a poor community such as Shahrak-i Masoudieh in South Tehran, or that on the north side of Ayatollah Kashani Boulevard, had to pay as much as Rls 1,000–Rls 1,500 for a tank of portable water that was hardly suitable for drinking.[35] Some spent as much as Rls 2,000 a week for unpurified water that "had caused kidney problems among the children."[36]

An alternative was local cooperation and self-help. Some communities got together to dig deep wells. This method, however, did not always work due to the short supplies of equipment.[37] The infamous squatter community of Zoorabad, 40 kilometers east of Tehran, was one such community. Spread out on the hillsides dominating the migrant city of Karadj, the settlement housed about 56,000 inhabitants in 1980.[38] Purchasing water from water carriers cost them up to ten times the cost of piped water to which only 12 percent of the residents had access.[39] Digging deep wells and installing sewer pipes proved extremely arduous. It was a tremendously hard job for women to carry heavy buckets of water up the hills every day. The settlers, therefore, turned to buying tank water and storing it in *aab-anbaar*s, underground water reservoirs constructed especially for this purpose beneath their houses.[40] The *aab-anbaar*s, however, harbored many sorts of bacteria and diseases. As the benefits of self-help proved limited, residents turned to local government to demand proper urban amenities.

Many locals publicized their needs in the form of petitions and open letters to the authorities in the daily papers. "Khaniabad-i Nou lacks safe drinking water," wrote the settlers of the community in South Tehran. "We are buying water from a well that a few profiteers dug some twenty years ago. . . . The water is full of calcium materials and salt . . . The shortage of clean water has caused problems for the people in observing their religious duties.[41] The inhabitants of Shahrak-i Valiye'asr, in South Tehran, protested: "We are using underground water which is unhygenic and causes disease . . . Now that this settlement has [officially] become part of the city of Tehran, we expect the honorable authorities to grant us a favor, the *mustaz'afin*, by extending piped water to our community."[42] The open letters covered all aspects of local life, ranging from garbage collection (in Khaniabad-i Nou), pavement of roads (in Afsariyeh)[43], electricity, power-cuts (in Afsariyeh)[44] and food rationing. The people of Islamshahr complained: "Rice has been distributed only once in the last three months; and no eggs have been brought to the locality at all during the last five months," demanding the authorities to "come and end this situation here."[45]

In the meantime people took to the streets in demonstrations and sit-ins in front of government offices and municipalities to pressure the authorities for results. In 1982 the women of Zoorabad, Karadj, following days of mobilization, forced city officials to extend the city's refuse collection network to their communities.

In the first year of the revolution, the women had organized themselves in order to acquire running water for each house. They went to the Water Board of the city and "refused to leave until they had been promised piped running water to all households."[46] Within two months, piped water gushed into the alleyways of a large part of the settlement. They had earlier campaigned, with the help of more educated women, to improve conditions in their local public bathhouse, whose owner had confined its usage to men only on the grounds that women would use a lot more water and take more time.[47]

Indeed the struggle for piped water in this settlement continued until 1985, when the growing community needed even more running water. That year the settlers managed to obtain the consent of the municipality to extend the supply. Yet without waiting for the initiative of the bureaucracy, they themselves began to dig ditches and lay pipes. In doing so, they offended officials. In a bloody confrontation between the people and the Pasdaran, some settlers were arrested and a number injured.[48]

In 1984 in Arak, an industrial town in the central province, hundreds of squatters from Zoorabad marched toward the town hall to demand running water. Rattling metal containers, they chanted: "water, water, we are thirsty." The protesters were forced to retreat after the Pasdaran were sent to control the situation.[49] Women of Mehdiyeh in South Tehran (in June 1985), Shahrak-i Fardis in Karadj (in June 1984), and elsewhere began similar struggles in the hope of developing their communities.[50] The residents of squatter areas in Tehran-Karadj road demonstrated while chanting "*na sharqui, na gharbi; na aabi, na barqui*" (neither East nor West; neither water, nor electricity), sarcastically referring to a government policy that ignored internal crises, such as urban problems, in favor of a senseless foreign policy rhetoric that dogmatically rejected ties with both the East and the West.

When noisy demonstrations proved insufficient, households began, individually or collectively, to connect their homes to the main street water pipe or to the electricity poles, at times by ingenious methods. The people of the Husseini neighborhood, in the southwest of Tehran, having attempted through the necessary formal channels to secure running water, decided in June 1984 to take the matters into their own hands. One night they secretly broke the main water pipe in the street and connected their already prepared pipes. Although this brought the arrest of six participants and a fine of Rls 300,000, they managed to maintain the illegal flow of city water.[51] In Khak-i Sefid, a settlement of 4,000 inhabitants, the squatters acquired electricity by do-it-yourself tactics. "We requested so many times to the Ministry of Power to connect us; but they didn't," stated a settler. "Now, because we really needed electricity, the people cooperated with each other to bring power into the community."[52] Another *zaghehnishin* in Tehran had similar story. "When I came to this place [in 1985], things were bad. But then people collected money to pave the roads. We got electricity from the power poles. And as for water, we ourselves installed pipes from the main street water tap"; "but we are still waiting for a school and gardens."[53] In 1987 an extensive study of about fifty shanties with some 8,000 families in seven districts of Tehran concluded that the majority of these settlements utilized illegal running water and electricity, in some cases with the tacit agreement of the municipality.[54]

An alleyway in Javanmard-Ghassab district, in south Tehran.
Nasrullah Kasraiyan and Hamideh Zolfaghari, *Tehran*, a book of photos, Tehran,
1373/1994, p. 56.

An old house in Pamenar, south Tehran.
Nasrullah Kasraiyan and Hamideh Zolfaghari, *Tehran*, a book of photos, Tehran, 1373/1994, p. 54.

A poor household, Maidan South, south Tehran.
Nasrullah Kasraiyan and Hamideh Zolfaghari, *Tehran*, a book of photos, Tehran, 1373/1994, p. 50.

A shantytown in south Tehran, March 1980.
Reza Deghati/Imax

A shantytown in south Tehran, June 1981.
Reza Deghati/Imax

An informal dwelling in Tehran, November 1979.
Reza Deghati/Imax

An apartment building occupied in Nizamabad, in south Tehran.
Ayandegan, 13 Khordad 1385/June 3, 1979.

A scene from Islamshahr, an informal community in south Tehran, 1993.
Goft-o-gu, 1 (1993): 78.

Khak-i Sefid squatter settlement, Tehran, 1986.
By a student of the Faculty of Art and Architecture, University of Tehran.

Khak-i Sefid squatter settlement, Tehran, 1986.
By a student of the Faculty of Art and Architecture, University of Tehran.

A shantytown in south Tehran, March 1981. "President: Welcome to the gate of civilization!"
Reza Deghati/Imax

"Illegal tapping of electricity." Squatter community of Shahrak-i Shahid
Mutahari, Tehran, 1988.

Ettilaat-i Syassi-Iqtisadi 21 (Tir 1367/1988): 54.

Children of Gowd squatter settlement in south Tehran. The placard reads, "We, the people of the *gowds*, are in the forefront of anti-imperialist and anti-American struggles."

Faryad-i Gowdnishin 50 (18 Tir 1358/1979).

A tea house in Maidan Soush, south Tehran.
Nasrullah Kasraiyan and Hamideh Zolfaghari, *Tehran*, a book of photos, Tehran, 1373/1994, p. 50.

Unemployed workers demonstrating in Tehran, April 1979.
Tehran Musavvar 37 (12)(24 Farvardin 1358/April 13, 1979): 12.

Demonstrations of the unemployed, Tehran, April 1979.
Ayandegan, 29 Farvardin 1358/April 18, 1979.

A street vendor in the Tehran bus terminal.
Reza Deghati/Imax

A young vendor, close to Tehran Bazaar, March 1980.
Reza Deghati/Imax

Vendors packed in a bazaar alleyway, Tehran, mid-1980s.
Nasrullah Kasraiyan and Hamideh Zolfaghari, *Tehran*, a book of photos, Tehran, 1373/
1994, p. 54.

Vendors and an active crowd in a Tehran street, mid-1980s.
Nasrullah Kasraiyan and Hamideh Zolfaghari, *Tehran*, a book of photos, Tehran, 1373/1994, p. 54.

An old vendor selling prayer beads, Tehran, mid-1980s.
Nasrullah Kasraiyan and Hamideh Zolfaghari, *Tehran*, a book of photos, Tehran, 1373/
1994, p. 54.

"Give us jobs and we will give up street vending. Maintain our livelihood and we shall give up vending." Union of street vendors. Tehran, December 1979.
Reza Deghati/Imax

Clash between street vendors and the Pasdaran who attempted to dismantle their kiosks. Tehran, August 12, 1979.

Reza Deghati/Imax

At times the skills of young volunteers, mainly students and activists, were also utilized for development, education, and health purposes. Groups of young volunteers established libraries, tutorial and literacy classes in neighborhoods.[55] In 1980 the residents of the Dowlatabad settlement brought illegal light to their community when student activists hooked their homes to power lines that passed over the settlement. With the new electricity came a communal place to receive guests, a mosque, and a mobile clinic.[56] Volunteer work in specialized fields was even more prevalent. Many popular neighborhoods enjoyed the assistance of doctors, nurses, and engineering students. In the squatter areas of South Tehran (e.g., Arab gowds), a number of medical units were set up, where over a hundred patients were diagnosed daily for a meager Rls 30 (nearly U.S.$0.5) each. In this community some 1,000 medical files were organized.[57] The spirit of voluntarism, however, tended to diminish among the middle-class activists when revolutionary fervor began to subside and the police surveillance kept many youths from such activities.

Unlike scattered *zaghehs* built before the revolution, I found a number of squatter areas such as Khak-i Sefid or Islamshahr reasonably clean, green, and orderly, with wide paved streets and alleyways, and sizable one-story homes whose residents collectively self-managed the communities. In Khak-i Sefid, for instance, residents realized that "the area did not have a plan and the streets were all irregular. So we got an architect who did the job; and we helped to build the pavements. . . . We built our own mosque where every two weeks people go for *rowze-khani*."[58]

This appears to be the kind of community participation that many in today Third World, including the right and the left, favor. The right views self-help as reducing dependence on the state and its financial burden; community participation, in this sense, is hoped to consolidate the political system. For the left, community participation serves to raise the social consciousness and living standards of the poor, eventually producing social transformation. Based upon Latin American experience, others conclude that community participation serves the interests of the state better than it serves the poor.[59] The Iranian pattern deviated from the prevailing models, first because, in their struggles the Iranian poor often combined institutional channels with direct actions, legal with illegal methods. On the other hand, community participation was understood not simply as self-cost self-help but as communal activism that *incurred costs* (in terms of property, profit, and power) to the state and the rich—in short, others-cost self-help.

In the case of Iran, as the government confronted extensive illegal land occupation and unpaid consumption of urban amenities, it felt that it would be better off integrating parts of the settlements to ensure both state control and compensation for the use of collective services. As a result some squatter lands in South Tehran were placed under *awqaf*, which, although it tolerated settlers, required them to pay some annual rent. In this way, the authorities recognized and extended urban services to a number of poor settlements.

The immediate problem, so far as the government was concerned, was that over-consumption of water and electricity entailed lowering water pressure and daily power cuts, thus causing widespread dissatisfaction and protests.[60] For the settlers, on the other hand, the policy appeared to be a victory. Apart from securing the formal provision of city amenities, official recognition also greatly reduced their tenure insecurities. Yet the involvement of the authorities conflicted with the desire for autonomy and for life without state interference. Formalizing the settlements meant undergoing bureaucratic control and taxation. Formal subscription to water, electricity, and refuse collection meant that the poor were obliged to pay for these services, at specific times. The issues of payment, timing, and procedures were no longer negotiable. Although the poor had struggled to extend such services to their illegal homes, they soon realized that they could not afford to pay the bills and play bureaucratic games.[61] Some poor families ended up having services suspended due to delays in payment (as in District 16 in Tehran). Once again women made journeys to nearby mosques and neighborhoods to wash dishes and clothes, and resorted to oil lamps and burners instead of electrical power. The more persistent inhabitants resorted to manipulating meters as their short-term alternative.

In sum, to develop their communities, the poor utilized their own initiatives and efforts. When the effects of self-help proved limited, they pressed the government to assist them. When the authorities resisted, the poor redistributed collective goods to their own advantage—that is, they stole urban infrastructure. Once gains were assured in this unlawful fashion, the poor collectively defended them, eventually forcing the state to recognize the communities in exchange for their integration into the formal structures. Thus the disenfranchised laid further claims, consolidated their position, and secured wider concessions. In these attempts, creating local associations was particularly significant, since in their genuine forms, the associations represented a significant counterpoint to formal power.

Associational Life

In poor communities, association and networking served in the short run as the necessary mechanism for mobilization and defense. Although the encroachments of the poor were, by and large, quiet and individual, there were issues concerning everyone that were beyond the capacity of individual households. Dealing with floods, police raids, paving roads, digging ditches, collecting garbage, setting local prices, and other undertakings needed the cooperation of all settlement members. In the long term autonomous life under a modern state also required some kind of local affiliation and identity, which often assumed an organizational expression. Performing common cultural and religious rituals, resolving conflicts, and providing mutual assistance were among the more salient examples. The associational life was one of primordial and civil extra-kinship. Two associations particularly stood out in the poor neighborhoods—the Neighborhood Councils (NCs), and the Local Consumer Cooperatives (LCCs).

The Neighborhood Councils

The Neighborhood Councils (NCs)(*Shura-ye Mahallat*), or Neighborhood Committees (*Komite-ye Mahallat*) as some preferred to call them, were loosely structured local bodies that were formed, appointed, elected, or even self-designated in order to protect, regulate, and upgrade local communities. Their function ranged from negotiating with the authorities for urban upgrading to resolving conflicts in the localities. The terms "committee" or "council" referred interchangeably both to the appointed/elected executive body and to the totality of the organization including the executive body, the constituency, and finally its activities.

Along with the Factory Committees (*Shura-ye Kargaran*), Peasant (*Shura-ye Dehqanan*), University (*Shura-ye Daneshgah*), and City Councils (*Shura-ye Shahr*) (as in Kurdistan, for instance), and Pasdaran Committees (*Komite-ye Pasdaran*) in the early days following the insurrection, the NCs constituted the massive grassroots mobilization of the revolution. These organizations, along with other self-help activities, gave an organized expression to popular mobilization; they exemplified the social and civic (as opposed to purely political) aspect of the revolution.

A whole range of NCs sprang up in various lower-class neighborhoods. Some continued the activities of the Local Committees that had emerged during the last phase of the revolution. Others were established after the insurrection. Apart from the general mood of mobilization during the postrevolutionary period, certain material reasons also stimulated their emergence.

Confronting common crises such as flooding or earthquakes in the localities often necessitated collective mobilization. The gowd communities of South Tehran were the victims of frequent flooding due to their location some 50 meters below ground level (some places had 150 stairs). Any rainfall, flood, or sewage system failure would threaten almost every household. Only the cooperation and coordination of all of households was capable of countering such disasters. Protecting alleyways from flood, securing personal belongings, and diverting flood water from the community demanded highly collective efforts. Although these crises and their consequent social impact were periodic, they nevertheless implanted the seeds of a nascent yet durable and structured form of cooperation.

Prior to the revolution, a number of neighborhoods in the gowds formed informal local associations. They raised funds and managed to construct stairways connecting the underground settlements to the surface. They also succeeded in bringing communal water taps to their alleyways, and installed electricity poles. Soon electric light illuminated the narrow passageways and before long found its way into homes as well. The graveyards of the poor surrounding the area were transformed into picnic places with greenery and trees.[62]

Local mobilization aside, the competition of various political groups over mobilizing the poor also contributed to the formation of the NCs. The advocacy of the radical left and Mujahedin organization for the idea of "councilism" certainly played a significant role. Their sympathizers were involved directly in local mobilization, and their emphasis on the idea of *shura* forced eventually the authorities to give legal sanction to the idea.

One important figure who pursued shuraism quite vehemently was a popular liberal clergyman, Ayatollah Taleghani, whose death in 1979 brought the concept into public discourse. Radio, TV, and the print media, not to mention public speeches, began to focus extensively on the merits of shuraism, and on how this notion originated with Islam. For the most part shuraism was conceived of as some degree of popular participation, but its extent and mechanism remained vague. Some even went so far as to propose restructuring the country's political system along the principle of shuraism. The left joined many others to support Taleghani who had called in April 1979 for the constitution of local associations as well as city and regional councils.[63] Sympathetic figures in the municipality followed suit and began implementing the idea from above.

In the spring of 1980 the government of Isfahan, the second largest city in Iran, took up the initiative. Within a few months some 70 percent of the city was administered by the Neighborhood Committees. NCs elected the mayor and administered their locales. But the policy ceased to function in the summer of that year, when the budget allocated by the Governorate was halted due to financial difficulties.[64]

The city of Tehran followed Isfahan. Conditions of the war with Iraq had made the need for local administration and self-organization more urgent. People needed to get mobilized, remain vigilant, organize in self-defense committees, and participate in the local distribution of basic resources such as food and medicine. The capital was divided into twenty districts and 341 neighborhoods of 10,000 people. Each constituency was to "appoint" five representatives from among "trustworthy," "pious" (ba-taqwa) and "enthusiastic" people, who then needed to be approved by the imam of the local mosque. This restrictive selection of shura members shows that the Islamic state perceived local organizations as an extension of itself.

The early enthusiasm and pretense of officials with regard to the idea of councilism and decentralization was followed, before too long, by the monopoly of power and paternalistic and selective mobilization of progovernment individuals. Councils were incorporated into the Islamic Constitution, but they were not properly convened. It was a concession to Taleghani and the left, but once he died and the left was crushed, the promise was forgotten.[65] Despite the state's attempt to control local initiatives, people in certain neighborhoods managed, with the cooperation of the volunteers, to establish genuine local councils. The gowds of South Tehran, for instance, developed a highly active shura, which came to be known as the Shura-ye Aali-ye Eskan-

i Gowdnishinan (Council for the Resettlement of the Gowd People) or in short, the Council of Resettlement (CR).

The Council of Resettlement

In the early days of the spring of 1980 a group of young volunteers came to the gowd settlements to offer their help in improving the conditions of life in these neighborhoods. A few weeks later, on April 4, 1980, an election was held, with the support of the radical mayor of Tehran, Muhammad Tavassoli, to form the Council of the gowdnishinan. Fifteen out of sixteen gowd settlements took part in the elections, each sending three delegates to form the central council of the gowdnishinan. A combination of two representatives from the central council, two from the municipality, and one from the local Pasdaran Committee established the *Shura-ye Aali-e Gowd*, the supreme Council of the Gowds.[66]

Most of the elected representatives were local leaders who were factory workers in nearby industries such as SAKA on Tehran Karadj Road. Although the CR aimed, in the short term, to improve the conditions of life in the gowds, its prime concern revolved around the resettlement of the 46,000 residents into more decent housing.[67]

With the help of the council and the cooperation of the central municipality, the settlers, in particular the youth, established a clinic, a *husseinieh* (an ad hoc mosque), several libraries, and a soccer field. *Fishaari*s (street fountains) were erected; sewage ditches (*jouy*s) were dug, and the roads of fourteen settlements were fully paved.[68]

The council also set up mobile medical teams and clinics in the streets of South Tehran, providing general medical services and vaccination for infants.[69] Some cultural activities and sports facilities for youths were housed in the already occupied buildings of the previous regime,[70] while the morally deviant elements in the community, e.g., gamblers and drug dealers, were identified and isolated.

The outbreak of war with Iraq in September 1980, and the ensuing threat of air raids broke new ground for the activities of the CR and the local poor. The CR and the Mujahedin Organization in the gowds called for the creation of Local Resistance Groups (LRG) to respond to the wartime emergency situation. They were to link their activities with the local people through instructions on wall posters, pamphleteering, and assemblies in the local mosques. Although not entirely successful, some LRGs were formed in South Tehran with the participation of the youth. They identified local resources, especially medical services and basic needs, for emergency purposes, formed vigilante teams, engaged in military training, put up wall posters with information and war news, and provided instructions regarding security and self-defense.[71] A young volunteer described some of the functions of the LRGs in Yakhchiabad squatter settlement:

> Initially, we began talking to our local fuel-distribution branches about the problem of the fuel shortage, and suggested implementing a rationing system. They accepted the suggestion. We then talked to the people about the plan and they received it warmly and offered their cooperation. To implement the plan, we divided our neighborhood, which is quite large, into smaller zones. Then, we took a census of the households within each zone. With the cooperation of *Basij* [Mobilization Groups] brothers, we planned to issue rationing cards to each household, so that they could get their shares on the assigned days. This aimed to prevent long queues and hoarding. We now plan to ask the people to provide us with some help so that we can bring each household's share of fuel to their door steps. . . . About other basic food stuff, we have already prepared things like grain, eggs, rice, sugar, tea, and washing powder, which we supply to the people without making any profit. However, we're planning to ration these items as well in the future.[72]

Despite these activities, the CR considered its most important function to be relocating the gowd residents. Some significant steps were taken. The CR was able to compensate the owners of over five hundred run-down homes so that they could settle in other areas; it also managed to rehouse another six hundred households in already occupied apartments.[73] Some families needing immediate assistance were taken to emergency headquarters until permanent housing was available.[74] The CR also combined its policy of negotiations with the authorities with a more militant tactic of local mobilization. When necessary, the CR staged street demonstrations so that local people could make their demands to the authorities more forcefully.[75]

The activities of the CR came to an end after a year and a half, in the midst of growing political rivalry and intolerance. At the beginning it seemed that all the different local groupings—the *Komiteh*s, the Mujahedin, the leftists and the municipality—cooperated with one another on local issues. However, political and ideological differences soon surfaced, and alliances gave way to sectarianism both at the

national and local levels. The Pasdaran *Komiteh*s, which originally
emerged as a voluntary civic organization consisting of youths with
different political orientations, soon became a vestige of the ruling
Islamic Republican Party. In early summer 1979, the *Komiteh*s were
"cleansed" of those who refused to follow the IRP line. In Tehran
alone, some 40,000 to 50,000 members of about 1,500 *Komiteh*s were
sent home.[76] Many others had already left after becoming disen-
chanted with the monopolistic policies of their leaders. The *Komiteh*s
then began a sustained campaign against the growing power of leftists
and the Mujahedin.

Thus the CR became the target of mounting pressure on the part of
the local Pasdaran *Komiteh*, which by now had become a parallel
power in the community. Organized thugs supported by the local
Revolutionary Guards attacked the headquarters of the CR; the
Komiteh organized mass meetings to discredit the CR; and rumors
spread accusing its members of bribery. Finally, material support to the
council was suspended from both the municipality and, of course, the
*Komiteh*s. Not being able to cope with such a mounting pressure, all
members of the CR jointly resigned on May 14, 1980 as a gesture of
protest. A few months later the publication of *Faryad-i Gowdnishin*, a
weekly journal of the Mujahedin, devoted to the gowd community,
was suspended by the government. With this, the activities of one
autonomous local organization came to an end.

Beyond political pressure, internal problems also weakened the CR.
Political organizations lent their support to localities not so much to
promote people's welfare as to cultivate political support. For the
Mujahedin, for example, the "Local Resistance Cells not only play an
effective role, in the short run, in alleviating war damages, but in the
long run serve people's mobilization against imperialism."[77] On the
other hand, the elitist nature of such activism made residents rely
excessively on outside organizations, whose infighting ultimately
undermined local mobilization. Finally, the council was far from genuinely democratic institution; activists had only begun to experience
participatory democracy. To make a comparison, in postrevolutionary
Portugal, for instance, the neighborhood commission was an elected
body. Although activists spearheaded local organizations, ordinary
people were extensively involved in decision-making. Local power lay
in weekly general assemblies, with the votes cast by raising hands.[78] In
Iran formal polls were uncommon and lines of power and responsibil-

ities unclear. As regular, general meetings were rare, rumors more than correct information reflected local politics, in turn, fueling sectarian conflict and rivalry. Ordinary people only began to experience modern participatory democracy in these turbulent times when the state instituted its own brand.

Working Within the System

Like the Council of Resettlement, many of the independent *shuras* were dismantled and their members were purged. With the state-sponsored "new elections" more proregime members were put in charge, and in many ways the neighborhood councils turned into an extension of the ruling IRP. The poor had to adjust to the new phase of increasing political restriction and the absence of opposition groups. They needed to work within and against the official apparatuses. Patient and persevering, the poor struggled to gain from these paternalistic institutions as much as they could by exploiting the pro-*mustaz'afin* discourse of the government to exert pressure on local authorities.

As autonomous and grassroots institutions were gradually dismantled due to political pressure and their own shortcomings, the alternative government-sponsored organizations, Mosque Associations (*shura-ye masajid*) and Islamic Neighborhood Councils (INCs), rapidly filled the vacuum. They began to serve with more zeal and commitment, partially in order to demonstrate the efficacy of the alternative arrangements. The local Pasdaran *Komite*s first took the initiative, involving proregime local individuals who then centered their activities in the local mosques. These local councils became increasingly active after the outbreak of the war with Iraq, when local popular mobilization became a necessity. Thus the Mosque Associations were engaged in mobilizing the local population for the war effort, distributing scarce goods such as domestic appliances, and settling disputes. They were also charged with supervising and monitoring the rationing system involving local shops. The members of these associations, in the meantime, also acted as neighborhood watchdogs for the ruling IRP.

Hundreds of such associations functioned throughout the urban areas during the eight-year war. Their main strength derived from their official status, which enabled them to utilize government resources and political support. They cooperated with the Governorate of Tehran (Farmandari) to control the flow of rural migrants to the city, by controlling the issuance of ration cards within the localities.[79] In 1983, Mahdavi-Kani called upon the Mosque Associations to "furnish the ground for the stability of the Islamic Republic."[80]

The weaknesses of the INCs, however, remained more acute. Corruption, inefficiency in the distribution of the basic needs, bureaucratic incompetence, and overlapping functions with other agencies (such as *Komiteh-ye Imdad-i Imam*), tarnished their image before their constituencies.[81] Yet, given the conditions of war, scarcity, and government intolerance of autonomous association, the situation at the local level would probably have been worse without the Mosque Associations. With the war at a stalemate, and with the gradual relaxation of pressure on the distribution system, the conjunctural role of the associations began to subside. By the time the war was moving toward a resolution, the Mosque Associations were essentially withering away. Controlled by local elites, their function in the postwar period was relegated largely to ad hoc ceremonial activities.[82]

The Local Consumer Cooperatives

On May 24, 1980, a group of angry housewives from a lower-class neighborhood, Gorgan Street, forcefully closed down the fruit market of the Maidan-i Somaiyeh and the nearby stores. The women's repeated complaints to both local shopkeepers and the authorities over the high prices of food had been ignored. When one woman protested to a fruit-seller about his high prices, others rallied behind her, expressing their frustration and anger. A street demonstration of local people soon followed, as housewives proceeded to close down the market place, one shop after the other, by yanking down the metal gates (*kerkereh*) of each store. The police reported that the angry women wanted to set the market on fire but were persuaded to disperse only by an immediate repricing of the goods. The shops remained closed for the entire day.[83]

Like housing, food constituted a special commodity, one that the poor viewed in moral terms. When the satisfaction of these basic needs was left to the whims of the market alone, the poor resisted and attempted to subvert the market both by direct action, as evidenced by the angry housewives, and by institutional means, e.g., the consumer cooperatives.

Through Local Consumer Cooperatives (LCCs), poor urbanites attempted to secure easy access to inexpensive consumer goods by removing greedy middle men. Earlier attempts to set up consumer cooperatives had occurred during the few weeks before the insurrection (see p. 52). After an initial decline immediately after the revolution, LCCs resurfaced throughout lower-class and poor districts after the outbreak of the Iran-Iraq war. By December 1979 the constitution recognized cooperatives as one of the three main economic sectors. In 1981 some 60 LCCs were set up in the lower-class neighborhoods of Tehran. By 1985, 600,000 Tehranies cooperated in 530 LCCs with a total capital of Rls 4,000 million. These cooperatives, along with those in the provincial cities, were placed under the supervision of the Central Organization of the Cooperatives, a government agency.[84]

In general, the people themselves ran the cooperatives. In the more independent experiences, a number of individuals, the "constituent group," set up ad hoc cooperatives, inviting local people to purchase shares. The members subsequently elected executive committees (EC) and dissolved the constituent groups. The ECs then assumed the responsibility of managing the LCC in terms of purchasing, distribution, and book-keeping. A group of observers (*bazresan*) were responsible for monitoring the operation.[85] Middlemen were eliminated and the profit motive, when it existed, was only to cover the cost of hiring full-time administrators.[86]

Most of the LCCs, however, were dominated by local elites, the religious, community, and economically well-to-do leaders.[87] For these leaders the LCCs served more as their personal properties, at best functioning as typical charities and at worst as a source of local prestige and access to the high officials. Instead of *cooperation*, a spirit of *paternalism* prevailed. During the revolution ideas of solidarity and selflessness constituted the spirit of voluntarism. After the revolution principles of efficiency and profit- motive eventually replaced ideals of cooperation. As a result, some cooperatives, ended their activities.[88]

Yet the LCCs did contribute to the poor's access to basic commodities in the difficult times of the scarcity of consumer goods, war-time economic conditions, and high-priced black market goods. In addition to subsidizing basic goods and implementing a rationing system, the government contributed to the LCCs by allocating 10 percent of the total domestic production and imported goods directly to the LCCs to be distributed among members, with fixed prices and without profits. Moreover, the LCCs furnished a vehicle through which common people were activated socially and were directed onto a path of institution-building.

Nevertheless, when institutional channels such as LCCs were nonexistent or proved to be ineffective, the common people did not hesitate to take matters directly into the streets. Early plans to remove subsidies on bus fares provoked riots in Tehran and Mashad. Indeed, the postwar economic liberalization under President Rafsanjani witnessed widespread unrest on the part of the urban poor in the early 1990s (see below). The latest of these riots in April 1995 in Islamshar, a South Tehran squatter settlement, left at least one dead, dozens injured, and hundreds arrested. This three-day street protest was sparked by some two hundred youths who demanded better supplies of fresh water, as well as a decrease in the bus fare. It rapidly grew into a demonstration of 50,000 poor people protesting against price rises for public transport and fuel. The police used tear gas from helicopter units to disperse the crowd who attacked government buildings, banks, department stores, gas stations, and buses.[89] As elsewhere, poor housewives were major actors in the street politics that involved food prices and shortages.

In contrast to occasional food riots and collective actions (e.g., the housewives of Maidan-i Somaiyeh and the Islamshahr riots), public nagging was employed as an everyday form of protest by ordinary people. It involved people collectively voicing their complaints without the fear of persecution in public places—in taxis, buses, bakery queues, grocery shops, and so on—in the form of loud conversations about state policies including prices, rents, war, shortages, and the like. Public nagging represented an effective mechanism for expressing the public opinion of ordinary men and women; it became an epidemic and irrepressible source of dissent.[90]

Squatters and the State

In brief, squatters' struggles took place in three main arenas: First, resistance to existing hardship and aspiring to a better life. These were manifested in physical movement and migration and entailed a profound demographic change in the country. Second, struggles around the redistribution of public goods, including land and urban collective consumption. And third, attempts to extend autonomy from the state, relying on local norms instead of state legislatures, traditional and accessible institutions instead of modern official arrangements. These struggles, when cumulative, positioned the poor as a counter-hegemonic force against officialdom, as each practice captured an arena of control from the state and encroached on its power. These three areas accounted for the most important sites of contestation between the state and the marginal poor. Without intending to, the *mustaz'afin* had become an enemy of the Islamic state. How did the Islamic state, as the government of the poor, respond to these struggles?

The earlier official responses to squatters' actions were characterized by competition, confusion, and contradiction. Whereas prior to the Islamic revolution the poor had remained virtually unnoticed (see chapter 2), after the revolution their mobilization became the subject of competition among over twenty official and unofficial groups and organizations working within poor neighborhoods.

The ruling clergy, seeking a reliable social base, made the *mustaz'afin* the champions of struggle for Islam and the Islamic revolution. Within this broad category, urban marginals, or *koukhnishinan* (literally hut-dwellers, the destitutes), acquired a central position. "This Islamic revolution is indebted to the efforts of this class, the class of shanty dwellers," declared Ayatollah Khomeini. "These South Tehranies, these footbearers, as we call them, they are our masters [*vali-ne'mat*] . . . They were the ones who brought us to where we are."[91] To the dismay of Prime Minister Mehdi Bazargan, Khomeini declared only a few days after the revolution that "everyone must have access to land, this divine endowment," that "no one must remain without a dwelling in this country," and that water and electricity should be supplied free of charge to the poor.[92] Bazargan, like President Bani Sadr and Muhammad Tavassoli, the mayor of Tehran, feared that such statements would unleash uncontrollable migration and urban disorder. They called instead for rural development and improvements in agriculture, although they also favored the selective upgrading of existing poor neighborhoods. In 1980 the Revolutionary Council discussed, without results, ways to repatriate to the countryside some shanty dwellers, like the inhabitants of the gowd in South Tehran.

In the meantime, as I have already discussed, the Office of Housing for the Dispossessed led by Hassan Karrubi and the Housing Foundation of Ayatollah Khosrowshahi, opted for radical confiscation and allocation of homes and land for the homeless. The major leftist groups supported these measures. The Pasdaran opposed the confiscations, advocating the upgrading of poor communities instead. Yet they prevented volunteer groups, in particular Leftist and Mujahedin organizations, from undertaking similar activities there.[93]

This rivalry in practice and opinions had significant implications for the housing sector and the status of squatters. First, it offered new opportunities for the mobilization of the poor by encouraging them to make demands and further legitimizing their direct action. On the other hand, a profound policy confusion with regard to housing and land prevailed, rendering the systematic handling of homelessness and poverty impossible. Troubles eased slightly only when, in June 1980, Hassan Karrubi's Office was abolished and Ayatollah Khosrowshahi was sent off to be the ambassador in the Vatican.[94]

With the fall of the housing radicals, the government brought some legal and administrative order to the sector; its most important single step was the promulgation of the Urban Land Law whereby the Revolutionary Council nationalized and thus controlled *mawaat* (unused) land and later *baayer* (previously used) lands in urban areas.[95] Nevertheless, the government never formulated a consistent policy with regard to housing the poor. Even the new thinking, which advocated the elimination of government responsibility by leaving the housing of the poor to themselves and to their "savings," remained up in the air.[96] Indeed, throughout the 1980s the prevailing policy combined five strategies: selective housing provisions, halting rural-urban migration, integrating the informals, demolishing unlawful homes, and de facto tolerance.

Selective Provisions

The Housing Foundation continued to function with the aim of providing housing for the poor. In 1980, upon the invitation of the Foundation, more than 800,000 people sent in applications for land or housing. The foundation claimed to grant about 100,000 plots of land and 2,500 homes, most of them in rural areas.[97] Yet following the Iran-Iraq war, the bulk of the foundation's activities were directed to war reconstruction, and its function was limited to promoting self-help housing through interest-free loans and the provision of materials and technical assistance.[98] In addition to the Housing Foundation, the municipalities in the large cities cleared a number of slums, relocating their residents to more decent dwellings, or offered them aid and loans to build their own homes. The squatters of Khaniabad in South Tehran were to be relocated in about 1,000 two-bedroom, 72-square-meter flats the government planned to construct,[99] converting the settlement to public parks and recreational facilities. Some of the communities, such as the notorious gowd settlements in South Tehran, have had symbolic significance for officials as the embodiment of *istiz'af* (poverty and misery), and thus were incompatible with the self-image of the Islamic Republic as the government of the dispossessed.

Halting Migration, "This Social Catastrophe"

Yet the continuous flow of rural poor to the cities in search of a better life diluted the effects of such piecemeal measures. While the regime seemed to have succeeded in reducing the overall fertility rate,[100] cityward migration remained a major problem. By 1983 Iran had more people in cities (52.5 percent) than in the countryside. Despite the shortcomings, squatters were evidently happier in the city and were not prepared to return to the country.[101]

Whereas the poor viewed migration as a means to a better life, for the authorities it represented a "social catastrophe,"[102] "the most important problem beside the war,"[103] and "a major threat to the revolution and the Islamic Republic."[104] This was because the population flow was altering the urban order by bringing about communities, social groups, and social practices upon which the central authority would have little practical control.

By 1983 when the cityward migration was accelerating, officials frantically sought a solution. In February of that year, the mayor of Tehran, Habibi, pleaded with Ayatollah Khomeini to declare a "state of emergency" terming the migration one of the most crucial political concerns of the day. The state media subsequently began a campaign against the population drift; Friday prayer leaders were mobilized to discuss the vices of moving to cities and numerous seminars were organized to address this "major social problem."

The dominant discourse denounced migration as a social pathology that was infecting the whole of urban life. It was responsible for "land speculation," "unemployment," "parasitic occupations," "drug dealing," "disease," and urban unrest, and was also "destroy[ing] social and Islamic values."[105] In their turn, migrants were portrayed as the victims of this disorder. *Hamshahri*, the Tehran municipality daily, unknowingly invoked the spirit of Simmel, Park, and Wirth when it described rural migrants as "those who wander aimlessly around in the quicksand of the city . . . these victims of ignorance, naiveté, and propaganda—they live a particular sort of life; they represent the men on the margin."[106] The anxiety over squatter expansion also perplexed the community of experts: the rural poor were shaking their epistemological order. These experts viewed migration as "a phenomenon which is transforming the destiny of the cities, presenting itself as an urban and political challenge."[107] The roots of the disorder were to be found primarily in the "wrong policies of the past regime," notably in the Land Reform program.[108] At times the problem was even attributed to "a calculated plot by our enemies who lure the villagers into the cities."[109]

The migrant poor were not aloof from this discourse. Their reaction was bitter; as some squatters put it:

> It is ridiculous that they [the government] are treating us, the *mus-taz'afin*, like this, slandering us. They write [in newspapers] that we keep the water taps running, that we waste water. But then we don't even have running water! Or that we keep our gates open until very late at night, or that our boys refuse going to military service; whereas my own son is in the service! As a matter of fact, this community is being protected by our own *basij* boys; the municipality has done nothing for the security of this place. . . . Is this divine and Islamic government not supposed to protect us, the *koukhnishin*, the *hashiyenishin*, the weak?[110]

Beyond the ideological campaign, the state also devised some concrete measures to stop the population drift. The Mosque Associations were instructed to deny food ration cards to migrant families. The government also attempted to restrict the purchase of homes or land by the migrants in cities by controlling all relevant transactions.[111] These legislative measures had little impact, however, precisely because of the informal and autonomous way in which the poor tend to operate and subsist. "These migrants simply need not and do not apply for any permits; as a matter of fact, they do not deal with us at all," the housing minister acknowledged.[112]

In the long run the government aimed to improve agriculture and rural communities as necessary measures to deter cityward migration. The Construction Crusade achieved considerable success in rural electrification and the construction of roads, which in practice facilitated traveling to cities. Nevertheless, urban bias remained the practical policy of the Islamic government despite its ruralist discourse.[113]

Formalizing the Informals

Given these conditions, few options remained available to the government. One was to formalize or integrate the illegal communities into the state structure by recognizing their status and incorporating them in urban collective consumption. This strategy would not only ensure popular support and state control of the poor, it would also make residents pay for the services that they would otherwise tap informally.

For the poor, informality served both as a means of coping and of livelihood, and as an end in itself. In the settlements the poor evaded the institutions of the state and governed their own lives, tacitly rejecting bureaucracy, taxation, the discipline of time, and the regulation of space. For instance, over 80 percent of Islamshar inhabitants did not see any role for the municipality in regulating their community.[114] And in the surrounding settlements, over half of the people avoided the state bureaucracy.[115] Instead, extending kinship through intercommunal marriages served to expand cooperation and mutual responsibility. "One of the advantages of living here" said a resident of Aliabad, Khazaneh, "is that I am next to my village fellows [hamshahri]. And since my work requires me to travel a lot, I always feel relieved that my family is secure among them."[116] Others felt happy that "everyone is related in here, and they help each other out."[117]

The poor contested the dominant spatial policies and perceptions. They built their dwellings according to their own needs, taste, and resources (e.g., raising domestic animals), avoiding police control concerning how to appear or assemble in public, and when to pay bills and return loans. For instance, when relocated to the apartments of the Shahrak-i Shoush, squatters of the gowd settlements built courtyards around their apartments by making the alleyways private domain and erecting a wall or fence around the apartments. A number of them returned to their old squatter dwellings. Some of the settlers of Pol-i Mudiriyat and Halabshahr of Tehran Pars, who had been given homes in new apartments, eventually moved and settled in other squatter settlements.[118] The relocation project of Kouy-e Nohom-i Aban in South Tehran before the revolution had a similar problem. Many squatters who had been relocated into the government housing either sold or rented out those homes and moved back into shacks. In Bandar Abbas, the 2,500-unit government housing turned after a while into a spontaneous settlement primarily because such government housing patterns did not meet the needs of the poor.[119]

Yet integrating these communities was crucial for the Islamic state. The populist regime could hardly tolerate diversity, let alone autonomy. It was adamant about molding an obedient Islamic *umma*—a concept totally in contrast with that of the squatter settlements, which some officials viewed as bastions of lawlessness, deviance, and potential dissent. Some marginal neighborhoods in Tehran were granted official recognition when the government was forced to change the administrative boundaries of the city. Yet integration was not so simple, since it could foster further migration; it would also require massive infrastructural facilities, as well as a reorganization of the cities. Furthermore, as the experience of Islamshahr in Tehran shows, any practice of integration with which the subjects could not afford to cope, sows the seeds of new marginality. In the early 1990s the settlers of Islamshahr campaigned for the official recognition of their community. Once that was achieved, however, new marginal communities sprang up around the settlement in Akbarabad and Soltanabad through the illegal construction of agricultural and *awqaf* lands.[120] It was partly these constraints that would push the authorities to resort to forced eviction and demolition of unlawful dwellings.

Demolishing Communities

Squatters suffered intermittent attacks by the security forces throughout the 1980s and the early 1990s. The intensity and frequency of assaults shifted depending on national political conditions, the policies of particular mayors, and the reaction of the squatters. The earlier (1979–1984) demolitions seemed haphazard and unsystematic, with the Pasdaran mainly in charge of urban order. The pressure on the squatters increased after the summer of 1981, following a widespread government crackdown on the opposition. From 1984 on, demolition work became more systematic. In July 1984 the Tehran municipality built a 300-man task force composed of the army and municipality agents, who patrolled the streets to catch violations before they actually occurred. The task force was made up of seventy-six units who covered mainly the peripheral areas of South and Northwest Tehran around the clock in three separate shifts.[121] By September 1985 the task force had increased to 1,000 men.[122]

Numerous communities were attacked throughout the 1980s, often by paramilitary gendarmes escorted by trucks and bulldozers. The earliest reported attempts in Tehran included those in Dashtak, Shahrak-i Mamazan, Shahrak-i Qiam, Shahrak-i Karoun, Shahrak-i Kianshahr, Qal'eh Hasankhan, Shadshahr, Nizamabad, a community in Varamin road, all in the south, and Khak-i Sefid in the east of the city. Squatters in provincial cities such as Mashad, Arak, Tabriz, Isfahan, Bakhtaran, Kradj, Khoramabad, Ardabil, and others did not remain immune from eviction attempts. While selected homes were destroyed, settlements were under constant surveillance by the vigilant Pasdaran and special task forces, who drove around in military jeeps to make sure that no new shacks were put up and that none of the existing ones were consolidated.

The total number of homes and business places destroyed is unknown. But a report quoting the municipality of Tehran suggested that during summer 1992 alone, some 2,000 unlawful homes and business places were torn down.[123]

In an earlier well-known incident in Khak-i Sefid, in Tehran Pars, east of the capital city, where illegal housing grew rapidly after the revolution, some 1,000 Pasdars and army soldiers encircled the settlement from the north on January 11, 1980, intending to level the community once and for all. At 4 A.M. they halted traffic in the area; the operation began at 7 A.M. By the end of the day, thirty homes had been destroyed and more than forty people detained. "The day after when I went there, the scattered debris pointed to what had happened," recalled an eyewitness and activist. "It was clear that people had not slept through the night. They had anticipated the assault. Women with sleepy eyes were busy taking their belongings out of rubble, while swearing at the regime, especially the municipality and the Pasdaran."[124] "It was also obvious that the security forces had been unable to destroy them all; people had resisted."[125]

Resistance against the destruction of squatter areas was confirmed repeatedly by the authorities.[126] The Pasdaran's routine warnings and deadlines were missed, renewed, and invariably ignored. Corruption among government agents made things even harder. "A few years ago [1990], the municipality sent its agents to evict us from here. They came, got some money, and left."[127] The intermittent offensives often entailed bloody confrontations and street unrest. On many occasions the assaults were offset by women and children refusing to leave their dwellings, and by others laying themselves down in front of the bulldozers. In the Khak-i Sefid incident, once the security forces withdrew, the inhabitants staged a demonstration, chanting, "We built homes with our blood, and they destroy them so easily." They marched on to convey their anger at the local municipality office. The day after, when the municipality trucks returned to collect the debris, the residents attacked them, inflicting heavy damages. A new march was organized,bringing some four hundred people to the municipality office once again. The demonstrators staged a sit-in and demanded that they be compensated for the damages to their homes. Three members of the Neighborhood Council began negotiating with the authorities, agreeing on a plan to identify the opportunist developers from the "real homeless" who deserved to keep their homes.[128]

Noisy resistance of this sort made the government try different tactics, including buying off certain residents and divide-and-rule tactics—as is evident in the case of Shahrak-i Kianshahr. The government's attempt to evict over seven hundred households in this shahrak failed, despite the destruction of some one hundred homes in March 1990.[129] When its compensation offer was collectively rejected by the squatters, the municipality divided the latter by persuading a group of them (who worked for the municipality) to accept the offer. It then began to put pressure on the rest to comply, while threatening to cut off water and electricity and destroy shacks. By December 1992 it succeeded in evicting about 80 percent of the squatters in exchange for a payment of Rls 1,500,000–Rls 2,500,000 to each household.[130] The squatters of Pol-i Mudiriyat, in Tehran, however, rejected a similar deal in 1987, arguing that the compensation offered was not sufficient to purchase new homes. But to offset police provocation, they consciously prevented newcomers from joining the settlement.[131]

The prevalent spirit immediately after the revolution contributed to the militancy of the squatters in defending their gains. The urban riots some ten years later demonstrate the continuing collective passion with which the squatter poor defended their communities. During 1991 and 1992, five major incidents of unrest took place in Tehran, Shiraz, Mashad, Arak, and Khoramabad, in addition to frequent minor clashes in many urban centers. In August 1991 the squatters of Bagherabad, a district in South Tehran, rioted against the municipality agents who had begun demolishing their illegal shacks. The protesters threw stones at police and set the government cars on fire.[132] The Shiraz riots came less than one year later in March 1992, when some three hundred disabled war veterans staged street protests against the mismanagement of funds at the state-run Foundation of the

Dispossessed. They were immediately joined by squatters protesting their forced eviction from their illegally built homes. The protesters went on a rampage of looting, burning city buses, banks, and police stations. During this one-day riot, two protesters and six police were killed, many injured, and three hundred arrested; four were subsequently executed by the government.[133]

More widespread riots occurred in the industrial city of Arak, 240 kilometers southwest of Tehran, which lasted for two days and resulted in "hundreds" of arrests and detentions. The riots broke out in May 1992 when a dump truck being chased by a municipality pickup hit and killed a young boy. "Neighbors stopped the truck and set fire to the municipality pickup." The following day "up to 3,000 people marched on the city center chanting 'down with the mayor,' setting fire to several bank branches and three municipality buildings."[134] The city remained under martial law for several days.

The most dramatic of these events took place in Mashad, a holy city of three million people close to the Afghanistan border. Mashad's disturbances on May 30, 1992, began in a squatter area, Kouy-e Tollab, where the municipality had refused to grant construction permits to the illegally built dwellings. When local representatives returned home from the municipality office where they had made their requests, they encountered bands of demolition squads and security forces with trucks and bulldozers who had come to destroy the unlicensed homes. Many inhabitants resisted by assaulting the officers, others by refusing to leave their dwellings. A temporary lull in the skirmishes ended when the local children returned from their schools. The crowd grew larger, and in the ensuing clashes with the security forces, two young boys were shot and killed. The indignant rioters then "went on an orgy of looting and arson, burning the city hall, the main library, several police stations." "By the evening the city was in the hands of the rioters, with the police and Islamic guards standing back and letting the crowd get on with it."[135] "The army could not quieten the city, so the government sent in units of *basij* (voluntary militia)" in the hope that they could calm the crowd.[136] Among the crowd were eight masked gunmen who led the looting and attacks on the government buildings.[137] In the end the riot left over one hundred buildings and stores destroyed and thirty-five cars burnt, with an estimated total damage of Rls 10 billion.[138] Over three hundred people were arrested,[139] six police officers were killed, and 4 rioters were hanged. Government officials blamed the "religious hard-liners ousted from the parliament," "foreigners," "opportunists," and the Mujahedin for the unrest.[140] While it is likely that some professional activists took part in the incident, it seems evident that squatter discontent lay at the core of the unrest.

Following each attack, things seemed to go back to normality before long. In the Khak-i Sefid settlement, "soon after the departure of the demolition agents, people began to rebuild their homes once again . . . Women helped their husbands in rebuilding their dwellings . . . And I pursued my work on a self-help plumbing project to bring running water to the community."[141]

Despite the intensity of these riots, they were not extraordinary political events. Rather, they were the logical corollary to the politics of the squatter poor in their everyday lives, which maintained no line separating struggle from life; they represented the vocal facet of the silent movement of the poor, in the backstreets of the urban peripheries, in pursuit of a better life.

Given the resistance of the poor, it seems that the limited available options made a de facto tolerance of the informal communities an undeclared state policy, leaving the task of deterrence to "nature"— a recent method employed by the municipality of Tehran is the forestation of vacant land around the city as a way to halt the creeping advance of the squatters. This measure represents the quiet response of the state to the quiet encroachment of the homeless. Indeed this policy, along with forceful eviction and economic exclusion, has to a large extent succeeded. During the late 1980s and early 1990s Tehran experienced outmigration. However, the people driven from one spot are likely to end up settling in different, usually more distant places. Not surprisingly, informal communities, as we saw earlier, spread at an unprecedented rate not within the big cities but just outside their administrative boundaries, by turning hundreds of the nearby villages into low-income urban settlements.[142] The silent movement of the poor in the backstreets of their insecure communities is likely to continue. But if and when the captured gains are threatened, the silent movement of the backstreets is likely to turn into open and audible street action.

Six

Workless Revolutionaries: The Movement
of the Unemployed

The victory of the 1979 revolution resulted in a sudden and "unprecedented high level" of urban unemployment in Iran.[1] Hundreds of companies, businesses, and factories suspended their work. The owners
and managers of these ventures, foreign and Iranian alike, had left the
country months before the insurrections of February 10–11, 1979.
Those who remained in the country shut down their enterprises in the
midst of chaos, waiting to see what economic policy the new revolutionary government would pursue. Labor strikes, which escalated after
October 1978, had almost crippled industry, large-scale services, and
the government offices. Hardest hit was the construction sector, which
resulted in hundreds of projects being abandoned mid-way. Cranes
and tools stood idle on the lots of half-finished building complexes,
and worksites remained deserted. In the end thousands of laborers
who had withdrawn their labor for the victory of the revolution found
themselves without jobs on its morrow.

To these was added a new army of unemployed: those working in
ideologically unfit occupations. Western-type restaurants, cafeterias,
cabarets, liquor stores, red-light district theaters, and brothels were all
closed down, not only because they were incompatible with the Islamic
Revolution but also because they were considered symbols of the deca-

dence of the ancien régime. In Tehran alone, an estimated 3,000 employees of such establishments lost their jobs.[2] The lottery ticket company was shut down entirely, laying off 200,000 low-income street ticket sellers. The entry of about 150,000 high school graduates, *diplomeh*s, gradually added a new weight to the army of the jobless. Thus in the very first year of the revolution, some 2.5 million Iranians, 21 percent of the workforce, were out of work.[3] About 55 percent of the jobless, according to an official survey of Tehran unemployed, were laid off owing to closures; 10 percent were casual laborers who left their jobs because of low income and hardship; the rest were migrants and school graduates who sought work for the first time.[4] In short, between 1.5 to 2 million people lost their work within the few months of revolutionary events.

The preceding two chapters have focused on the politics of the everyday life of ordinary people in their sphere of living space. In this chapter, I shift my attention to the domain of work. Here, I show how the ordinary unemployed utilized the revolutionary situation by resorting to collective action to demand jobs and maintenance. They set the ground for the birth of a movement of the unemployed in postrevolutionary Iran.

The jobless were not a heterogeneous group. While factory workers and high school graduates played the leading role in the movement, the articulation of differing interests and discontent at the extraordinary conditions, brought many poor unemployed, casual laborers, and rural migrants into an audible and collective street politics.

In developing countries an unemployed movement that struggles for jobs and protection is extremely rare, despite high rates of visible and invisible joblessness. Family, kinship, patron-client relationships, and especially the informal sector provide essential mechanisms of protection and survival; in addition, the lack of organization prevents sustained protest movements from developing.[5] In this chapter, I argue that what distinguished the Iranian case was a conjunctural articulation of resources and political opportunity that underlay the movement. The resources included the creation, after the revolution, of a *massive* and *sudden* loss of work, along with a revolutionary ideology among the jobless. The simultaneous *sudden* decline in the standard of living and damping of expectations generated a moral outrage. The movement was perceived as the continuation of a broader revolutionary struggle. Expectations among the poor and the unemployed had been raised dramatically; in addition, the intense competition of the ruling clergy and the left opposition to gain the support of the poor further heightened expectations. This ideological dimension served as the engine to the massive body of the jobless, who utilized both the existing relative political freedom and the skills of mobilization they had learned during the revolution.

The Onset

Some three months prior to the victory of the revolution, over 13,000 seasonal or "project" workers in the city of Abadan, a large oil port city in the south, were made redundant when their companies ceased operations. The workers had lost their jobs but they considered their situation of joblessness insignificant compared to the revolutionary struggles around them. Even those who had maintained their jobs were on strike. Yet for these workers the extraordinary days of unity and sacrifice were coming to an end. The revolution was entering into a new stage where groups and personalities began revealing their true colors. The factionalism and struggle for power among the new leaders was growing as the clerical leadership started exhibiting its intolerance of dissenting political voices.

As the days passed, these workers began thinking about their precarious present and uncertain future. During the unsteady premiership of Shahpour Bakhtiar, the last prime minister appointed by the Shah, a small number of these workers gathered frequently in local teahouses to discuss their plight and decide on a course of action to take. Out of these and subsequent meetings emerged the Syndicate of the Unemployed Project Workers of Abadan (SUPWA). This marked the onset of collective actions taken by the unemployed. Within five months campaigns successfully secured jobs and unemployment benefits.[6] Several demonstrations, all confronted by the Pasdaran, were organized to secure these objectives. Two months later, on April 13, 1979, as social struggles intensified, some four hundred laborers resorted to a sit-in in the syndicate headquarters, threatening to go on a hunger strike.[7]

An unemployed protest movement was well underway in several big cities including Tehran, Isfahan, Tabriz, Ghazvin, Gachsaran, as well as in the province of Kurdistan. In the capital city several laid-off and expelled worker groups (*kargaran-i bikaar-shudeh*) had initially been mobilized by the leftist organizations. Before long they came together to form a loosely knit Organization of Unemployed and Seasonal Workers, which included laborers made redundant in manufacturing, construction, and other industries.

Campaigns in Tehran

On March 2, 1979, a group of laid-off workers gathered in the Ministry of Labor to publicize their plight. The labor minister, Dariush Foruhar, a liberal follower of Mosaddeq, spoke. Disappointed with his response, and due to their small number, the workers ended their protest action by reading a resolution calling for job creation, a meeting place for a syndicate organization, a forty-hour work week, and unemployment benefits. The group returned soon, better prepared and with over 2,000 members. Over the next two weeks they visited the ministry more than five times. In the subsequent meetings two further demands were made: that their organization be recognized, and that the national radio and TV broadcast their grievances.[8] Facing mounting pressure in its first few weeks in office, the Ministry of Labor decided to establish an "unemployed loan fund."

The plan envisioned granting loans of Rls 7,500 to Rls 9,000 (U.S.$110–U.S.$130) per month for a maximum of six months. Workers between the age of twenty-five and sixty years who had paid social security for at least one year, would be eligible,[9] effectively excluding casual laborers and recent high school graduates. In the debate that followed, the unemployed turned down this concession, demanding that age and contribution to social security requirements be removed. They further insisted that the payments be based on family size and that the program be implemented and supervised by unemployed representatives. Most important, they called for the idea of "loans" (*vaam-i bikaari*) to be changed to "benefits" (*haqq-i bikaari*). In the meeting, a laid-off employee of Tehran bus services, *Sherkat-i Vahid*, echoed the concern of those who considered the loan concept to be a sell-out for the working-class struggle as a whole:

> We are representing all of the suffering Iranian workers. Our demand is not an individual demand. Unfortunately, it was announced today that everybody gets one thousand *tuman*s[10] and leaves . . . Is it really fair to spoil the spirit of workers' struggle with these few pennies? . . . How can they call themselves "workers," those whose character is not worth more than one-thousand *tuman*s? . . . One hundred thousand were killed [for the revolution], and still we cannot get what we want?[11]

A representative of the unemployed offered his support in rejecting the plan. Addressing the laborers he said:

> You are the source of our power. We will act according to your decisions. I am glad that the group, with a complete awareness, declared its criticisms and hatred on accepting the offer. By this decision, we proved that we are not just concerned about our stomach . . . It is your consciousness that must rule. It is your faith, belief, and consciousness that give us power.[12]

The issue of loans versus benefits became the fundamental source of confrontation between the unemployed and the Provisional Government. Undoubtedly, the left played an instrumental role in articulating and radicalizing the workers' demands. As people who had supported and endured hardships during the revolution, this group of unemployed considered it their right to make demands on the new leadership. That their movement was influenced by the left held no bearing on their conviction that their demands were legitimate.

The Provisional Government, however, considered their demands unacceptable. For the Prime Minister, Mehdi Bazargan, this was connected to Communist currents to undermine his government, especially after the left had characterized the government as "liberal" and "procapitalist."[13] Moreover, the government did not want to bear the huge burden of permanently feeding the unemployed.[14] The Labor Minister insisted that the term "loan" could not be changed. "I do not want," he stated to the workers' representatives on March 12, 1979, "to give the impression that this is a grant without a repayment. Workers' honor is above all this. I want this plan to be understood merely as a loan."[15] Consequently, following a meeting on March 17, over 3,000 jobless laborers began a sit-in in the labor ministry compound. When nothing came out of subsequent negotiations with the ministry, some 700 participants went on a hunger strike in the late afternoon in a state of frustration and anguish.[16] To mobilize support from other citizens, they issued a statement three days later, which was distributed in Tehran:

> We are the unemployed workers who have staged a sit-in in the Ministry of Labor. Since the authorities have not responded to our demands, we have been on a hunger strike since March 17 (1 A.M.), and are prepared to continue our strike to the point of our death, unless our grievances

are considered. We request our laboring brothers to distribute this note, and publicize our situation among the working people, so that they can all join us. As we write, at the end, [the authorities] have come to us shooting their guns.[17]

Immediately after the hunger strike started, the Labor Minister met with the workers' representatives at 1 A.M. After negotiating for one hour, there was still no agreement. According to a strikers' spokesperson, the minister had insisted on the loan issue—a point that was unacceptable to the strikers.[18] A further attempt was made to appease the strikers, this time by a clergyman who tried to utilize his religious authority. His appeals, however, were to no avail, and the sit-in carried on.[19] On the first night, *hizbullahi*s (proregime street thugs) marched on the ministry to attack the strikers.

Outside the compound leftist students joined groups of unemployed to express their support of the strikers, despite repeated clashes with the proregime thugs.[20] Inside, however, the mood surrounding the protesters was one of frustration and determination to fight on. Workers felt as if they had been betrayed and cheated by the new politicians whom they had trusted. They felt a kind of moral outrage that their leaders had violated a tacit social contract that had evolved in the course of the revolution. They expected respect as well as material rewards. They felt they had gotten neither.[21] One of the women strikers, Zahra Dorostkar, angrily echoed this feeling publicly at the compound:

I want to know why the radio and TV do not broadcast our grievances, so that people can understand how much we suffer, and appreciate how little [the authorities] are offering us. If they broadcast this, the people will no longer be misinformed [by the government] who pretend that they are giving us our rights. We have gathered here, and have gone on hunger strike, because we want unemployment benefits (*haqq-i bikaari*). We don't ask for charity. If there are jobs, we are prepared to work. Otherwise, our living expenses must be secured. We all shouted that we wanted Mr. Khomeini; we supported the religious leaders. Now we expect them to tackle our problems. I have two children; my husband has worked for the last six months, but has not been paid; they say, "We don't have any money"! And I myself used to work in the Vitana [biscuit factory in Tehran]. I was forced to resign because they did not accept my children in their nursery. Now, [the Labor Ministry] tell us "take one thousand *tuman*s for the time being"! I have not paid my rent for the last six months; we hardly have any food at home; my children are without clothes . . . What can I do with this one thousand *tumans*? So, I am telling you, I will not leave this place unless they consider my life situation.[22]

While the hunger strike was underway, negotiations with the authorities continued. The strike leaders had sensed that the Provisional Government was not prepared to back down. Some pro-government elements had begun to spread seeds of division. The loan offer undoubtedly fed into the division between the political and non-political laborers. Adding to this, sustaining a hunger strike against a government that had just come out of a victorious revolution was not easy. On New Year's Day, March 21, 1979, the Pasdaran broke into the compound, attacking the strikers and terrorizing them by continuously shooting in the air.[23] A number of hunger strikers passed out and were taken to hospitals; others were given glucose.[24] The strike leaders softened their positions and eventually accepted the loan principle. The remaining differences revolved only around the provisions of the loan. A compromise was finally reached on March 22, 1979. According to the agreement, each unemployed person was to be granted a monthly payment of Rls 9,000–Rls 12,000, with an advance payment of some Rls 10,000. The conditionality of the payment was substantially modified. In addition, the unemployed succeeded in having *Khane-ye Kargar* (House of Labor) recognized as their organizational headquarters in Tehran.[25]

The Escalation of Collective Actions

The government hoped that the compromise would bring an end to the protests of the unemployed. Peace, however, never came in the lifetime of the Provisional Government. Both the government and the unemployed knew that loans were not a solution to the misery of joblessness. The government made the concession primarily to pacify the jobless crowd. Privately it assumed that the workers would not pay back the loans but hoped that the measure would defuse their protests. Similarly, the unemployed and their left-wing leaders did not consider the payment as a loan but as a mere piecemeal monetary gain. In addition, the Tehran agreement had left a large number of casual laborers and recent high school graduates out of its provisions.[26] The agreement ended the hunger strike in Tehran but failed to halt the protest actions of the unemployed in general. The campaign would go on.

The following three months saw an escalation in the protest movement of the jobless in different parts of the country. In some regions the organizations of the jobless flatly rejected the Tehran compromise; others, notwithstanding their desire to obtain the loan, continued their protests. In the meantime the migrant poor and the school leavers not covered by the loan became even more aggressive.

Thus, less than two weeks after the initial agreement, on April 1, 1979, more than 3,000 jobless held an open meeting in Labor House, the outdoor loudspeakers carrying the debates into the streets. The meeting condemned the loan plan once again and resolved to continue the campaign. An unemployed speaker angrily echoed the mood of the crowd:

> Swear by my conscience I would have never accepted the promise of the [labor] minister; would have never agreed to be on TV even to the point of death, if I had sensed that [ending our hunger strike] would lead to this hopeless situation. I would rather die than face this situation. . . . We don't want a free ride, don't want charity. Give us work."[27]

The crowd subsequently staged a sit-in within the Ministry of Justice for five days. It ended only when the liberal Justice Minister, Asadullahi, promised to take the issue to the cabinet. He also facilitated the unemployed's publicization of their grievances on national radio and TV.[28]

The Syndicate of the Unemployed Project Workers of Abadan focused its campaigns on consolidating its position and struggling to dislodge the rival Union of Workers and High-School Graduates that had been created by the local authorities to undermine the SUPWA. At the same time it continued negotiating with local and national officials to win concessions from the government. Some three weeks after the Tehran agreement, in the same region, the Unemployed Workers of Ahwaz and the Vicinity rejected the Labor Ministry's plan and demanded "unemployment benefits" instead.[29]

In the southeastern city of Khorram Abad, only a few days after the Tehran agreement, hundreds of jobless laborers took over the headquarters of the Governorate demanding jobs, an unemployment fund, and a headquarters for their assemblies. The protesters were attacked by progovernment forces, especially the Pasdaran of Komite-ye Imam, violently assaulted, and fired upon.[30] The unemployed in the industrial city of Ghazvin began their collective action by electing representatives to negotiate with city authorities. Demoralised by the response of the authorities, who had asked them to "wait for two months," they went on protest marches and later organized gatherings in local mosques to discuss their strategy.[31]

In the northwestern Azari city of Tabriz, on March 28, hundreds of unemployed and laid-off workers staged a sit-in of several days on the premises of the Workers' Club.[32] Another group marched on Tabriz's radio and television station to force the authorities to publicize their grievances. Some two weeks earlier the jobless had already been mobilized by left-wing activists and had voiced their grievances in a number of gatherings. One of the meetings issued a resolution calling for an immediate return to work, the creation of an unemployed benefit fund, and the assignment of a permanent headquarters.[33] Similar sit-ins and protest marches took place in Shahr-i Kord and Sari during April and May.[34]

In each city such protest actions would often be prolonged primarily because the authorities would either reject the demands or delay their responses to them. The violent reaction of the security forces resulted in further escalation of protests. The Union of the Unemployed Workers of Isfahan and Vicinity (UUWIV) established in March 1979, had also rejected the minister's loan provisions and made a number of other demands, giving the officials two weeks to respond. When a favorable response did not come, some 7,000 unemployed and their sympathizers staged a protest demonstration on March 26, 1979. They carried slogans that read "The burden of the revolution was on the toilers, but the outcome has gone to others." The banners called for the government recognize the Council of the Unemployed Workers and their right to assemble.[35] The demonstrators were blocked by the Pasdaran and *hizbullahi*s who were carrying clubs and knives. The governor rebuffed the demonstrators and Pasdaran arrested a number of organizers. In an effort to put further pressure on the authorities, another protest march of some 10,000 marchers gathered in front of Isfahan's House of Labor less than two weeks later to demand direct talks with the governor. The talks produced no tangible result, and the marching continued. A rumor was spread accusing the demonstrators of intending to attack the police station. In the violent confrontations with the security forces that followed, one demonstrator, Naser Tawfiqian, was killed, eight others injured, and nearly three hundred detained.[36]

These collective protests were not always in vain; at times desirable outcomes followed. In the Kurdish towns, for example, where the left and Kurdish nationalist organizations enjoyed mass support, the protests were more fierce and more successful. In the capital city of the Kurdistan Province, Mahabad, the employees of the power and water supply who had been laid off during the revolution managed to regain their jobs following a bitter struggle. The Fedaii Organization appears to have played a crucial part in this success and began appeals to jobless in other areas.[37] In another town, Sanandaj, following intense negotiations with various authorities of the city, some temporary measures were taken to assist the jobless who numbered nearly 7,000, including the immediate employment of 500, payment of benefits to those laid off, and loans for others until they found reemployment.[38]

Toward the end of May 1979 the unemployed of Kermanshah were mobilized by young socialist activists. Recent high school graduates, the unemployed poor, some parents' groups, and other sympathizers joined together in street demonstrations and sit-ins. They organized some of the largest protest marches in the city, with the participants in one demonstration reaching 5,000.[39]

In one incident in May the demonstrators intended to launch a sit-in in the Governorate headquarters. Despite opposition from the guards, the demonstrators broke the gate and seized the building for a few hours. This forced the governor, who had already fled the building, to return and listen to the crowd. The protesters agreed to end their sit-in only when the governor assured them that he would seriously consider their demands. Before long, joint planning by the governor and the Union of the Unemployed, an elected body, resulted in the reopening of a house-building factory, which was able to employ some one hundred people. The plan also included jobs for another group of the unemployed at Kashmir Factory. The remaining jobless were to be compensated between Rls 7,000–Rls 15,000 per month until they found work.[40]

Although the unemployed were mobilized in almost every town where some workers had been laid off, the movement remained dispersed and isolated for the most part, but the protest actions of the unemployed culminated in a massive show of unity and force on May Day 1979. Some 500,000 people marched in the streets of Tehran, and many more in other provincial cities. The rally, organized by the Coordinating Council of May Day, a committee composed of various socialist and labor organizations, was the biggest independent gathering of lower-class people in years. Groups of men and women, parents and children marched hand-in-hand through the city's main streets chanting slogans. May Day was a show of the strength of the working class, but even more so of the left. It was their forces who had been mobilized in such a massive numbers. Young male activists held hands along both edges of the march, creating a human chain in order to protect the demonstrators from the occasional assaults of organized thugs—the informal groupings under the protection of this or that powerful mullah. A number of state organizations, such as *Sepah-i Pasdaran, Jihad-i Sazandegui* (the Construction Crusade), and the Islamic Republican Party, also made statements on May Day; some took part in the marches. However, they focused more on the "danger of Communism," the "agents of the U.S." (referring to socialist activists), and *Wahdat-i Kalameh*, or the unity of the Islamic ummah, and less on specific labor issues.[41]

The unemployed made up a substantial portion of the demonstrators. The slogans reflected the strategy of the organizers: "The struggle of the unemployed is not separate from that of the employed workers." The march ended with the reading of a resolution praising Ayatollah Khomeini and calling for, among other things, the nationalization of industry and banking, changes in the labor law, and the expulsion of foreign experts.[42]

The Variety of Street Protests

As would be expected, jobs constituted the major concern of the jobless. During the first five months after the revolution, eighty-six major worker collective actions protested lock-outs and layoffs, and campaigned for their return to work. This made up the largest proportion (some 20 percent) of the industrial actions waged by the working people.[43] Yet the variety of demands reflected the strategy of the leadership of the unemployed movement to relate the struggle for jobs to other political and social concerns of the working class. Socialist leaders drew attention to such well-known demands as the forty-hour work week, better working conditions, equal pay for men and women, and the right to strike. It is not clear if the possible implications of the demands were well thought out or if they were made simply in order to radicalize the movement. Certainly the insistence in almost every campaign on having a headquarters pointed to the urgency of organizational work among the actors. Some of the demands (such as the expulsion of foreign experts) contradicted the central concern of saving jobs; the withdrawal of foreign companies was partly responsible for many closures and layoffs.

The protest actions mainly assumed the form of demonstrations, sit-ins, and issuing resolutions. The demonstrations focused on voicing the plight of the jobless both to fellow citizens and to the authorities. Some groups forced the local radio and TV stations to publicize their grievances. Demonstrations were also staged as a method of practicing collective action and protest. But in the postrevolutionary conditions, when street marching had become a common practice, the immediate impact was less than satisfactory. Sit-ins (*tahassun* and *ishghal*), or temporarily occupying public premises and causing disruptions, became the most prevalent method of bringing pressure to bear. The buildings of the Labor Ministry, local labor offices, the governorates, and the Ministry of Justice served as the major targets. At times the sit-ins were combined with hunger strikes, which resulted in some immediate gains.

Although *tahassun* seems to have a long historical tradition in Iran, it is unlikely that the practices of the unemployed drew on this history. In the traditional form, *bast-nishini*, the actors seek refuge in holy places, such as shrines or mosques, in an attempt to seek forgiveness, wage a protest, or pursue justice. The act represents a defensive cry for clemency and justice, normally by one suffering under arbitrary rule.[44] Thus those who had committed a crime would seek refuge in a shrine where they would be immune so long as they remained in asylum.

The connotations of contemporary actions are essentially different. The unemployed referred to their acts not by the traditional term, "*bast-nishini*" but in the terms "*tahassun*" (sit-in) and "*ishghal*" (occupation, squatting). For the unemployed, the terms had a different meaning. They signified a form of collective action through which the actors seek either publicity for a cause or, more often, a method of disruption to bring public pressure to bear on the authorities.[45] Nevertheless, some symbolic elements of the traditional idea remain. For instance, the unemployed did organize sit-ins in such places as the headquarters of Workers' Syndicates or House of Labor, which were not intended to disrupt. Similarly, staging a sit-in in front of the Ministry of Justice signified a cry for justice in a more traditional sense.

In spite of the large number of sit-ins, there is no evidence of such direct actions as mob looting or rent riots. In Iran such actions historically result from a sudden drop in income and a lack of alternative sources for survival. Rapid, massive, and unexpected unemployment may produce such phenomena in any country, as evidenced during the Depression in the U.S.[46] In Iran, though, as in most developing countries, people are better prepared to adopt survival strategies in a relatively short time. Kinship, friendship, patronage, and especially informal economic activities offer the most handy mechanisms. In Iran those who had already been unemployed were equipped with coping techniques, and those who were laid off could partially rely on the support of their kin members while searching for another job.

Although it was quite limited, the unemployed also launched a fundraising campaign. The contributions came largely from working people who had not lost their work. Significantly, the bazaar, a major source of funds during the revolution responded negatively.[47] Unemployment loans, however meager, provided immediate relief. So long as the jobless believed they could gain ground through collective resistance, they refrained from limiting themselves to individualistic acts and survival strategies. And so long as the unemployed poor lacked any institutional setting in which they could exercise direct action, such as workplace occupation, they needed to resort to collective protest. This interest in collective activity, encouraged by the leftist groups, paved the way for some degree of associational activities among the jobless.

Getting Organized

The struggle of the jobless was somewhat chaotic. For one thing, the unemployed did not constitute a homogenous group. They originated from different backgrounds, which gave them different capacities for mobilization and collective action. As I have already pointed out, three main groups made up the jobless population: laid-off and expelled workers, recent graduates, and already jobless and casual laborers. No organizational link between them was conceivable. Laid-off workers had largely worked in the factories or on construction sites. Whereas a common workplace gave this group some basis for communication, the other two groups were generally atomized and dispersed, lacking even a common physical space. Within these categories, individuals met each other accidentally and only for a short while. Leaders of the groups were often chosen spontaneously without much deliberation or competition. At times excitement outweighed rational decisions and calculated actions. As one participant commented, "We had not decided to occupy the Labor Ministry; it just happened. We were only demonstrating in the streets; chanting slogans; people got very excited, and all of a sudden we found ourselves jumping over the fences."[48]

Nevertheless, some degree of organization and coordination could be observed. Two factors played a key part in this: simple necessity, and the role of mobilizers.

Organizational Necessity

Before all else, before demonstrations and sit-ins, and instead of looting or rioting, the unemployed relied on the disposition of the new authorities. They initially preferred to negotiate. This required that representatives be appointed (as in the cities of Ghazvin, Tehran, Isfahan, Tabriz, and Kermanshah). If negotiations did not bring a result, they made sure to maintain some kind of communication and network in order to continue their campaign. To achieve this, they needed first a place to assemble and then recognition of their representatives by the authorities. Such recognition, they believed, would serve to protect them from the arbitrary assaults of the Pasdaran and others. These formal groupings of the unemployed workers were given different labels depending on the perception of the leaders. Among the most common names were *shura* (council), *sandika* (syndicate), and *kaanun* (center).

Some groups went beyond merely appointing representatives, attempting instead to give a more durable structure to their organizations. In Isfahan, when the jobless realized that securing jobs was not as easy as they had initially thought, they began to consolidate their organization by involving the unemployed workers of the entire city and its environs in the Union of the Unemployed Workers of Isfahan and the Vicinity. In Tehran, when the initial negotiations with the Ministry of Labor failed, jobless leaders gathered (on March 5) in the House of Labor to begin plans for a more structured organization. This was followed by the formation of a Steering Committee of Casual/Seasonal Workers and (on March 22, 1979) official recognition of the House of Labor as their permanent headquarters. The latter became a significant institution for the laboring poor.

The House of Labor was originally taken over quite spontaneously by the unemployed. Its early meetings, open to all, revolved around diverse topics. These general meetings were often both dynamic and chaotic, drawing crowds of three to four hundred people. To remedy this problem, separate workshops were sometimes held. As political groups became more involved, some disciplinary standards were introduced: discussions became more organized, speakers more articulate, and, simultaneously, ideological divisions more pronounced. Speakers affiliated to a particular political line were heckled by opponents and cheered by sympathizers. It was as if the huge slogans hanging on the background wall—"The Only Solution for the Toilers is Unity and Organization" and "Workers' Democracy Is Limitless"—had lost their resonance. The debates introduced by militants tended to center on such issues as "democratic versus socialist revolution," and "economic versus political struggles," which seemed less relevant to the daily concerns of the unemployed.[49] Whatever the debates, official recognition of the House of Labor signified a victory for the laboring poor both in practical and symbolic terms: it provided a space for their organizational activities and a symbol of their capacity for independent collective action. For many it was an intimate shelter: "Some would spend the nights there; would bring food and share with other fellow laborers. Others spent their lunch break in the House, while discussing topics of interest. In this way so many simple-minded lads experienced class solidarity. The House had practically turned into a school for collective action."[50]

The organized activities of the jobless were not limited to the House of Labor, however. A number of unemployed associations were also created. Unemployed workers in the oil and port city of Abadan, in southern Iran, developed a more elaborate organization known as the Syndicate of Project/Seasonal Workers of Abadan (SPWA). As I discussed earlier, the embryo of the syndicate was formed weeks before the insurrection in the casual gatherings of laborers in the local teahouses (*Bushehri-ha*), where preparatory registering and campaigning began. These were followed by an assembly of a group of workers in the Oil Industry College, where they formed a steering committee (*shura-ye muassess*). The committee began recruiting members by using teahouses as their meeting points. At this time the priority was to obtain a permanent headquarters. Following intense negotiations and confrontations with city officials, they succeeded in getting the state-owned premises of the former Workers Union as their headquarters.[51] They also registered the SPWA with the *Komite-ye Imam*, the local Pasdaran, and the office of the Governorate.[52] The SPWA managed to organize over 13,000 unemployed workers from twenty different trades, with various skills and income levels.[53] The steering committee produced a set of by-laws based on the union experiences in postindependence Algeria, postrevolution Nicaragua, and Iran during the 1940s. The most pressing tasks comprised negotiations with employers to require them to reemploy the laid-off workers. They also included finding jobs for the rest of its members and securing unemployment benefits.[54] In the long run, the SPWA aimed at establishing unions of unemployed workers in other provinces, and ultimately creating a unified national union.

During its lifetime the SPWA won a number of concessions through negotiations with the Provisional Government, including reemployment of groups of workers and securing unemployment loans.[55] A conflict arose between the SPWA and the authorities on the method of allocating these loans. While the Ministry of Labor recognized the role of the SPWA in the allocation process, the local clergy and the Pasdaran refused it, insisting that the loans be distributed through the local mosques. The SPWA, however, did not give in. In a compromise solution both sides agreed on schools instead of mosques as the place of loan payment.[56]

The Role of Mobilizers

Young activists, mainly students with radical Islamic and socialist orientations, played a significant part in mobilizing and organizing the unemployed. Activists often initially targeted recent high school graduates, *diplomeha-ye bikaar*, who were better prepared for mobilization; the revolution had given students much experience in group work. The activists then linked the concerns of these young job-seekers to those of the general mass unemployed. The social skills, literacy, and mobility of the high-school graduates made them potential mobilizers in their own right. A socialist organizer described how this tactic was effective in creating an unemployed organization in Kermanshah, a city in the East of Iran:

> We gathered the others (*diplomehs*) and asked them to express their views [on matters of protest actions]. We concluded that each of us who was present there should take a responsibility. We should, for instance, inform our friends, relatives, neighbors, and classmates of such an action. We should also think of preparing flyers to be distributed throughout the city.[57]

The *diplomeh*s in Kirmanshah initially insisted on having their own exclusive organization. They were later convinced, however, that they had a common cause with other jobless people.[58] Thus their recruiting began among the unemployed poor, construction workers, and casual workers in the lower-class neighborhoods. In their first collective effort they managed to bring one thousand unemployed together. In this assembly the speakers stressed the importance of setting up an association of the unemployed and uniting all the jobless. Following a street march, the organizers called for a sit-in on the premises of the Governorate. It was during this occasion that the crowd appointed seven representatives, including four *diplomeh*s (two men and two women), two unemployed laborers, and one representative from among the parents of the *diplomeh*s. A few days later the representatives met in a public park with a group of fifty participants to adopt an official name for the organization and to propose by-laws for discussion and adoption. Thus was the Union of Unemployed People of Kermanshah created.[59]

Although widespread, the organizational activities of the unemployed remained largely localized and isolated around different parts of the country. Most were so involved in their daily struggles for survival that they hardly paid attention to the outside world. The vital tasks of recruitment, confrontations with the Pasdaran, and sustaining morale consumed much of their energies. Talk of creating a national coordinating association came by and large from left-wing activists.[60]

One crucial attempt was made to link these individual campaigns in a national context. On April 23, 1979, delegates from over twenty cities and towns gathered in the House of Labor in Tehran. Their aim was to unify their stands and strategies, to create eventually a nationwide organization of the unemployed. Delegates also discussed the conditions of jobless people in different parts of the country, especially the ramifications of accepting the unemployment loan.[61] The meeting lasted three days, and no reporter was allowed into the meeting hall. A statement issued at its end instructed all unemployed masses in the country to stage demonstrations on May Day 1979 and to direct their demands toward the government. The resolution warned that if the authorities did not respond positively, the national organizers "will take harsher and more resolute measures to ensure that the Iranian working people will achieve their just objectives."[62]

Indeed, the speed with which organizational efforts were carried out was quite extraordinary. The Tehran Meeting on April 23, the climax of the organizational activity, came only two months after the revolution. Setting up a structured association often constitutes the last stage of a campaign. If mass action, spontaneous protests, and an unstructured mobilization have not produced results, then a structured organization is required to ensure continuity. In Iran the line between mass action and organizational work seemed blurred. For one thing, people had just come out of a successful revolution and were prepared to be mobilized. Second, the mobilizers highly valued association-building and considered it as a measure of success. The left especially insisted on organizational work, viewing institution-building as an essential element for creating a sustained working-class base for itself. Yet for the most part these associations remained loosely structured, often serving only as ad hoc coordinating committees to mobilize the campaigns. They rarely employed any elaborate organizational procedures or advocated electoral campaigns and competition in appointing representatives. Despite intensive efforts, lack of time did not allow these organizations to develop and confront the test of efficacy. The unemployed movement soon came to an abrupt halt.

The Demise

The movement withered away as quickly as it had come to life. May Day marked the climax of the collective action of the jobless. The slowdown began gradually afterward, until its virtual demise by mid-autumn 1979. The war in Kurdistan in summer 1979 undermined the activities of the movement. During its clampdown on Kurdish nationalists, the government used the opportunity to quell other dissent. Although a number of jobless protest marches did take place their scope remained limited. On October 1, a crowd of 1,500 jobless, the second march of its kind organized within a week, demonstrated outside the prime minister's office. Pasdaran fired over their heads and the government warned of tough action against the protesters.[63] In the dramatic atmosphere associated with the seizure of the U.S. embassy in Tehran in November 1979, the concerns of the unemployed were lost in the noisy campaign of "Islam against the Great Satan." Indeed, on the very same day that the Muslim students climbed over the walls of the embassy, a large group of unemployed were marching in the streets of the capital. But the desperate voices of these marchers were stifled by the nationalist outcry of the mass demonstrations that began to unravel from the Embassy compound.

Why did the movement disappear so rapidly? First, political pressure intensified. Progovernment paramilitary organizations stepped up psychological and physical attacks, raiding and ransacking the headquarters of the jobless. The leaders of the movement were stigmatized as "infidel communists," or "*munafiqs*" (hypocrites), referring to the Mujahedin-i Khalq, a left Islamic group. Almost any sit-in by the unemployed was assaulted violently by the armed Pasdaran, especially when they were convinced that the radical left and the Mujahedin were behind the troubles that they believed were aimed at undermining the revolution. Various attacks were reported in Tehran, Isfahan, Abadan, Ahwaz, Gachsaran, and Khorram Abad, most within the first two months after the victory of the revolution. In addition, worker gangs were set up by employers to harass laid-off workers who voiced their protests, especially those calling on the government to take over industry.[64] Friday prayer leaders would often denounce the unemployed activists as agents of a counterrevolution, provoking the praying crowd, often from lower-class backgrounds themselves, to attack and disrupt gatherings of the jobless. The Islamic leaders were able to mobilize the poor against the poor. Whatever their differences, the various factions within the ruling elite all favored ending the unemployed protest. Radicals and conservatives, liberals and Islamists, all considered the activists as impatient opportunists who aimed at harvesting the fruits of the revolution before they were ripe.[65]

Second, an internal battle among the leaders, especially those with strong political convictions, further weakened the movement. Whereas Muslim activists along with nonpolitical workers tended to compromise for immediate gains, radical left leaders and "political" workers insisted on prolonging the campaign, making it part of a general struggle to undermine the Provisional Government.[66] In addition, despite the attempts of the mobilizers to unite jobless graduates and unemployed laborers, the rift between the two remained.

Undoubtedly the left played a significant part in publicizing the plight of the jobless masses. It was particularly adamant that the movement be radicalized and be given a distinctly political character. Most leftist publications,[67] especially those of the Maoist groups, known as *khatt-i sevvum*, carried diverse reports on the struggles of the unemployed. They provided analyses of the causes of layoffs, often relating them to the "crisis of capitalism," followed by prescriptions for how to combat joblessness. One particular weekly, *Alaihe-i Bikaari* (Against Unemployment) of the Razmandegan Organization,[68] was well known for raising these issues. A number of militant workers, such as Ali Adalatfam, Hassan Lur, Asad, and others, mainly with Maoist tendencies, led the campaign in Tehran; their counterparts mobilized job-seekers in the provincial cities.[69]

While the idea of helping out the poor was a prime motive of the left activists, they nevertheless utilized the campaign for their own political ends—first, to undermine the "liberal bourgeois" Provisional Government and, second, to build popular support for the left. This meant that the interests of the movement could in practice be sacrificed to favor the political strategy of the individual socialist groups.

Finally, and perhaps most important, the exceptional conjuncture and conditions (i.e., sudden and massive loss of work in a revolutionary situation) that had fostered the birth of the movement began gradually to be transformed. A number of the factories resumed operations, reemploying some of their labor force. Within the first six months of the revolution, some 50 percent of industries and small units had returned to production.[70] The labor-intensive construction sector, which had previously employed some one million laborers, still needed to be revived. To this end, the provisional government extended Rls 12,000 million credit to contractors to enable them to pay back wages and to rejuvenate the whole sector.[71] Construction activities began to rise slowly in the second half of 1979 as small and inexpensive housing units were built.[72] By May 1979 some 21,000 jobs were created in this sector.[73]

On occasion laid-off workers took over their workplaces, appointing a *shura* to run them. At times they requested that the government appoint professional managers in order to resume work.[74] On May 6, 1979, for instance, ten workers at the Metusak factory attempted to regain their jobs by staging a sit-in in the factory. They continued their occupation for twenty-five days, after which they issued a statement: "25 days sit-in with four days hunger strike! The result? . . . Nothing!" "What could we do?," they went on. "There was only one way left. And that was: taking over the workshop, operating it by ourselves." So, "on Sunday 9 Ordibehesht [May 1, 1979], we went into the workshop and, after repairing the machines and dividing responsibilities, began to produce and sell the products."[75] Similarly, laid-off workers in Plastou Masourehkar reopenend their plant and resumed work.[76] While these tactics were effective in regaining jobs in some cases, they were ineffective in many others. The former employees of such "un-Islamic" occupations as cabarets, nightclubs, and the lottery business, for example, had no chance of reemployment.

Under intense pressure from the movement, the Ministry of Labor attempted to create some temporary jobs, including public works such as road construction and planting trees in public places. Although Bazargan's government officially banned any further state sector employment, a number of new revolutionary institutions (*nahadha-ye inqilabi*) such as *Pasdaran Komitehs* (Revolutionary Guards), *Jihad-i Sazandegui* (Construction Crusade), *Nihzat-i Savad Aamuzi* (Movement for Literacy), and *Bonyad-i Maskan* (Housing Foundation) nevertheless did absorb a good number of the jobless population. For instance, the Construction Crusade, established in June 1979, had 327 centers in the country, employing 14,800 persons in 1979, with 4,700 volunteers.[77] A small percentage of the 200,000 lottery ticket sellers were hired by the local *Pasdaran Komitehs* to sell cigarettes in the streets as a way to combat hoarding.[78] A job creation project for the high school graduates, ratified in December 1979, involved establishing production cooperatives throughout the country.[79]

In the end, the unemployment loan offered by the government, however meager, proved a temporary solution for some poor unemployed. The offer undoubtedly created a rift within the ranks of the jobless. By July 6, 1979, within three months of its institution, about 182,000 unemployed workers had received an average monthly loan of Rls 9,500.[80] But the whole scheme ceased to exist after six months, at the end of the summer 1979, on the grounds that "industrial investment has started, and workers are returning back to their jobs gradually."[81] As for the unemployed *diplomeh*s, the government planned to extend an "honorary loan" (*vaam-i sharafati*) from a fund made up of 1 percent of the monthly salaries of any citizen wishing to contribute. The contributions were to be paid back by the state in five years time.[82]

In the meantime the institutions of family, kinship, and traditional networks continued to protect the jobless. Young unemployed depended on their families, and older ones relied on networks of kinship and friendship to secure some sort of work, loans, and assistance. In the end the traditional method of reliance on informal networks as opposed to politically oriented associations, coupled with the force of political pressure and changes in the economy, resulted in the demise of the movement. Traditional institutions made the unemployed less desperate; economic changes eroded the constituency of the movement; and political repression deprived it of its leadership. The beginning of the war in Kurdistan inflicted a heavy blow to the weak body of the movement, while the euphoria over the seizure of the U.S. embassy drowned out its presence.

Despite organizational weaknesses, the movement of the jobless in Iran did make some important inroads. It forced the Provisional Government to grant loans and aid to over 180,000 unemployed for six months, and to create a number of temporary jobs. In some provinces the authorities were forced by the campaigns of the unemployed to reopen shut-down factories. At some point groups of laid-off workers themselves began reopening their own workplaces without the consent of the employers. Most important, the movement prompted the Provisional Government to rush to reconstruct the economy, especially the crippled industries where most jobs had been lost. But these very achievements undermined the movement itself. The laid-off factory workers who were in the forefront of the organizations and campaigns of the unemployed began to return to work. Others either found jobs, went back to their old occupations, or began to search for alternative means of survival. In short, the unemployed movement began to decline primarily because it was to some extent successful.

For many of the people without work the problem of joblessness remained, in particular as new groups of job-seekers entered the labor market. Concessions neither reduced unemployment significantly nor ended the plight of many of the jobless. From the start the movement failed to win unemployment benefits as it had originally demanded, and accepted an unemployment loan. The loan, although never expected to be paid back, covered only some 10 percent of the unemployed[83] and was discontinued after six months. Job creation schemes remained limited. Not only did thousands of the remaining jobless fail to find work, but a new wave of rural-urban migration in the following years inflated the size of the jobless population even further. In short, the exceptional circumstances (massive and sudden unemployment and an ideological element) that facilitated the development of the unemployed movement began to change, even though unemployment persisted. The jobless population needed to adjust their activities to the new political and economic reality. The Islamic regime began to stabilize and seize control of popular struggles. The critical mass of unemployed, the laid-off factory workers, mostly regained their work and exited the movement. For the remaining jobless, activities in the informal sector, petty-trade, and street vending served as the most common recourse.

While involved in their movement, many workless revolutionaries never stopped their individual search for alternative sources of income. There were probably many like Ahmad Mirzaii, a *diplomeh* who described his position as "owing to unemployment, I take care of the electrical problems of my neighbors and get paid for it; some times, I work on my brother's taxi."[84] Some were convinced that they could secure some kind of work if only they would make a little effort. Ali Golestani, a *diplomeh* who was on the job market for six months, believed that "if people are only a bit clever, they can do thousands of things; they can sell fruits in the streets, do vending, be sales persons, or engage in part-time and casual work."[85] Indeed, thousands of jobless resorted to street subsistence work, occupying spots on the sidewalks, public parks, and busy thoroughfares of the big cities to erect kiosks and stalls.

The unemployed movement came to an end, but street politics continued. It simply shifted from the jobless onto the street subsistence workers, notably the street vendors. By changing the agency, street politics assumed a different form and dynamics, involving different political ground—the subject of the following chapter.

Seven

Street Rebels: The Politics
of Street Vending

[From the Islamic viewpoint] the occupation of thoroughfares by the vendors is *haram* [not permitted].

—Ayatollah Khomeini[1]

Why does the municipality want to prevent us from our [vending] work? We don't earn our living in a *haram* way.

—A woman food vendor in Tehran[2]

The authorities think in such a way as if they have inherited the streets from their fathers.

—A fruit peddler[3]

By the close of the first year of the revolution, thousands of unemployed urbanites realized that they had to come to terms with the state of their joblessness. Neither the movement of the unemployed nor the efforts of the new government were sufficient to ameliorate the situation. With industry and construction stagnant, recruitment in the state sector frozen, an annual release of thousands of school leavers and soaring urban migration all combined to inflate the number of jobless. In Tehran, open unemployment had jumped from 3 percent in 1976 to some 14 percent in 1979.[4] One year later it rose to 16.3 percent.[5] By 1984 the rate for the whole country was 18.7, or 2.2 million people out of work.[6] Over 60 percent of the jobless in cities were new entrants, including high school graduates (30 percent).[7]

While joblessness grew in the postrevolutionary years, no protest movement emerged to address the issues of jobs and social protection. The particular sociopolitical circumstance that had caused the emergence of the unemployed movement in 1979 began to change. The bulk of the movement's leadership, mainly experienced laid-off workers, returned to work. In addition, the subsequent political restrictions curtailed independent popular mobilization as well as the activities of militants who had influenced the earlier jobless collective action.

The jobless, consequently, resorted to individual and quiet encroachment strategies. In addition to relying on family, friends, and patrons, most found opportunities in casual work. The black market, largely free from the bureaucratic control of the state, offered the only space in which individuals could exercise their own initiatives to better their lots. Despite its own costs, this sector offered such a versatility that many individuals, even many unskilled rural immigrants, were able to secure a job, earn a relatively decent income, and enjoy some degree of autonomy in their working lives. Street subsistence activities constituted the largest segment of such activities. They were the productive, service, and distributive activities that took place in the social and geographical space of the street corners. Among them, petty-trade, street vending, and stall-holding (*dakkeh-daari, dast-foroushi, basaati* and *charkh-daari*) proved to be the most flourishing occupations.

In Iran just as elsewhere, street vendors are rarely the subject of serious scholarship, despite their growing significance. Available studies focus mostly on their economic activities. For instance, De Soto's well-known work, *The Other Path*, is interested not in vendors' politics but in their perceived enthusiasm for and practice of a free market.[8] On the other hand, officials often regard street vending as a social *problem*, a side effect of "maldevelopment"; it is rarely considered as a possible *solution* to certain economic and social ills. And, finally, sympathizers often look upon street vendors with pity and patronage, perceiving them as powerless and wretched.[9] All of these diverse views share one thing—they deny any agency to the street subsistence workers.

This chapter attempts to examine street vendors not simply as a by-product of economic shift but also as agents of social change. It shows how economic necessity made the poor appropriate public space as well as (business) opportunities that had been primarily generated by the rich and powerful. Both the use of public space—physical and social—and the opportunity cost became the subject of intense contestation. As the vendors spread out their business in the busy alleyways, public thoroughfares, and corners of the public parks, their activities inevitably came into conflict with the prerogatives of both the state, which tends to control the public order and space, and the merchant class who felt their business opportunities appropriated. While the state insisted on the passive use of public spaces, the vendors needed to use them actively and participatively through their own initiatives.[10] The conflict between the street rebels and the state over the use of public space, the meaning of order, and the aim of economic activity characterized the street politics in postrevolutionary Iran. In this conflict, the state sided with the business class, since both power and profit were contested.

Spreading Out in the Streets

Street vending was not a novel phenomenon in Iran. Indeed, it was characteristic of the premodern urban quarters where local street traders exhibited their merchandise in public thoroughfares, usually in the vicinity of the established Bazaar.[11] Local norms and local authorities regulated the use of the streets, which varied according to the local culture, and a kind of Durkheimian organic solidarity (reciprocity, social control, primordial ties, and norms) prevailed in the neighborhoods. If the state seemed to lie far away from the local life, the street vendors were at its center, performing a highly significant function of distributing goods in the local markets and providing services for the communities. Street vending represented perhaps the most salient feature of street life as it kept capturing the imagination of the writers, artists, and historians.

Street vending, peddling, and cart-carrying continued throughout the prerevolutionary years both before and after the establishment during the 1930s of Reza Shah's centralized state. Along with construction work, street vending offered rural migrants and unskilled urbanites easy access to urban employment. Indeed, throughout the century, street life was defined very much by the activities of the chanting peddlers and vendors who operated side by side in the busy thoroughfares and local market places. Although the state began as early as 1896 to regulate their activities,[12] nevertheless many hawkers simply continued to operate unlawfully, often by being scattered, invisible, and thus tolerable. Nevertheless, bribing and/or befriending the local police also helped them carry on their work. Indeed, more often than not, the vendors and the local police were brought together. Although they diverged in their roles, they nevertheless shared many traits—they operated and interacted on daily basis in the same geographical area and shared more or less similar economic needs and probably living standards. Out of this developed a complex relationship in which the line between favor and friendship, bribe and assistance, control and cooperation was often blurred.[13] What underlay this state of affairs was the small size of the vending population and its apparent invisibility, which in terms of both state regulation and shopkeepers's interests made it tolerable if not legitimate. Nevertheless, by the mid-1970s over 15,000 vendors were spread out both in the southern and central areas of the capital (especially in the streets of Lalehzar, Ferdowsi, and Saadi).[14] Insecurity, nevertheless, remained a lasting cost of this informality.

The postrevolution period brought new changes to the vending sector. In addition to a sharp increase in their size, a new form of political vending emerged, thus rendering the group more susceptible to control by the state. During the period between February 1979 and mid-1981 political vending enjoyed very high visibility as educated young men, mainly supporters of the opposition political groups, traded intellectual merchandise such as books, newspapers, and cassettes. Political vending, however, represented only a transitory phenomenon, comprising a small portion of the total number of street traders. More important were the ordinary vendors, whose main concern was to make a living.

The collapse of the Shah's regime brought with it a temporary halt in bureaucratic control of economic activities. The breakdown of police and municipal control opened the way for thousands of young, educated, unemployed, and rural migrants to utilize their own initiatives in economic life. Many conquered new territories in the public space. Scores of new handcarts, kiosks, and stalls mushroomed in the busy thoroughfares of the major cities. Between 1976 and 1986 the informal economy became the fastest-growing sector, second only to the public sector, attracting over 300,000 new entrants. By 1986 these activities made up some 18 percent of urban employment, or close to one million people.[15] Of this, about 320,000 were petty-traders and street subsistence workers, and the rest were workshop workers or family and domestic laborers.[16]

The streets of the capital experienced the largest groups of street workers whose number is estimated to about 40,000 in 1981.[17] Between 1981 and 1984, at the height of urban migration when 1,500 persons migrated to greater Tehran every day, street subsistence work spread like a brush fire in the capital and in other cities and towns. The authorities were apprehensive of its political ramifications. Within these three years, about 80,000 new vendors began working in the capital[18] providing support for an estimated 400,000 Tehranis.[19] In August 1984 a Tehran daily acknowledged that "Today, vending as the most widespread street activity. . . . attracting a major segment of the labor force. It seems that the *mashaghel-i kazib* [fake occupations] have in the long run established themselves, and cannot be dismantled."[20]

Political Vending

In the late afternoon of one hot June day in 1979, about thirty young men and women in the garden of the Teatr-i-shahr in Tehran were involved in an intense discussion. They had gathered there to explore ways of dealing with the official threats against street book-sellers. They discussed the procedures for establishing a street association, and where it should be, putting its by-laws to the vote. Four men and one woman were elected as members of the executive committee.[21] The Association of Street Book-Sellers would fight to secure the position of street book-sellers against the municipality's attacks. It also planned to put pressure on the authorities to create permanent jobs for its members. "In fact, we are seasonal street workers," explained a woman book-seller. "The municipality and the Labor Ministry must feel responsibility for our situation. Bad weather does not allow us to work in the streets during the fall and winter. . . . The municipality must give us a place [for the Association], and the Labor Ministry should give us jobs."[22]

Street vending as a political issue began to unfold from the very first days of the postrevolutionary period. Politicized young unemployed, school and college graduates took advantage of the chaotic freedom and began to set up stalls and kiosks along the sidewalks of the main streets of the capital city. They filled the pavements with their merchandise, mostly in the better-off central districts—Tehran University, Park-i Farah, Park-i Mellat, the streets of Kargar and Keshavarz, and those surrounding the major public parks. Some simply spread their handful of goods on a piece of newspaper on the ground. Others preferred to stand by a single table, trading their major items—books, newspapers, music cassettes, and tapes of political speeches. Some supplemented this merchandise with a variety of sandwiches, hot tea, and cold drinks. The more ambitious vendors installed permanent structures, metal kiosks and wooden shacks, and felt free to tap into electricity from the nearby power lines, which illuminated the surroundings with colorful lights. Thus every evening the occupied sidewalks turned into exotic fun-fairs, with vendor-shoppers and passers-by browsing amid jeers, jokes, music, and plenty of politics.

For these young men, vending served multiple purposes. Primarily, it was a job, serving as a means for the young unemployed to make a living. A fixed business location provided them with a base to assemble, a place to discuss politics, to socialize, and to have fun with friends and mates. The *dakkeh-daari* (kiosk-holding) for them also meant doing political work. Besides their cassettes and cold drinks, these young vendors also traded dissenting newspapers, pamphlets, and books, and distributed tracts and flyers. In this role they were the most important agents for disseminating, in a relatively open fashion, the publications of the opposition groups up until June 1981, when the major crackdown of the opposition began. This role became even more crucial afterward, as their street businesses acted as covers for continuing distribution of underground literature and maintaining a base for public communication between political activists. It was essential for them to maintain the captured spaces, and to help other vendors to do so as well. It was under the initiative of the political vendors that the two vendor associations, the Association of Street Book-Sellers (ASBS) and the Association of the Vendors of Fatemi Avenue were set up. During the first few months the ASBS gathered some two hundred vendors together. To prevent obstruction of thoroughfares, it advised its members to place standard one-by-two-meter stalls on the edges of the sidewalks.[23] But the municipality did not seem to agree to such a project. The associations were dismantled during the first government attacks against the street vendors later in the summer of 1979.

Ordinary Vendors

Despite its salient political presence, political vending was only a short-lived phenomenon and made up a small portion of the total street subsistence activities. More important were those ordinary vendors who continued their prerevolution business, as well as the many who joined them by thousands following the revolution. The newcomers were composed of rural migrants, war refugees, young Tehrani unemployed, and low-income state employees seeking a second income. While the political vendors centered in more affluent areas, the typical street squatters spread out in the most heavily trafficked thoroughfares and big *maidan*s such as Valiye'asre Street, Maidan-i Inqilab, Maidan-i Imam Hussein, Maidan-i Khomeini, Mawlavi Street, Maidan-i Shoush, Maidan-i Azadi, Lalehzar, Istanbul, Imamzade Hasan, and in the vicinity of Park-i Shahr, as well as the neighborhoods in lower-class South Tehran. In 1980 over 1,850 stall-holders were concentrated in Mosaddeq Avenue and 686 along Inqilab Street.[24] Their means of trading ranged from simple carton boxes or tin plates to wagons, handcarts, and kiosks. Many peddlers carried their merchandise in baskets that hung down from their necks.

Their business activities ranged from selling goods to providing services and producing objects. Their merchandise extended from fresh produce, old clothing, cigarettes, and washing powder to domestic appliances, car parts, medicine, stale bread, and their own bodies. Some ingeniously traded phone coins, Xeroxed car application forms, and rationed gasoline coupons. Indeed, the wartime rationing of basic commodities boosted their business, as their genuinely free market offered almost anything restricted by the state. They produced and sold food, kitchen appliances, and handicrafts. They offered entertainment, performing as magicians, enacting passion plays, displaying animals, telling fortunes. Or they remained in silent despair next to their handcarts, waiting for someone to buy their muscle power. The more desperate did almost any and everything that they thought would ensure their survival. This did not exclude begging, theft, drug-dealing, and prostitution.[25] For these men and women, neither their underdog status nor the morality of their enterprise hindered them so long as they made a living. "Hawking is a disgraceful [abirourizi] job. You see, I really get embarrassed when sometimes my relatives or friends pass by this place. If they [the government] would provide for my livelihood, I would never do this work."[26]

This panorama of individuals, objects, and activities, this street culture, marked the social space of the street sidewalks, creating an image of a social whole that embodied a seemingly harmonious division of labor—beggars begged; shoppers and traders bargained; the village traveler ate from the cheap food stands; porters carried heavy loads; young men flirted, and believers broadcast loud religious chantings. But these busy thoroughfares became so clogged with screaming traders and street shoppers that moving through became a troublesome venture. It was as if this universe of hurrying individuals, shifting events, and constant noise had turned these streets of Tehran into a boundless macrocosm of its great old bazaar, with its densely packed little shops and narrow alleyways seemingly filled with everyone and everything.

The street subsistence workers came from diverse social and economic backgrounds. Political vendors apart, the bulk of them were urban youths without work, high school graduates who failed to get into college or find office positions, war refugees, disabled war veterans, low-income state employees seeking second jobs, and—the largest group throughout the 1980s—rural migrants. Some three-quarters of the vendors in Shiraz were migrants from other regions; one out of three was a war refugee.[27] Similarly, the bulk (over 80 percent) of Tehrani street vendors originated from unskilled peasant migrants, most of whom (about 75 percent) became vendors for the first time after the revolution.[28] Many had migrated from the Turkish-speaking provinces of Azarbaijan, Zanjan, and Hamadan—the origin of many of the squatter settlers in South Tehran.[29]

Vendors often embarked upon their new venture individually and quietly. Perceiving it as a natural way to make a living, they encroached on public spaces by rolling their pushcarts around, spreading their basaats, or setting up their stalls, often without being aware of the legal implications of their actions. Those who knew the laws justified themselves both privately and publicly by referring to the moral principle of necessity. "I don't see this as unlawful. [Because] only the needy and the poor do this job, not the rich; only those who are embarrassed before their families because they cannot afford to provide for them—these do the street vending. Otherwise, they would have to resort to theft and pickpocketing."[30] But some viewed the streets simply as public property. "Look," they often argued "the authorities have not inherited the streets; have they? It is not their private property! They belong to all."[31] To escape from police control, some became "invisible" by scattering to the less strategic locations. But once the vendors gained some degree of security, stalls were replaced by permanent kiosks. Security could be ensured by the legitimacy of continual occupancy.

Relatives and friends often offered advice on the quality of the "spot," the desirability of the merchandise, police harassment, possibilities for bribes, and the like. The vendors also thought about the cost-benefits of travel-peddling (dast-foroushi), stall-holding (basaati), or kiosk-owning (dakkeh-daari). Peddling offered versatility in finding customers and escaping police harassment, but it required the physical fitness to walk long distances. Possession of basaats in fixed locations in the busy thoroughfares was a highly competitive enterprise. Informal norms among the vendors regulated who possessed which location. Key money of certain sites was calculated in terms of square meter sidewalk tiles and the sites were at times traded for hundreds of dollars.[32]

On occasion vending began and operated collectively when groups of relatives and village-mates would take over a public space, a *maidan*, or a vacant piece of land by hurriedly constructing stalls, kiosks, and booths to form collective markets. These group vendors often specialized in single commodities. In Tehran, for instance, a large number bought used clothing and appliances from affluent homes and sold them in the poor southern districts. Most residents of the poor areas of Ghal'eh Morghi, Khazaneh, and Darvazehghar purchased their clothing from the second-hand street markets of Gumrog, Maidan-i Sayed Ismail, and the Baagh-i Azari neighborhood.[33] This trend continued after the revolution, but some of these markets moved further north, to Maidan-i Golha, Maidan-i Fowziyeh, and Amirabad Street.[34] Similarly, a large number of clothing vendors in the southern part of Inqilab Square and Khiaban Kargar-i Jonoubi came from the Caspian Sea area. They benefited from the support of the Caspian-origin merchants of the Tehran Bazaar.[35] While group vending offered street traders an established network, mutual assistance, and a high measure of security, it also made them more visible to authorities and reduced their flexibility in dealing with the local police in times of removal.

Why So Much Growth?

Three major factors contributed to the massive growth of street vendors in postrevolution Iran: *unemployment*, a possibility of earning *higher income*, and *autonomy* from state regulations and institutions.

Unemployment remained a salient feature of the economy through the 1980s. The total unemployment rate jumped from 10 percent in 1976 to 18.7 percent in 1984[36] or some 2.2 million people. From 1976 to 1986, on average, some 302,000 (ten-years-old and over) entered the job market, while about 224,000 jobs were created.[37] More than 64 percent of the unemployed lived in the cities. Of these, 40 percent were previously employed and 60 percent were new entrants into the job market. In the cities, open unemployment increased from 5.1 percent in 1976 to 15.2 percent in 1986.[38] Rural migration placed a heavy strain on the urban job market. For instance, during 1982 to 1983, the twenty districts of the capital were receiving an average 1,500 daily new immigrants. This excluded those who migrated to and settled on the margin of the city.[39]

Many of this jobless crowd, including unskilled village migrants as well as educated Tehranis, moved into the street subsistence sector.[40] Muhammad Ali Kehzadi, a young man (twenty-seven years old in 1980) arrived in Tehran immediately after the revolution from a village around the city of Khorram Abad. He ended up in the streets of South Tehran, making a living by entertaining children with a toy gun (*tufang baadi*):

> I used to do farming in the village. It's been now some two months since I've arrived in Tehran. What made me come here was the pressure of making a living in the village: unemployment, debt, and the [danger] of the starvation of my family. Maybe there is a way out here in Tehran. My brother and I have two hectares of land which we inherited from our father; and we divided the income between us. . . . Swear to God, both of our families would work the land for over nine months to produce only two tons [of wheat]. And that, we would consume all [without being able to sell any portion]. . . . At times, toward the end of the year, we would even be short of that amount; so, we had to buy some extra flour. In addition to that, we still needed to buy clothes, shoes, sugar, tea, meat, cooking oil, etc., etc. We barely made it . . . Now, I am in debt for 15 to 16,000 tumans. . . . I came to Tehran to make this money to pay my debt back. . . . At the beginning, I didn't want to do this work at all. I tried the fruit retail markets; I tried the bazaar. No way! nobody wants to hire labor. There are just no jobs around. So, I borrowed 700 tumans, and bought this "gun" to make a living with.[41]

Abbas Ismaili, 40 years old (in 1980), had left his village near the town of Tawiserkan years before the revolution, in 1973, after the death of his wife:

> In fact, I do not have a regular job. I will do anything that is offered to me. In the past, when I [was young and] had some energy, I used to do construction work. I was also a porter for some time. But when my health deteriorated, I began doing lighter work. I said to myself, "I don't have [anybody or] anything in this world. So, let's not suffer more than this in these couple of days remaining of my life." Now, it's been a month or so since I've begun selling *tasbih* strings.[42] Before doing this, I was a vendor. If I had enough money, I would go to the business of buying and selling rings or things like this.[43]

The stories seem to reflect the stereotypical image of the vendors as a desperate and destitute segment of the urban underclass. Postrevolutionary developments in fact produced greater diversity among the vendors by introducing people with diverse social attributes of age, income, education, and ambition into this subaltern group.

Many unskilled as well as skilled *men* joined street work because it offered them a relatively high income. In 1990 about 60 percent of Tehrani vendors, with one out of three being high school graduates, made between 3,000 to 10,000 rials a day.[44] The mayor of Tehran claimed in March 1984 that some of the street bread traders in the capital earned as much as Rls 5,000 a day.[45] About 20 percent of skilled people preferred the high income from vending to making use of their expertise.[46]

Finally, for some the idea of running a business autonomous from government regulations and bureaucratic discipline made street vending an attractive option. Despite the low status attached to the trade (considered as *hammali* and *abirourizi*) many street hawkers seemed to prefer remaining in similar activities.[47] As a worker put it in 1983, "working in large industries like car factories is very draining; one would always be under someone's thumb. That is why, I think, work like street vending is more suitable and worthwhile."[48] The vendors did suffer police harassment, income irregularities, low status, and the physical hardship of working in the streets during the cold winters and hot summers. High income, autonomy, and easy entry for many, compensated for these costs of informality. Nevertheless, they never stopped their efforts to offset these costs while maintaining the benefits. This meant demanding security, shops, kiosks, and credit, which involved the petty business of the street in a major sociopolitical conflict.

Consequences and Contradictions

With expansion of street vending, three main areas—urban employment, urban physical space, and urban social space—became sites of contestation and conflict between vendors and the state. By engaging in street subsistence activities, some 320,000 people managed to earn a living. Many unskilled migrants, laid-off workers, disabled poor, recent high school leavers, and even university graduates moved into these occupations, primarily because they did not see any other alternative.[49] "What is our fault that we have no other opportunities but these jobs?," vendors argued when confronted by belligerent officials.[50] As an old man stated:

Well, this is the way I make my living. I sit here, and some people bring me goods; I add a percentage to the price and sell them . . . I know the government has said that we shouldn't cause inflation. The municipality agents came a few times to stop my work. I told them, "What do you want me to do instead, go around and beg? Give us opportunity, then we would stop this kind of work."[51]

Official discourse perceived street work as a "social disease" (*bimari-ye ijtimaii*), an "afflicting malaise" (*bimari-ye mosre'*) "parasitic" (*mashaghel-i angali*), and "fake and pseudo-occupations" (*mashaghel-i kazib*)—which caused nuisance and obstruction in public sites.[52] Street vendors were represented as opportunists, lazy bums (*tanparvar*), political conspirators, military service escapees, and drug dealers. Those who "have set up food stalls in the streets are in fact rebuffing the Revolution," stated Tehran's radical mayor, Muhammad Tavassoli, in 1979. "If the municipality does not stop these activities, it will practically encourage idleness and indolence."[53] The terms "*mashagel-i kazib*" and "*sadd-i ma'bar*" became the most widely used terms in these discursive campaigns.[54] "Fake occupations" were defined as the "unproductive" and "consumptionist" jobs that "create no value-added."[55] They were responsible for shortage and inflation. Ironically, most revolutionary officials, from radical clergy to conservative and liberal politicians, shared the modernization theory and ideology of urban duality. Their concept of *insan-i hashiye-ii* (marginal man) did not diverge much from the cultural type constructed and shared by many late nineteenth- and early twentieth-century Western urban sociologists.[56]

On the other hand, street vending had an obvious impact on urban space. Once the individual vendors established their simple *basaat*s or kiosks on the street sidewalks, they began gradually to extend their spatial domain by putting chairs, benches, tables, and plants around their spots and covering their stalls with shades or umbrellas. Before long, and often illegally, the kiosks were connected to the city's electricity supply, allowing colorful lights, fans, and music, which, for some, had become an inseparable component of vending life. Every morning and late afternoon, vendors became responsible for sweeping and wetting down the areas surrounding their lots. When some security was achieved, fringe areas were tiled and stalls cemented to the ground.

Vendors were involved in an active use of the public space by directly participating in its utilization, organization, and change. But such participative use came into sharp conflict with the tendency of the state to restrict public space for a passive use. The state reserved for itself the prerogative to determine how the space should be organized. In Iran, early attempts to regulate public space began in the late nineteenth century. In 1896 the state made systematic provisions to police the movements of hawkers, street workers, pimps, prostitutes, mules, carriages, loiters, and street children.[57] Darughehs enforced the laws until 1926, when it was replaced by modern municipalities and the police, a policy that has continued to the present.[58] All modern states share this tendency, since the issue of space is simultaneously an issue of order and ultimately an exertion of power.[59] An active use of space means, in a sense, the state relinquishing some degree of control over the activities of the populace.

The Islamic authorities viewed street work as having a destabilizing effect, threatening the social fabric. They invariably expressed fear about the "cancerous" spread of street activities, this "contagious malaise." One can visualize how they saw cities being sunk into the chaos of an uncontrollable mass of "fake" elements with their quarrels, complaints, and rumors.[60] Vendors were seen to cause obstruction, harass women, provide cover for draft dodgers, drug dealers, and opposition conspirators, and present a squalid and chaotic image of the capital to foreign visitors.[61]

Vendors were also involved in creating a new *social* space in the streets, which the Islamic state could not tolerate. The jubilance, jokes, music, assemblies of youths, colorful lights, and the brisk atmosphere together created an alternative cultural aura. This generally secular, cheerful, and colorful street culture was in sharp contrast to the prevailing somber and dark religious mood. Street vendors, in particular the political breed, had indeed created a highly visible counterhegemonic street subculture that seemed to challenge the state's notions of governance and its meaning of order. Beyond this, vendors had appropriated the favorable business conditions that merchant class had created. Many potential customers of stores were attracted to street vendors who offered more affordable and convenient bargains. Merchants thus joined the government in combating the street vendors.

In short, what was at stake was the relative autonomy and fluidity of vending life, outside and against the surveillance of officialdom. In their capacity as autonomous or informal individuals, vendors were seen as promoters of disorder, immoral behavior, and political conspiracy.[62] For this, they had to be curtailed.

Confrontations

To outmaneuver the street vendors, the authorities resorted to institutional mechanisms, exerted moral pressure, and waged violence. Several agents and institutions were involved in combating street subsistence activities. Beyond the *hizbullahi* groups—the Pasdaran and the municipality authorities—the Anti-Vice Court (*Dadgah-i Zedd-i Munkarat*) served to give legal cover to the demolition policies and to offset the legal struggles of the vendors. The Committee for Guild Affairs (CGA), a nongovernmental body administering business affairs in Tehran, also intervened by issuing antivending warnings and instructions on professional and legal grounds. In June 1980 for instance, the committee refused to recognize street vending as a legitimate trade by "those who have taken advantage of the revolution by setting up tents, basaats, and trading ventures in the public thoroughfares."[63] On many occasions the attorney general and the General Commands of the Revolutionary Committees directly authorized the Pasdaran to intervene, as in Karadj in November 1984 and Shiraz in December 1984.[64]

Despite the operations of these agents, there was still a need for a central authority to manage the crisis systematically. Increasing rural migration and urban unemployment made this task even more urgent. In May 1983 the mayor of Tehran, Engineer Seifian, formed the Committee Against Obstruction of Thoroughfares (CAOT)(*Sitad-i Raf'-i Sadd-i Ma'bar*), an interdepartmental group composed of representatives from the central municipality, police, revolutionary committees, traffic, and a few others.[65] Authorized by the attorney general, the CAOT instructed its special agents to evict the street vendors.[66] The CAOT created special antiobstruction squads, which, in cooperation with the Pasdaran, replaced the street thugs. By May 1984 six mobile units were set up to provide surveillance over the twenty-one districts of the capital city. Agents drove around in their vans and pickup trucks; any illegal vendor they encountered was evicted and his property confiscated. The merchandise might be returned or not, depending on certain procedures, including the extent of illegality and the payment of fines.[67]

Yet even this proved inadequate to contain the crisis. In September 1985, some eighteen months later, CAOT became the Committee for Continuing Mobilization Against the Obstruction of Thoroughfares (CCMAOT) (*Sitad-i Basij-i Payguiri va Raf'-i Sadd-e Ma'bar*). The change of name pointed to an emphasis on long and sweeping campaigns, with antiobstruction squads stationed permanently in the major trading locations, including the maidans of Inqilab and Tajrish in the north, and those of Imam Hussein, Khorasan, Shoush, Rah-i Aahan, Gumrok, 15th Khordad Avenue, Serah-i Azari, and streets off Lalehzar, in the poor neighborhoods of South Tehran.[68]

In addition to systematic institutional mechanisms, many politicians resorted to religious leaders to exert moral pressure on the vendors.[69] Urban migration, squatter settlement, and street vending were discussed in Friday prayers and local mosque sermons. Preachers often instigated their audience into violent actions against vendors.[70] The mayor of Orumieh proclaimed that "obstruction and unemployment are *haram* [unacceptable] according to *shari'a*."[71] Attorney General, Ayatollah Muhammad Gilani requested Ayatollah Khomeini to issue a *fitwa*, forbidding street vendors from "causing obstruction."[72] The *fitwa* was sought not only to put moral pressure on the street vendors but also to silence the few officials who cast doubt on the viability of violent crackdowns.[73] The resort to violence pointed to the fact that institutional and moral pressure was having little practical effect.

The early antivending policies and actions were directed largely against the political vending. On March 17, 1980, only one month after the revolution, "the Tehran central municipality instructed all other districts to remove as soon as possible all the recently erected stalls."[74] This was followed by harsher instructions. The warnings in part functioned as a green light to the informal street thugs, the *hizbullahi*s, to get on with the dissenting vendors. Groups of thugs, often escorted by the Pasdaran, went around kicking down stalls and *basaat*s and confiscating merchandise and other belongings.[75] Subsequent scuffles and fistfights resulted in many injuries and deaths. In the first year of the revolution, demolitions tended to be random, concentrated mainly in the streets around Tehran University, Mosaddeq (then Valiye'ahd), and Inqilab avenues in the capital city. Large-scale violence also took place.

The largest antivending operation in Tehran coincided with the first widespread attempt to quell the Kurdish autonomy movements in the late summer of 1980. In the late afternoon of one of those days, I ventured to the area around Tehran University. The locality, once celebrated for its brisk and energetic feeling, had turned into a lonely and joyless area. Pasdaran and the *hizbullahi* thugs were patrolling on foot or in military jeeps, driving victoriously up and down the deserted streets. The pavement and the streets resembled a battle zone, with piles of scattered newspaper sheets, ripped books, torn flyers, broken tables, and wrecked vending stalls littering the ground. The occasional passers-by looked bewildered, resigned, and silent; among them were local vendors who had returned with dismay, anguish, and anger to learn the fate of their spots.

Small-scale and random attacks, demolitions, and the removal of the street traders became an everyday practice, one that continued through the late 1980s. Almost any national crisis was used by the government to crack down on street enterprises. On May 25, 1981, in the midst of the clerical confrontation with President Bani Sadr and the Mujahedin, a group of fifty *hizbullahi*s attacked the kiosk holders of Fatemi Avenue in Tehran. The thugs turned on the stall holders, using iron clubs, knives, and similar objects. Some thirty kiosks and stalls were badly damaged or totally destroyed, and seven vendors were seriously injured. The attackers returned the following day to finish off the remaining *dakkeh-daars*, this time leaving ten to fifteen wounded.[76]

There were similar, though not as devastating attacks in the provincial cities. Between 1982 and 1984 the authorities in Shiraz, Tabriz, Urumiyeh, Khorram Abad, Masjid Soleyman, Ghazvin, Langroud, Kirmanshah, and Karadj gave the go-ahead to both Pasdaran and club-wielders to destroy kiosks and remove the peddlers. Everyday surveillance seemed to have a marked impact in reducing street activities. In April 1984 officials announced they had removed over 90 percent of the 120,000 illegal vendors and kiosk holders from the streets of Tehran. "The remainder," they promised, "will be dealt with harshly in accordance with law."[77] Some 1,865 street cigarette sellers were arrested by July 1985 in Tehran alone.[78] In the words of the mayor "the obstruction of thoroughfares which could have major social and political ramifications is on the verge of total resolution."[79]

Although street violence did force some vendors to retreat, the removal policy in the capital affected mainly those centered in Maidan Azadi, the margins of Valiye'asr Avenue (a major shopping center of the well-to do), and Inqilab Avenue. Four years into the campaigns a mood of resignation replaced the language of aggression. In March 1983 the mayor of Shiraz pleaded with the citizens to "offer us a solution."[80] In Tehran the head of the CCMAOT, Muhammad Malayeri, acknowledged that "our [demolition] agents are operating in the most difficult and dangerous conditions. Every day a number of them get beaten up and injured by the vendors, and after a while they get tired and worn down."[81] Some vendors stood and defended their enterprise; many owners of the less versatile kiosks moved to less noticeable locations; the more flexible peddlers took up a guerrilla-type tactic of resistance.

Resisting the Eviction Policy

Vendors resisted the eviction policy in different ways. They organized street demonstrations, withstood the eviction agents on the spot, took legal actions, and publicized their plight in the press. The most enduring method was the everyday guerrilla-type tactic of "sell and run."

What determined these diverse tactics had to do with the differing types of vending and the changing political circumstances. Vendors did not rely solely on informal association or active mobilization; these tactics were less useful after the state repression began. The enduring factor was the operation of "passive networking" among vendors. Passive networking is the instantaneous and silent communication established among atomized individuals with common interests by virtue of a visibility that is facilitated through common space. Those individual vendors who worked in the same street and saw one another on a daily basis could develop latent communications merely by the fact of their common interest, even though they might not know or speak with one another. When a common threat arrived, they came together spontaneously to act collectively.

Demonstrations and sit-ins were organized largely by the political and immobile vendors. They took place in the early years of the post-revolution, 1979 to 1981, when this method of protest enjoyed a wide legitimacy. The vendors demonstrated either in order to hinder their forced removal or to publicize their plight and express their anger after an eviction had already occurred. Thus, on December 16, 1981, a small group of Tehrani vendors responded to a demolition raid by assembling in front of the municipality. A representative was sent to plead with the mayor, who pledged to provide them with a space to set up an off-street market. Similarly, in Kirmanshah (Bakhtaran), some three hundred vendors staged a march on the city hall to protest against an attack by the Pasdaran who two weeks earlier had destroyed their kiosks. They asked the authorities to allow them to sell all their merchandise and establish a permanent off-street market for them. The mayor agreed to both their claims.[82]

For most part, however, demonstrations remained isolated, small-scale, and loosely organized. They occurred mainly during 1979 and 1981, when a freer political climate allowed left-wing activists to mobilize street dissent. They often encountered violent reactions from the Pasdaran, who considered such activities as a ploy to delegitimize the revolution. A joint march organized by the Union of the Street Book-Sellers and the Union of the Kiosk Holders of Mosaddeq Avenue in July 1980 was dealt with very harshly. It lasted a few days, involved marching to the presidential office and city hall, and resulted in many injuries and the killing of one demonstrator by the Pasdaran.[83]

Because of their mobilizing role, political vendors were more susceptible to violent reactions than others. They were not only defending their jobs, they were also exposing the government's violation of freedom of expression. While their forms of resistance tended to be more elaborate and loud, their successes proved limited. By the summer of 1981 the political vendors had been driven off the streets, leaving the ordinary vendors on their own, with some resorting to on-the-spot defense of their enterprises.

On December 15, 1985, CCMAOT squads, along with groups of Pasdaran, raided a fruit market located in the Falake-ye Dovvom-i Khazaneh, a poor neighborhood in South Tehran. They began to collect handcarts, scales, and similar belongings, throwing fruits into the sewage ditches running through the market. The vendors responded with their fists, inciting the Pasdaran to shoot into the air. One cart owner reacted by throwing a heavy scale weight at the agents, knocking one down. They beat him up and dragged him to the Security *Komiteh*. Reportedly, the women present defended the vendors, screaming at the agents and blaming the troubles on them.[84]

Despite open resistance of this sort, the outcome for the vendors was not always favorable. On-the-spot resistance certainly made the removal policy very costly and slow. In particular, the involvement during each confrontation of scores of sympathizers and passers-by would frustrate police operations, leaving the agents embarrassed and indignant. Yet the vendors also felt the cost of their constant vigilance and the insecurity of everyday clashes with the demolition agents. One vending stronghold around Tehran University resisted the eviction policy until April 1990; despite their bitter resistance—eighty were detained—they were eventually driven off the streets by Pasdaran and by local shopkeepers.[85] The scattered nature of street work, the localized nature of their operation, and the fact of self-employment rendered a large-scale resistance (similar to that of the factory workers or the squatters) difficult. As the threat of demolition persisted, vendors had to think of alternative solutions. From mid-1981 they turned to other forms of struggle. Some took legal action against the CCMAOT, bringing complaints to the courts, the Committee of Act 90 of the Majlis, the Presidential Office, the speaker of the Majlis, and the Administrative Justice Court (*Divan Idalat-i Idaari*). Lawsuits piled up to the extent that the head of the CCMAOT expressed his frustration at the time and energy they consumed.[86]

Others resorted to a campaign of publicity and appeal in the press. The two major Tehran dailies, *Ettilaat* and *Kayhan*, carried letters of the vendors that combined cries for justice with desperation and urgency. Ahmad Islami, a vendor from the city of Karadj wrote:

> For the last eighteen years, I have been making a living and supporting my seven-member family by selling daily papers in a kiosk. But some time ago, the municipality in the city of Karadj began to collect the kiosks on the ground that they obstructed the public thoroughfare and they are doing this in the conditions where the cold winter is on its way. We, the newspapers sellers, cannot do our business in the streets without shelters. So, we appeal to the honorable mayor to allow us to carry on our work through this winter. Otherwise, we will have no recourse but to stay at home [doing nothing].[87]

Rahim Rezaii, a peddler from Tehran, appealed:

> I am a *faludeh*[88] hawker, a tenant, and a breadwinner for a family of five. I would like to request the honorable mayor to think of the families of the vendors when he orders their eviction from the streets. If they [the municipality] allocate us a market site anywhere in the city, we will remove our business off the streets promptly and without any hesitation.[89]

Although these nonconfrontational campaigns proved effective in changing the attitude of some policy-makers, they failed to deter the immediate danger of eviction. These struggles represented largely the tactics of the kiosk holders and immobile vendors, whose fixed location had become a liability. The method served as the last attempt to which the kiosk holders could resort under the conditions of repression. The situation for the mobile and more versatile vendors, however, seemed quite different.

To survive the immediate threat of removal, the more versatile and mobile vendors turned from an open confrontation to a war of attrition through a hidden and everyday resistance. The fluidity of the operation of the *basaati*s, peddlers, hawkers, wagon holders, lorry keepers, and van owners made it possible for them to pack up their merchandise once the antiobstruction squads appeared, and to resume their operation as soon as the agents left the scene. The passive network, which is facilitated by mere visibility and proximity, as well as the active informal communication among the street vendors rendered this quiet form of resistance highly successful. The vendors often appointed a few peers to guard the vicinity of their work by informing the others of the arrival of eviction agents, by shouting: "the agents are coming, run away."[90]

On many occasions even the immobile kiosk holders followed similar tactics. In the course of the six months following their first removal in summer 1980 from Fatemi Avenue in Tehran, a group went back several times to build their stalls, after being driven away each time. On one day in February 1981 a number of them returned and hurriedly erected some seventy-five kiosks in a few hours.[91] *Ettilaat* concluded that, given this guerrilla-type campaign, the activities of the demolition squads "have no outcome, except to waste time and energy."[92]

The antiobstruction vans and trucks drove around in the streets, supposedly clearing away the unauthorized vendors. But as soon as they moved away, "in a few minutes, everything gets back to normal as if nothing had happened . . . It appears that the Municipality is simply unable to do away with this highly extensive network."[93] A large number of the vendors individually went "invisible" by scattering to less noticeable and less strategic positions. Some vendors stood by in strategic locations where they displayed not merchandise but a piece of cardboard that carried a list of potential items. Prospective customers would then be guided to backstreets where the actual merchandise were stored. This method reduced the risk of losing capital by enhancing vendors' ability to confront the police.

To be more agile and mobile, vendors had to transform from kiosk-owning to stall-holding, push-cart vending, and to simply carrying cardboard signs. While this maneuver reduced vendors' active use of both public space and business conditions, it ensured their continuing presence in the street economy and politics.

In the end, the antiobstruction operations did not reduce the number of the venders as mush as they redistributed them. The problem remained. In 1984 an Azari vendor, commenting on antivending policies, stated: "I have been a vendor for the last twenty years. Different governments have been trying to remove us since the time of General Razmara [1950–1951]. But they couldn't. I think, this regime also won't be able to force us off the streets."[94] As late as April 1990 a new mayor of Tehran, Gholam Hussein Karbaschi, summed up the state of affairs. "The problem of vending and obstruction in the large cities," he stated, "has always existed and will continue to persist. But the approach to this problem should not be 'sitadi' [what the CCMAOT adopted]." He then disclosed the new strategy of the government to incorporate the more mobile vendors by establishing off-street collective markets throughout the city.[95] Having failed to end street activities, the authorities decided to bring them under their own control.

Incorporation, Diffusion, and Back to the Streets?

By early 1986 the authorities had acknowledged that street activities were there to stay. Their hope that at least the "seasonal" street peddlers would return to their villages[96] also appeared to be a fantasy. It was widely accepted that the remedy to this "disease" must be sought not in the cities but in the countryside, by tackling the development problems in the rural areas. The official press carried articles, reports, and debates on the predicament of street trade, wondering where these desperate people would go if and when the removal policy succeeded.[97] The question now was how to accommodate them without letting the situation to get entirely out of hand.

In October 1985 the Tehran municipality began a survey of street activities to identify those "who deserved to continue their activities," including the old, sick, and disabled, and those with at least ten years in the business. Lawful vendors were required to get official permits, to be issued by the Union of the Kiosk Holders and Ice Traders of Tehran (UKHITT), which cooperated with the CAOT. This method replaced an earlier policy whereby the "deserving vendors" would have to apply through and be recommended by the local mosques.[98] According to the new directives, street activities were restricted to selling flowers, fresh fruit juice, machine-made bread, and foreign newspapers.[99] The rest, the unlawful kiosk holders and peddlers, were to be removed within forty-eight hours.

Municipality plans to construct formal street and off-street markets had been entertained, two years earlier, to accommodate some 30,000 to 40,000 vendors and stall-holders in Tehran, placing them in such street markets as Tangeh Chezabeh in Valiye'asr Avenue; Bazaarche-ye 22 Bahman in Nizamabad, which had about 200 stalls; and similar units in Maidan-i Inqilab, Naser Khosrow Street, and especially in districts in South Tehran.[100] The plan barely got off the ground until the early 1990s, as street vending kept growing undeterred.[101]

With the coming to office of Karbaschi, a young, Western-educated mayor, incorporation overcame confrontation. In the winter of 1992, seven flea markets began operating at different localities in the capital city.[102] Each of these "traditional markets," as they were called, was organized on a different day of the week. They accommodated up to three hundred vendors. The markets were located in places such as parking lots and blocked streets for a limited time, and no fees were charged. In addition to professional vendors, households were also allowed to sell their used items, and a special market was set up for artists to exhibit and trade their creations. Some thirty-five markets were planned to operate during 1992. The vendors were encouraged to establish *shura*s with the elected representatives serving the general interests of the trade, negotiating with the authorities, and supervising the tagged prices. The *shura* issued a special I.D. card for the "committed" vendors, recognizing them as members of the lawful vending community.

Government officials stated that their objectives in setting up the markets were to coordinate the activities of the street vendors and to reduce city traffic by localizing the supply of goods available to the public at fair prices. Whatever the true aim, the project served to integrate the scattered street vendors into a controllable structure by regulating the time and space of their operation. Both the place and the timing of the markets were ad hoc, rotating in different parking lots or blocked streets for a limited period of time. By bringing the vendors collectively into designated places, officials could maintain surveillance more efficiently. They could also prevent the vendors from developing any sense of territoriality by moving them around to different locations at different times.[103] Newspaper sellers also came under surveillance through the standardization of their space. The municipality relocated them into fixed kiosks, which it designed and that were given only to licensed vendors. More than 650 of these official kiosks were installed throughout Teheran.[104] Nonstandard kiosks, easily recognized, remained illegal.

Vendors nevertheless asserted their determination to remain in their occupations, albeit in different settings. They won recognition, but had to function in a controlled structure. How long can such a bargain last? It depends probably upon the extent to which the markets will respond to the long-term needs of the street's economic activities—to secure a competitive income and to respond to the possible increase in the size of street work. Otherwise, as it often happens in many places such as Cairo, a return to the original patterns is a likely scenario. Already by the mid-1990s, indications were that the flea markets in Iran had begun to wither away, and many street rebels were on their way back to the streets.

Eight

Grassroots and State Power: The Promise and Perils of Quiet Encroachment

This book has been about the struggles of ordinary people to survive and improve their lives. I have been concerned with a type of informal politics, which I have termed the quiet encroachment of the ordinary—the lifelong, everyday, small-scale, and often silent strivings of the Third World poor, which at certain historical moments assume a collective character, giving rise to major conflicts in society. At a different level I have attempted to explore the relationship between social movements and social change. In this concluding chapter I would like to assess the significance of this type of grassroots activism, exploring its implications both with reference to the specific case of Iran and more broadly in relation to a number of theoretical issues.

Significance

The preceding chapters discussed in detail how the urban poor in Iran strove to extend their social and economic space both where they lived and in their working lives. The chapters chronicled the way in which squatter migrants brought urban land under development both long before the Islamic revolution and after, creating new communities; the way in which they demanded urban amenities from the authorities, or acquired them unlawfully. Street subsistence workers took over the main public thoroughfares, putting up stalls, driving pushcarts, and erecting kiosks. Taking advantage of the opportunities provided by the revolution, poor families appropriated vacant homes and hotels and the unemployed strove to secure jobs or else demanded social protection. The justification for action was based invariably on the moral principle of necessity. Nevertheless, rational calculation was also part of the game.

Many of these efforts involved organizing, marching in the streets, and scuffling with security forces. Others involved community mobilization, identity politics, and struggles for communal and cultural autonomy. Undoubtedly the Islamic Revolution of 1979 provided the poor with an exceptional opportunity for collective and audible mobilization. Yet, for the most part under normal circumstances, the actors, these "informal people" without any institutional structure, were individuals and families who made their advances steadily, individually, and without much clamor.

From these considerations alone a number of simple but important conclusions emerge. First, given the limited opportunities available to the poor (in terms of income, education, skill, and connections), such direct actions constitute the most viable method for their self-development. Most commentators, focusing on the structural processes of social exclusion and poverty, neglect those on the receiving end of the process—the excluded—or else regard them as victims. However, I have looked at the everyday life and social activities of the excluded groups in terms of a particular type of grassroots *movement*, showing that the poor are not simply passive recipients of change but are also actors in its making. I have shown that, contrary to the prevailing stereotypes that portray them as "passive poor," "fatalistic Muslim masses," or "disoriented marginals," the disenfranchised do not sit around to wait for their fate but are actively engaged, within their constraints, in shaping their own destiny. In this context the Muslim Middle Easterners, despite cultural differences, are no different from other low-income groups in the developing world.

This raises a second point. There is a widespread assumption that the appeal of political Islam is to the masses, especially the recent poor migrants to cities. A deep religiosity, along with shared language and institutions, are said to bring the masses and the clergy together, rendering them close allies. The accounts in this book (and my current research in Egypt) show that the relationship between the poor on the one hand and the Islamic movements and the Islamic state, on the other, is much more complex. There is no such a thing as a natural ally for political Islam. The activities of Egyptian Islamists among the urban poor are very scattered and pragmatic, and so is the reciprocal support of the poor; the underclass in urban Egypt is left predominantly on its own. In Iran, on the other hand, the ruling clergy never established total hegemony over the poor, despite its pro-*mustaz'afin* discourse. Rather, the disenfranchised were polarized. Some segments—including groups within the revolutionary guards, *Basiji*s, the Construction Crusade, and the like—were incorporated into the state structure. Others remained outside, and their struggles for self-development brought them into conflict with the Islamic state. These include those hybrid elements whose ideological affinity with the Islamic government did not deter their daily struggles against the same government's agents (Pasdaran, the municipality and so on).

The fact is that the disenfranchised cannot afford to be ideological. As the historical narratives in this book evidence, the political ideological class par excellence is not the poor but, as usual, is the class made up of students, teachers, and other sectors of the intelligentsia, who seem to be initiators and leaders of most radical and oppositional politics, including the Islamic. Most of the poor seem to be uninterested in any *particular* form of ideology and politics, whether governmental (e.g., Islamic as in Iran) or oppositional (e.g., leftist). Their interests lie in those strategies and associations that respond directly to their immediate concerns. Their attachment to informal primary relations and solidarities seems to be the best form of protection. This, I should emphasize, is not meant to imply an essential lack of interest on the part of the poor in abstract thinking or planning for distant futures. On the contrary, many poor people *live* on the dream of a better future. In the Middle East the particular attention that poor families pay to the well-being and education of their children is a proof of their foresight. My point is that such forethoughts may be internalized only if they are immediately concrete and meaningful in the poor's cultural worldviews.

Of course, when opportunity arises, as in multiparty democracy or under political patronage, attempts are indeed made to articulate the politics of the state and/or oppositional groups and the interests of the poor. However, this articulation of interest does not usually last long, since the poor's stake in the immediate and the concrete distracts them from the abstract ideology and long-term program of both the opposition and the state. Perhaps more than any other social groups, the poor tend to rely on themselves to survive and improve their lot.

Yet in their endeavors to survive—and this is my third point—these ordinary people with their ordinary ways bring about significant social change—the kind of changes that at times are comparable to those a revolution may (or may not) produce for them. Beyond affecting their lives, these localized practices, meanwhile, entail critical social changes at the broader level—in national demography, urban structure, law and order, and public policy. The actors' efforts in redistributing social goods and opportunities, together with their struggle for autonomy, tend to lay a heavy economic and political cost on the dominant groups, tilting the balance of power in society.

Some may equate these localized struggles with desperate acts of survival in conditions where a nationwide reform movement is lacking. Thus a revolution sympathetic to the poor is expected to end their quiet encroachment. However, such a formulation raises some difficult questions. To begin with, why is a nationwide reform movement lacking in the first place, and how can one be brought about? How often does a revolution sympathetic to the cause of the poor take place, and what are the poor to do in anticipation of such a reform or revolution? After all, the Islamic revolution in Iran did not entirely end the quiet encroachment of the poor. What it did was alter its dynamics by facilitating collective mobilization and extrakinship association. Yet when the revolutionary uproar subsided and the Islamic regime consolidated, the disenfranchised returned to the same strategy that they had pursued in the years before the revolution. This was not because the Islamic regime was anti-lower class. In fact, its pro-*mustaz'afin* language was clear. Furthermore, the state based its legitimacy on Islam as a religion of justice, and on its ardent support of the downtrodden.

Rather, for the poor, localized struggle, unlike an abstract and distant "revolution," was both *meaningful* and *manageable*—meaningful in that they could make sense of the purpose and have an idea about the consequence of those actions, and manageable in that *they*, rather than some remote national leaders, set the agenda, projected the aims, and controlled the outcome. In this sense, for the poor, the local was usually privileged over the global/national. In addition, the flexibility and perseverance associated with such grassroots activism enabled the poor to extend their social space and to respond to political constraints more effectively. In authoritarian political conditions, family-centered and free-form activism often substitute for and prove more durable than structured and formal organizations.

More broadly, and precisely because of this largely silent and free-form mobilization, the current focus on the notion of "civil society" tends to belittle or totally ignore the vast array of often uninstitutionalized and hybrid social activities—street politics—that have dominated urban politics in many developing countries. To be sure, there is more than just one conceptualization of civil society, and of course it is crucial to understand what one means by the term. Jillian Schwedler's review of the literature on the Middle East reveals the tremendous diversity of perceptions not only between the classical and contemporary variants but also within the latter. Some perceive of civil society as organized life that lies outside the state. Others exclude from this, family, tribe, and clan; others, religious institutions; others, by attributing moral qualities to the concept, leave out violent groups.[1] Yet all seem to agree that an associational core constitutes an integral element of civil society and is therefore essentially privileged over other forms of social expression.

Without intending to downgrade the value of "civility"[2]—central to the notion of social capital—my point is that the reductionism of the debates on civil society excludes and even scorns modes of struggle and expression that, in some societies such as those in the Middle East, are more extensive and effective than conventional independent institutions.

Shortcomings and Costs

Recognizing the merits of grassroots activities associated with quiet encroachment, however, should not blind us to their costs and failures. Some have already reminded us of the danger of "the romance of resistance."[3] The sad truth is that not everything in the life of the poor is rosy, and that the poor face enormous obstacles in bringing about fundamental change in their lives. Nor, on the other hand, is a lifelong struggle necessarily a virtue, even if it eventually yields the desired results. The recent history of the poor in Iran is witness to this. The unemployed, despite a powerful show of force and visibility in the streets, failed to realize fully their demands for jobs or social security benefits. Many homeless families failed to retain the homes and hotels they had seized and were forcefully evicted. Squatters faced violent counterattacks by security forces; water and electricity supplies were cut, hundreds of informal homes were demolished, communities were dismantled, independent neighborhood councils fell apart, and activists were arrested and jailed. Street vendors endured similar setbacks. After some ten years of confrontations, it was as if they had disappeared from the streets. Of course, these contenders were not eliminated altogether. Yet although most of them resisted, they had to bear with constant insecurity and despair. Indeed, for some time in the late 1980s it was as if street politics had simply waned. What caused these costs and setbacks? What do they all mean?

Some obstacles had to do with the poor's own dynamics, and some were structural—notably those relating to the role of the state. But before elaborating on these, let me make it clear that, despite occasional overlaps among the actors, each of these particular grassroots activities (i.e., home/hotel occupation, informal home construction, unemployed protests, and street vendor struggles) had their own specificities, which affected the degree of their success. The composition of the actors, the internal organization, the nature of demands, and the identity of the enemies were the most salient factors. For instance, unlike in land-squatting and street vending, radical students also participated in both home takeovers and the unemployed protests. This was both a strength and a liability—a strength because of their support, and a liability in that it would make the movement more susceptible to government suppression. On the other hand, such radical demands as *seizure* of private homes and hotels, or unemployment *benefits* had a highly political dimension; the state's reactions against them were much more swift than against the unemployment loan or the squatting on state land or on properties belonging to agents of the past regime. Furthermore, the Islamic regime showed a greater hostility toward the political vendors, the students occupying hotels, and the rich developers squatting on urban lands than toward their urban poor counterparts. And finally, the movement of the unemployed was more a *protest* movement, whereas the squatters' and the vendors' direct actions served as the *solutions* to their problems.

Specificities apart, the internal shortcomings of the movements expressed themselves in various ways. First, as a lifelong, sustained, albeit silent encroachment, they were broadly independent and largely unlawful and thus constantly involved the risk of suppression. Second, quiet encroachment is a fluid, scattered, and unstructured form of activism. Surely this feature overrides Piven and Cloward's concern about the danger of "organizational oligarchy" that, according to them, defeated the poor people's movements in the U.S. during the 1930s.[4] Yet, while quiet encroachment may have the advantage of decentralization, flexibility, and endurance, it suffers from the lack of structured organization as well as legal and technical support. In addition, both the scattered individual initiatives (rather than collective action) and the repressive conditions under which they usually operate are detrimental to solidarity and democratic association. Loyalties are restricted primarily to families and kinship. Extrakinship mobilization and campaigning do not usually develop under repressive conditions, unless the actors feel a common threat to their gains.

When the possibility of organized struggles and association immediately surfaced in postrevolution Iran, the urban poor generally found themselves lacking the experience of modern organization and group work; they therefore relied heavily on local student or professional activists. Horizontal links among the contenders remained scattered and feeble. Thus the major associations concerned with the mobilization of the urban poor—i.e., those set up in the occupied homes/hotels, in neighborhoods, among the unemployed, and among the street vendors—were considerably influenced by the leftists or radical Muslims. At times political investment as well as rivalry among these largely-middle class agitators distorted both the local organizations of the poor and the process of democratic decision-making. And eventually the Islamic government's crackdown on the professional activists seriously curtailed much of the organized mobilization of the poor.

The wrath of repression also subsumed the poor's independent associations by either forcefully dismantling them or incorporating them into the ruling groups. As the regulator of urban land, public space, and order, the state forged a tacit alliance with the "legitimate property owners," shopkeepers, and bazaaris in confronting street politics. Here the ruling clergy mixed a policy of repression with populistic reforms. Evicting home squatters, bulldozing informal settlements, and removing street vendors went almost hand in hand with job creation schemes, resettlement projects, urban land allocation, and the creation of flea markets. However, these reform measures proved insufficient to respond to the growing demands of the urban disenfranchised.

Given these internal weaknesses, it was the state that in the end posed the major challenge to street politics throughout the 1980s. The crackdowns on the independent movements became more systematic and widespread when, following a short period of revolutionary chaos, normality returned and the Islamic regime was consolidated. The seizure of the U.S. embassy in 1979, and the escalation of the war with Iraq during the 1980s facilitated the suppression of internal complaints, including those of the urban poor, in the name of national unity, national security, and the anti-imperialist campaign. Thus open, collective, and audible mobilization was seriously undermined, and the disenfranchised withdrew into backstreet politics, only to reappear in the streets once again in the early 1990s.

Foucault's insistence that power is everywhere, that it "circulates," and is never "localized here or there, never in anybody's hands"[5] is surely instructive in transcending the myth of the powerlessness of the ordinary and in recognizing their agency. The stories in this book are a testimony to this. Yet, this "decentered" notion of power, shared by many poststructuralists,[6] underestimates state power, notably its class dimension, since it fails to see that although power circulates, it does so *unevenly*; in some places it is far weightier and more concentrated than in others. In the context of our discussion, this means simply that like it or not the state does matter: despite the current prevalence of neo-liberal ideas, it continues to be the major political player.

The role of the state is not limited to control. It also undertakes the responsibility of coordination, of which national, regional, and local planning is a principal function. It is, indeed, an old question as to how far the quiet or even open encroachment of the poor can proceed given the omnipresence of the state and the market. John Friedmann is right that although alternative development must begin locally, "without the state's collaboration, the lot of the poor cannot be significantly improved."[7] The fact is that if grassroots development initiatives and direct actions are to succeed, they cannot remain isolated from planning systems. Beyond simple shelter, the poor also want (and struggle for) schools, roads, and public parks; in addition to a spot in the street, vendors also need security, credit, and market information. These, plus jobs and social security, can hardly be achieved without the cooperation of the state.

However, planning as such is not a neutral territory; rather, it is a matrix of conflicting interests and struggles. Development plans tend not only to ignore local diversity and difference but also to overlook the particular needs and concerns of the low-income population.[8] Perhaps a concept of a *democratic* planning might accommodate multiplicity and specific concerns within a broad planning mechanism. Democratic planning is projected and implemented with effective participation from those who are affected, in particular, the poor. It is only through struggle that the interests of the poor may be effectively asserted. Quiet direct actions and grassroots movements are likely to continue so long as the needs of the disenfranchised are not met. A continuous grassroots activism of this sort, despite its costs, not only ensures that some basic necessities are fulfilled but in the long run may compel the state to take account of the concerns of the poor in its broader policies.[9]

Notes

ONE   The Quiet Encroachment of the Ordinary

1. For documentation see Shorter, "Cairo's Leap Forward"; Soliman, "Informal Land Acquisition and the Urban Poor in Alexandria"; Soliman, "Government and Squatters in Alexandria"; Soliman, "Housing Consolidation and the Urban Poor"; El-Kadi, "Le Caire: La ville spontanée sous contrôle"; Tawfiq, "Discourse Analysis of Informal Housing in Egypt"; and *Al-Ahram Weekly*, September 1–7, 1994.

2. See Abdel Taher, "Social Identity and Class in a Cairo Neighborhood."

3. Cited by Alexandria Water Authority, in a conversation with Samir Shahata, May 1995.

4. For instance, out of 104 spontaneous settlements in Cairo and Giza only 6 have been relocated. However, as a study suggests, the new state-sponsored settlements have in large part failed to respond to the needs of the inhabitants who, in turn, have persisted in organizing their own space. See Tawfiq, "Discourse Analysis of Informal Housing"; Ghannam, "Relocation, Gender, and the Production of Urban Space in Cairo."

5. See Bayat, "Cairo's Poor: Dilemmas of Survival and Solidarity"; also see *Al-Wafd*, January 17, 1995, p. 3; *Al-Wafd*, December 9, 1994; *Al-Ahram Weekly*, February 11–17, 1993; see also reports by El-Adly and Morsy, "A Study of Street Vendors in Cairo." Tadros, Feteeha, and Hibbard, "Squatter

Markets in Cairo" offers a very useful description of vendors' day-to-day activities in Cairo.

6. The report appeared in *Far Eastern Economic Review*, June 18, 1992, p. 68.

7. See, for instance, De Soto, *The Other Path*; Cross, "Organization and Resistance in the Informal Economy"; Bienen, "Urbanization and Third World Stability"; Leeds and Leeds, "Accounting for Behavioral Differences."

8. Documented in Leiva and Petras, "Chile: New Urban Movements and the Transition to Democracy," p. 117.

9. Ibid, p. 113.

10. See Stiefel and Wolfe, *A Voice for the Excluded*, p. 201.

11. From a lecture given by Professor Gail Girhart on new South Africa, The American University in Cairo, May 3, 1995.

12. These loaded terms are often incorrectly attributed to Marx who had a different understanding of them. Marx used the term "lumpen" to point to those people who lived on the labor of others. The exploiting bourgeoisie, the well-off classes, were, of course, in this category. By the "lumpen proletariat," Marx referred to those nonbourgeois poor elements who did not produce their own livelihood and subsisted on the work of others. The agents that are the subject of this book, the urban disenfranchised, are not of this group. For a detailed discussion see Draper, *Karl Marx's Theory of Revolution*, vol.2.

13. By giving agency to the urban disenfranchised, I do not mean to discard classical working-class struggles. I have already dealt with this subject in the case of Iran. See my *Workers and Revolution in Iran*.

14. See Scott, *Domination and the Arts of Resistance*, pp. 150–151; also Colburn, *Everyday Forms of Peasant Resistance*; Scott, *Weapons of the Weak*, and his "Everyday Forms of Resistance," published in *The Journal of Peasant Studies*, vol. 13, no. 2, 1986. This volume of the journal contains several pieces discussing this theme.

15. The major exponent of the "culture of poverty" thesis is Oscar Lewis; see his "Culture of Poverty," and his introduction to *Children of Sanchez*. For a critical appraisal of this thesis see Leacock, ed. *The Culture of Poverty: A Critique*. The notion of "marginal man" goes back decades earlier: Simmel, "The Stranger"; Park, "Human Migration and the Marginal Man"; Stonequist, "The Problem of the Marginal Man"; Wirth, "Urban Way of Life," and other sociologists adhered to Chicago school. For a strong critique of the "marginality thesis," see Perlman, "Rio's Favelas and the Myth of Marginality" and her *The Myth of Marginality*.

16. For this perspective see Power, *World Hunger: A Strategy for Survival*; Morrison and Gutkind, eds., *Housing Urban Poor in Africa*.

17. Arturo Escobar advances his argument specifically in relation to poor women; see Escobar, *Encountering Development*.

18. On the right see Huntington, *Political Order in Changing Society*; Nelson, "The Urban Poor"; and Huntington and Nelson, *No Easy Choice*. On the left see Fanon, *The Wretched of the Earth*; Bienen, "Urbanization and Third World Stability."

19. Most of these works originate from Latin American experience, of which the institutionalization of community participation is a salient feature that carries significant political implications. On the "revolutionist" position see, for instance, Garreton, "Popular Mobilization and Military Regime in Chile." Frantz Fanon's *Wretched of the Earth*, is a well-known example of this position. For a "passivist" approach see Cornelius, *Politics and Migrant Poor in Mexico City*.

20. For instance, Stokes, "Politics and Latin America's Urban Poor" represents a "centrist" approach.

21. At the same time, Scott's work on the peasantry seems to have moved many scholars to another extreme of reading too much politics into daily life of ordinary people. In an otherwise excellent work, Singerman's *Avenues of Participation*, attempting to deduce politics from daily lives of popular classes in Cairo, virtually mixes up resistance/politics and the coping techniques adopted by these people. James Scott is very clear about distinguishing between the two.

22. Scott, "Everyday Forms of Resistance," p. 6.

23. See Castells, "Is There an Urban Sociology?", "Squatters and the State in Latin America," and *Cities and the Grassroots*.

24. See Schuurman and van Naerssen, *Urban Social Movements in the Third World*.

25. See Friedmann, "The Dialectic of Reason" and "The Latin American Barrio Movement."

26. For a brilliant analysis of "archaic" social movements see Hobsbawm, *Primitive Rebels*. I understand the term "primitive" or "archaic" in the particular *historical* context that Hobasbawm deals with (mainly nineteenth-century Europe) and not as a theoretical category necessarily applicable to social activities that *appear* to resemble to those he examines. Some critics of Hobsbawm seem to ignore this historical dimension, leaving therefore no empirical possibility for certain activities to be in fact prepolitical or archaic. Such a perception is implicit in Scott, "Everyday Forms of Resistance," p. 22; see also Abu-lughod, "The Romance of Resistance," p. 47.

27. In general there is not an agreement on the definition of the New Social Movements. For a discussion of the prevailing controversies see Wignaraja, ed., *The New Social Movements in the South*. André Gunder Frank has shown many overlappings between the old and the new movements; see Frank and Fuentes, "Nine Theses on New Social Movements." Nevertheless, many authors have stressed the struggle for identity and meaning as the focal point of the new social movements; for example, Mellucci, "The New Social

Movements"; Touraine, *The Voice and the Eye*; Friedmann, "The Dialectic of Reason" and "The Latin American *barrio* Movement."

28. Gramsci, *Prison Notebooks*, p. 109.

29. This sort of moral justification, which I believe largely guides the activities of ordinary men and women, distances my perspective from those of others such as James Scott who seem to base their analysis on rational choice theories. For a sharp critique of Scott's framework see Mitchell, "Everyday Metaphors of Power." However, as I will argue later and show in the course of this book, I do not deny the fact that actors react also rationally to the structure of opportunities. In other words when social and political context change, the form and rationale of their activities may also shift.

30. See Sidney Tarrow, *Power in Movement*.

31. See Piven and Cloward, *Poor Peoples' Movements*, p. 24.

32. Here I use the concept of legitimacy in the Weberain sense.

33. For the case of Iran see chapter 6 of this book; for India see Lessinger, "Nobody Here to Yell at Me"; and Spodek, "The Self-employed Women's Association (SEWA) in India"; for Britain see Hinton, "Militant Housewives"; for the Peruvian experience see De Soto, *The Other Path*, 1989; and for Mexico City see Cross, "Organization and Resistance in the Informal Economy."

34. See Nelson, *Access to Power*; Leeds and Leeds, "Accounting for Behavioral Differences"; Bienen, "Urbanization and Third World Instability."

35. For the case of Iran see the following chapters of this book. For Cairo see Abdel Taher "Social Identity and Class in a Cairo Neighborhood"; also see Oldham, et al., "Informal Communities in Cairo." By the early 1990s Imbaba, a Cairo slum, had developed, according to the media, "a state within the state" as a result of the influence of Islamic militants who were playing on the absence of the state from the community.

36. Durkheim's *The Division of Labor in Society*, and Freud's *Civilization and Its Discontents* represent early commentators on the issue. Others include Simmel, "The Stranger"; Park, "Human Migration and the Marginal Man"; Stonequist, "The Problem of Marginal Man"; and Wirth, "Urban Way of Life."

37. Perlman, *The Myth of Marginality*; Castells, *Cities and the Grassroots*. See also Velez-Ibanez, *Rituals of Marginality*.

38. De Soto also finds the "mercantilist" structure of the state and the "bad laws" in many developing countries to be responsible for the growth of informals. He refers to mercantilism as a state of affairs in which the economy is run by political considerations, thus concluding that the informal sector reflects people's desire for a free market as an alternative to the tyranny of the state; De Soto, *The Other Path*. However, De Soto's fascination with the free market as a solution to the economic problems of the Third World appears to blind him to other factors that contribute to the creation of informality. For

instance, in the U.S., where mercantilism hardly exists, informality has appeared. In addition, he ignores the fact that the very market mechanisms he cites (on land, for instance) have contributed to the creation of informal communities. For a more comprehensive analysis of the informal economy, although not of informality as such, see Portes, Castells, and Benton, eds., *The Informal Economy*. On the autonomous character of informal activities see also Hopkins, ed., *Informal Sector in Egypt*.

39. See Friedmann, "The Dialectic of Reason"; for a critique of Friedmann's romanticization of the *barrios* movement see Palma, "Comments on John Friedmann's 'The Dialectic of Reason' "; Roberts, "Comments on John Friedmann's 'The Dialectic of Reason'"; and Touraine, "Comments on John Friedmann's 'The Dialectic of Reason.' "

40. See Gilbert and Ward, "Community Action by the Urban Poor."

41. Interestingly, similar language seems to be used in Latin America. As Miguel Diaz Barriga reports, "for many colons [in Mexico City] involved in urban politics, understandings of culture and power are articulated through *necesidad* [necessity]." See Barriga, "*Necesidad*: Notes on the Discourse of Urban Politics," p. 291.

42. For the literature on the moral economy of the poor see Thompson, *Customs in Common*.

43. For instance, chapter 7 of this book. On the cancerous growth of spontaneous settlements see various issues of *Al-Ahram*, analyzed in Tawfiq, "Discourse Analysis of Informal Housing in Egypt."

44. The term was brought to my attention for the first time by Professor Aycé Uncu of Boghazichi University, Istanbul, during a Joint Conference of Turkish-Egyptian scholars held in Cairo in spring 1991. Although my definition is entirely different from hers, I am nevertheless indebted to her for the use of the term in this book. See also her "Street Politics."

45. See Foucault, *Power/Knowledge*.

46. See Lis and Soly, "Neighborhood Social Change in West European Cities," pp. 15–18.

47. See Abraham Marcus, *The Middle East on the Eve of Modernity*.

48. During the early 1990s the backstreets of Imbaba, a poor neighborhood in Cairo, were practically been taken over and controlled by the Islamist activists and the rival local *futuwwat* groups. To counter the perceived Islamic threat in the locality, not only did the government attempt to cleanse it of the Islamists, it also had to transform these types of localities by opening them up (e.g., widening alleyways), thus making them transparent to state surveillance. This policy of opening up and transparency was also practiced during colonial times; see Mitchell, *Colonizing Egypt*, pp. 46 and 66.

49. See Tilly, *From Mobilization to Revolution*, pp. 62–69.

50. See Bourdieu, "What Makes a Social Class?" and "The Social Space and the Genesis of Groups."

51. Indeed, explaining the link between structure/interests—> conscious-ness—> action is still a major preoccupation of sociology; for a review of the debates see Crompton, *Class and Stratification*. Among the contributors to the debate are Tilly, *From Mobilization to Revolution*; Barrington Moore, *Injustice*; Smelser, *A Theory of Collective Behavior*.

52. According to Tarrow: "Transforming a grievance into a collective action is never automatic; a great deal of communication and conscious plan-ning is involved as well"; see his *Power in Movement*, p. 49. Like Tilly who develops concepts of opportunity/repression and resource mobilization, Tarrow also introduces element of structures of opportunity to mediate between organization and action.

53. Tilly's concept of collective action is very much conditioned by his notion of repression. Thus in his scheme governments, for instance, can easily seal off the streets or declare martial law to suppress public demonstrations. This may indeed happen. However, because his model lacks a concept of "pas-sive network," it cannot envisage the possibility of mass action by ordinary peo-ple on the streets unless they have developed intense interpersonal interactions.

54. Regional estimates by the ILO for 1975 put open unemployment at 6.9 percent for Asia (except for China and other centrally planned economies); 10.8 percent for Africa, and 6.5 percent for Latin America; see Gilbert and Gugler, *Cities, Poverty, and Development*, p. 67.

55. See for instance Vandemoortele, "The African Employment Crisis of the 1980s."

56. Cited in Sethurman, ed., *The Urban Informal Sector in Developing Countries*, p. 5.

57. See World Bank, *World Development Report, 1995*, p. 108.

58. Vandemoortele, "The African Employment Crisis of the 1990s," pp. 34–36.

59. In 1991 the rate of open unemployment for 45 developing countries (excluding the former communist and newly industrializing countries) was at an average of 17 percent. In this year the unemployment rate reached 12 per-cent in Latin America (19 countries), 17 percent in Asia (14 countries), and 21 percent for 12 African countries; (statistics compiled from CIA, *The World Fact Book 1992*).

60. See Leeds and Leeds, "Accounting for Behavioral Differences"; al-Sayyad, "Informal Housing in a Comparative Perspective"; Lessinger, "Nobody Here to Yell at Me"; Cross, "Organization and Resistance in the Informal Economy."

61. See al-Sayyad, "Informal Housing in a Comparative Perspective"; Nelson, *Access To Power* and "The Urban Poor."

62. See Nelson, "The Urban Poor"; Geisse and Sabatini, "Latin American Cities and Their Poor," p. 327; Cross, "Organization and Resistance in the Informal Economy"; De Soto, *The Other Path*.

63. For a detailed discussion of this point see Piven and Cloward, *Poor People's Movements*.

TWO   Mapping Out the "New Poor"

1. I draw this from the way Peter Worsley has identified the urban poor in his *Three Worlds*, pp. 195–196.

2. The protoganists include Park, "Human Migration and the Marginal Man"; Stonequist, "The Problem of Marginal Man"; Wirth, "Urban Way of Life"; and, more recently, Oscar Lewis, "Culture of Poverty."

3. This is how Janice Perlman and Manuell Castells use the term; see Perlman, *The Myth of Marginality*; Castells, *Cities and the Grassroots*.

4. For operational purposes, in this study I take the category urban poor as consisting of urban squatters, the unemployed, and street subsistence workers, who all seem to share similar residential conditions. Some of them might be involved in all of the four movements—of squatters (homes and land), the unemployed, and street vendors—I examine in this book.

5. See Katouzian, *The Political Economy of Modern Iran*.

6. See Shahri, *Tehran-i Qadim*, 1:9—10; Ashraf, "Marateb-i Ijtemaii dar Dowran-i Qajariye"; Marcus, *The Middle East on the Eve of Modernity*.

7. See Floor, "Political Role of Lutis in Iran," pp. 84–85; and Abrahamian, *Iran Between Two Revolutions*, p. 22.

8. Ashraf, "Marateb-i Ijtemaii dar Dowran-i Qajariye," p. 84; Saidnia, "Sakhtar-i Tehran," p. 324.

9. *Takiyeh* represents ad hoc Islamic gatherings; *Ta'ziyeh* is religious passion play, and *Muharram*, an Arabic month when Imam Hussein, the second Imam of the Shi'ites, was killed in the battle of Karbala. There are numerous forms of commemoration by the Shi'i community during this month.

10. See Ashraf, "The Roots of Emerging Dual Class Structure."

11. Banani, *The Modernization of Iran*, p. 144; Saidnia, "Sakhtar-i Tehran," pp. 324–428.

12.   See Khosrowkhavar, "Nouvelle banlieue et marginalité."

13. For a useful review of comprehensive urban planning see The Iranian Center for Urban and Architectural Studies (Markaz-i Motali'at va Tahqiqat Shahrsazi va Me'mari-ye Iran), *Hashiyenishini dar Iran: Elal va Rah-i Hal-ha*, report on phase 4, vol. 1, "Housing, Informal Settlements, and Spatial Development Planning." In the same series, see also the report on phase 5, "Recognizing the Low-Income as Citizens," pp. 16–21.

14. See Amirahmadi and Kiafar, "Tehran: Growth and Contradictions," p. 173.

15. Saidnia, "Sakhtar-i Tehran," p. 329.

16. See Husseinzadeh Dalir, *Tarh-i Tahqiqi-ye Hashiyenishinan-i Tabriz*, pp. 13 and 14.

17. See Danesh, *Rural Exodus and Squatter Settlements in the Third World*, p. 129.

18. Mashadizadeh, *Tahlili az Vizheguiha-ye Barnameh Rizi-ye Shahri dar Iran*, p. 129.

19. Iranian Center for Urban and Architectural Studies, *Hashiyenishini dar Iran*, report on phase 5, "Recognizing the Low-Income as Citizens," pp. 49–50.

20. See Kazemi, *Poverty and Revolution in Iran*, p. 48.

21. Ibid, p. 50.

22. See Danesh, *Rural Exodus and Squatter Settlements*, pp. 131–132.

23. See Jalili, 1356, cited in Piran, "Alounaknishini dar Tehran," in *Ettilaat-i Syassi-Iqtisadi*, no. 19, p. 52.

24. On Zoorabad see Tehran University, Institute of Social Studies and Research, *Mutale'e-yi Muqaddamati Darbare-ye Zoorabad (Islamabad) Karadj.*

25. It is notoriously difficult to give a precise figure on the number of the slum-dwellers. But if we take the density of people per room (five to ten people living in two rooms) as an important measure of slum dwelling, then it becomes clear that at least one million poor, accounting for 12.4 percent of the total households, inhabited these neighborhoods (*Tehran Census, 1359[/1980]*). This criterion fits well, for instance, with Khazane-i Fallahi slum in Southeast Tehran. According to a survey, 46 percent of the houses in this neighborhood had only one room and another 45 percent two rooms. The typical household in this area had between six and seven resident members (cited in Kazemi, *Poverty and Revolution in Iran*, p. 78). In addition, the relationship between density and poverty in Tehran is documented by Connell, "Tehran," and Bahrambeygui, *Tehran: An Urban Analysis*. See also Amirahmadi and Kiafar, "Tehran: Growth and Contradictions," p. 173.

26. According to the Tehran census, well over 80,000 units (9 percent) had been constructed with semidurable materials including a mixture of bricks and wood, mud, bamboo leaves, and similar materials. Perhaps of these, more than 48,000 settlement units (5 percent) lacked drinking water, instead depending on such sources as river, wells, underground water, and public street taps (*Tehran Census, 1359[/1981]*, p. 41). If one views these as informal units that housed five-member households, then some 400,000 people of Tehran lived in the informal settlements.

As I stated earlier, squatter settlements also grew in other main cities, among which Tabriz, Bandar Abbas, and Ahwaz had the highest ratio of squatters to total population; see Husseinzadeh Dalir, *Tarh-i Tahqigi-ye Hashiyenishinan: Tabriz*, pp. 13–14.

27. The Iranian Center for Urban and Architectural Studies, *Hashiyenishini dar Iran*, report on phase 5, "Recognizing the Low-Income as Citizens," pp. 49–50.

28. See Amirahmadi and Kiafar, "Tehran: Growth and Contradictions," p. 171.

29. See Planning and Budget Organization, *Census of Population*, for 1956; 1966; 1976.

30. See Saidnia, "Sakhtar-i Tehran," p. 334.

31. See Institute of Social Studies and Research, *Motale'e-yi Muqaddamati*, p. 6.

32. This information is based upon a recent comprehensive study, sponsored by the Ministry of Housing, on informal settlement in Iran, published in 7 volumes so far; see The Iranian Center for Urban and Architectural Studies, *Hashiyenishini dar Iran*, Report of phase 4, "Housing, Informal Settlements, and Spatial Development Planning," 2:29–35.

33. The Iranian Center for Urban and Architectural Studies, *Hashiyenishini dar Iran*, report on phase 4, 2:25–33.

34. Kazerouni and Qal'egolabi, "Tasvir-i Aamari-ye Hashiyenishinan." Mashadizadeh also gives similar picture of the occupations of squatters; see his *Tahlili az Vizheguiha-ye Barnamehrizi*, p. 133.

35. Kazemi, *Poverty and Revolution in Iran*, p. 53–56.

36. According to a survey, over 90 percent of Tehran's squatters expressed their satisfaction with their existing situation when comparing it to their past; see Mashadizadeh, *Tahlili az Vizheguiha-ye Barnamehrizi*, p. 145.

37. For instance, industrial workers seemed to distinguish themselves from the new poor whom they regarded as belonging to a fourth class. See Ashraf, *Iran: Imperialism, Class and Modernization from Above*, p. 345.

38. Interview with a squatter of Ali Abad, Khazaneh, in South Tehran; conducted in 1995 by sociology students, University of 'Allame-ye Tabatbaii.

39. Golesorkhi, a poet and journalist, was charged with plotting to assassinate members of royal family during the mid-1970s and was subsequently executed.

40. His short stories include "24 Hours in Dream and Awakening" (*Beest-o-Chahar Saa'at dar Khab va Bidaari*), and "The Sugar Beet Seller Boy" (*Pesarak-i Labou-Foroush*).

41. Such as "The Beggar" (*geda*), and "The Best Father in the World" (*Behtarin Baba-ye Donya*).

42. This theme is quite vivid in Ale-ahmad's well-known essay *Gharbzadegui*, translated into English as *The Plague of the West*.

43. See Akbari, *Lumpenism*, pp. 80–89.

THREE   The Disfranchised and the Islamic Revolution:
          "Our Revolution and Theirs"

1. *Jumhuri-ye Islami*, Farvardin 17, 1360/1981.

2. Quoted in *Faryad-i Gowdnishin*, no. 14, 1 Aban 1358/1979, p. 2.

3. This background section on the Iranian revolution is based on Bayat, "Revolution Without Movement, Movement Without Revolution: Comparing Islamist Activism in Iran and Egypt," memo, 1996. For a historical background to the Iranian revolution see Ervand Abrahamian, *Iran Between Two Revolutions* (Princeton, 1982) and Homa Katouzian, *The Political Economy of Modern Iran* (London, 1982). For literature on the Islamic Revolution, reflecting different perspectives, see Abrahamian, *Iran Between Two Revolutions*; Said Amir Arjomand, *The Turban for the Crown* (Oxford, 1988); Mansoor Moaddel, *Class, State, and Ideology in the Iranian Revolution* (New York, 1993); and Mohsen Milani, *The Making of the Islamic Revolution in Iran* (Boulder, 1988). The best account may be found in Misagh Parsa, *The Social Origins of the Iranian Revolution* (New Brunswick, 1989).

4. On the antidemocratic nature of the Shah's regime and its political implications see Fred Halliday on SAVAK activities in his *Iran: Dictatorship and Development* (London, 1977) and Habib Lajevardi, *Labor Unions and Autocracy in Iran* (Syracuse, 1985).

5. On guerrilla activities in Iran see Halliday, *Iran: Dictatorship and Development,* and Abrahamian, *Iran Between Two Revolutions.*

6. Eric Hooglund, for instance, asserts that the land reform of 1963 destroyed the traditional rural social structure without offering a workable alternative. Rural masses were thus forced to migrate to major urban centers such as Tehran where they became available for mobilization on behalf of the revolution; see Hooglund, *Land and Revolution in Iran.*

7. For an example see Rahnama and Nomani, *Secular Miracle.* In addition, Mohammad Amjad asserts: "The rural migrants' active participation in the 1977–1979 movement against the Shah eventually resulted in the overthrow of the Monarchy. . . . The populist ideology of Islam played a crucial role in mobilizing the masses"; see Amjad, "Rural Migrants," p. 35.

8. See Kazemi, *Poverty and Revolution in Iran*; Mottahedeh, *The Mantle of the Prophet*; Denoeux, *Urban Unrest in the Middle East.*

9. See Bauer, "Poor Women and Social Consciousness in Revolutionary Iran," p. 160. Mehdi Bazargan, the first Prime Minister of the Islamic Republic, who participated in most of the demonstrations in Tehran and recorded his observations, also arrived at similar conclusions; see Bazargan, *Inqilab-i Iran dar Dow Harakat,* p. 39.

10. See Amraaii, *Barrasi-ye Moqe'iyyat-i Ijtimai-ye Shohada-ye Inqilab-i Islami,* pp. 178–179. This unique work—"A Study of the Social Background of the Martyrs of the Islamic Revolution: August 23, 1977 to February 19, 1978"—reveals the socioeconomic background of those who participated in the Revolution, with a focus on the city of Tehran.

11. For the basis of this observation see my analysis in chapter 2 of this book. See also Banuazizi, "Alounaknishinan-i Khiaban-i Professor Brown," and Organization of People's Fedaii Guerrillas of Iran (OPFGI), *Mubarizat-i*

Daliraneh-ye Mardum-i Kharej az Mahdudeh. I have also utilized my own direct experience and observations for many years among the poor families that I grew up in and with. On this see the preface to this book.

12. See Banuazizi, "Alounaknishinan."

13. Hobsbawm, *Primitive Rebels*.

14. See the text of interviews in OPFGI, *Mubarizat-i Daliraneh*, pp. 38 and 34; see also Banuazizi, "Alounaknishinan," pp. 61 and 62.

To dramatize his story, the writer of the above letter seems to exaggerate about borrowing 100,000 tumans, which at the time was a relatively large sum.

Like the urban poor, the peasants and the rural poor would also make similar appeals to the *pedar-i taajdaar*, whom they considered as the benevolent monarch. During my student years in Iran, and as a part-time employee of the Ministry of Higher Education, I came across hundreds of similar appeals, or letters, which a mission of the Ministry brought back after a visit to the poor province of Sistan and Baluchestan. They had been sent by the poor to the Shah, asking for variety of assistance, including debt payment, building homes, and compensation for crop failure. One fine sunny morning the letters were disposed in a dustbin.

15. *Taaj-o-takht* refers to the crown, and royal leadership.

16. Interview with a poor resident of Serah-i Azari in South Tehran, in Autumn 1980.

17. See OPFGI, *Mubarizat-i Daliraneh*, pp. 10, 11, 21, 28, 31, 33, 35, 43, and 88.

18. In the same reports from which these statements are drawn, there were also a number of statements from younger inhabitants in the squatter communities, which directly referred to the Shah and the government as sources of their misfortune. If "political insurance" was a concern of the poor squatters, one would expect these residents also to pretend that the Shah was innocent, which they in fact did not. My reading is that no one acted tactically here. Most of the poor considered the Shah above politics; while only a few found him responsible for their poverty. Both groups expressed their position clearly.

19. For Chile see Castells, "Squatters and the State in Latin America"; for Peru, Stokes, "Politics and Latin America's Urban Poor," pp. 98–99; Burt, "Popular Struggles in Peru," and De Soto, *The Other Path*; for Turkey, Karpat, *The Gecekondu*. For Egypt I rely on the sample survey—"Social Response to Environmental Change in Egypt"—on four major Cairo poor neighborhoods—Kafr al-Elow (Helwan), Dar al-Salaam (South Cairo), Sayyida Zeinab (central Cairo), and the village of Abkhaz (about 50 kilometers north of Cairo), conducted by Social Research Center, the American University in Cairo, with the principal researchers, Sohair Mehanna and Nicholas Hopkins, 1996.

As for Iran, it seems that the class composition of the informal housing sector after the revolution is changing. That is, the members of the industrial working class and lower-middle classes are increasingly joining the marginalized poor in territorial terms; see chapter 5.

20. See Bauer, "Poor Women and Social Consciousness in Revolutionary Iran," p. 107.

21. This sharply contrasts with the pattern in Cairo where numerous squatter communities and slums (e.g., Imbaba, Boula' Abul-Alaa, Sayyida Zeinab, Dar Essalaam) are attached to wealthy neighborhoods (e.g., Zamalek, Garden City, and Maadi).

22. A general review of squatters' literacy states that "squatters are of low in literacy. Most of the older people are illiterate. Children are sent to work instead of school. Mainly boys attend school"; see N. Mashadizadeh, *Tahlili az Vizheguiha-ye Barnamehrizi*, p. 132.

23. See Bayat, *Workers and Revolution in Iran*.

24. See Portes and Walton, *Urban Latin America*, pp. 73–74.

25. See Burt, "Popular Struggles in Peru."

26. My survey of 150 factory workers in Tehran in 1981 showed that over 60 percent lived in the slums; see Bayat, "Poverty, Urbanization, and Development."

27. See Lajevardi, *Labor Unions and Autocracy in Iran*.

28. See Bayat, *Workers and Revolution in Iran*.

29. See Vieille, *Jaygah-i Kargaran-i Tehran*, pp. 38 and 39; Banuazizi, "Alounaknishinan."

30. See Banuazizi, "Alounaknishinan," pp. 59–60; see also Piran, "Alounaknishini dar Tehran."

31. *Ramadan* refers to the month of fasting when Ali, the first Imam of the Shi'ites was killed. *Muharram* is the month in which Hussein, Ali's son, the second Imam was martyred.

32. Both the *Husseiniyeh* and *Hey'at* are ad hoc Islamic sermons organized mostly in the months of Muharram and Ramadan. Janet Bauer has documented some of these activities in a poor South Tehran neighborhood during the revolution; see Bauer, "Poor Women and Social Consciousness in Revolutionary Iran."

33. See for instance Kazemi, *Poverty and Revolution in Iran*, pp. 90–96; Mottahedeh, *The Mantle of the Prophet*, pp. 350–356; Denoeux, *Urban Unrest in the Middle East*, pp. 157–58.

34. The terms he used to describe the poor included *badbakhtan* (unfortunate), *mellat-i bichareh* (desperate people), *mustamandan* (the needy), *tabaqat-i bichareh* (unfortunate classes) and *Kargaran* (workers); see Ayatollah Rouhollah Khomeini, *Sahife-ye Nour*, collected works compiled and edited by the Ministry of National Guidance.

35. He stated that: "It is intrinsic to the character of the lay people to

adhere to the past and the way that they are accustomed to; they do not distinguish between right and wrong. Common people usually label any new phenomenon as heresy or carnal desire; they do not understand the principal law of creation and the circumstances of nature and therefore they object to any new ideas and endorse the status quo." See Anonymous, ed., *Bahsi Darbare-ye Marja'iyat va Ruhaniyat*, p. 183. The translation is by Professor Ali Mirsepassi.

36. See Shariati, *Jahatguiri-ye Tabaqati-ye Islam*. On the middle-class constituency of the Left and the Mujahedin-e Khalq Organizations, see Abrahamian, "The Guerrilla Movement in Iran, 1963–1977" and his *Radical Islam: The Mujahedin of Iran*.

37. See Ayatollah Khomeini, *Sahife-ye Nour*, ibid.

38. See OPFGI, *Mubarizat-i Daliraneh*; Bakhash, *The Reign of the Ayatollahs*.

39. Cited in Banuazizi, "Alounaknishinan," p. 59. The above cited statement by the young squatter—"Nothing brings us together more than the love of Imam Hussein; my personal view is that these *hey'at*s have a positive role in uniting us and keeping us informed about each other's affair"—is quoted in many major writings on the Islamic Revolution to establish the ideological role of Islam in the revolution and to prove how the *hey'at*s acted as the mobilizing medium between the clergy and the poor (see for instance: Kazemi, *Poverty and Revolution in Iran*; Mirsepassi-Ashtiani, "The Crisis of Secularism," p. 59; Mottahedeh, *The Mantle of the Prophet*; Arjomand, *Turban for the Crown*, p. 92.) None of these writers, however, have paid attention to the remainder of the statement made by the same squatter who suggests that what the clergy preached in these *hey'at*s were, in fact, far from political education and agitation; rather they focused on strictly religious prescriptions and mournings.

40. Khaleh Fatimeh, an old resident of Halabiabad, the Community of Tins, cited in *Kayhan*, Esfand 12, 1361/1982, p. 2.

41. The demands are discussed in Kazemi, *Poverty and Revolution in Iran*, pp. 77–80.

42. Cited from interviews in OPFGI, *Mubarizat-i Daliraneh*, p. 42.

43. These reports were part of the activities of the Marxist-Leninist OPFGI. Although produced by an ideologically committed organization, the content of these rare interviews does seem to reflect the mood of the field. The politics of this organization does not seem to have influenced the outcome of the interviews.

44. Cited in OPFGI, *Mubarizat-i Daliraneh*, pp. 98 and 118.

45. From interviews in OPFGI, *Mubarizat-i Daliraneh*, p. 19.

46. See OPFGI, *Mubarizat-i Daliraneh*, p. 34.

47. Ibid.

48. See *Ettilaat*, Shahrivar 23–27, 1357/1978.

49. *Ettilaat*, Shahrivar 26, 1357/1978.

50. It is worth noting that demonstration in Maidan-i Zhaleh (later known as Maidan-i Shuhada, or the Martyrs Square), was initiated by the activists who came largely from Gholhak area in north Tehran. The day before the "black Friday" a large collective prayer had followed a demonstration that had been stopped by the police. On that occasion a middle-aged, bazaari-looking activist had said "Tomorrow Morning, at 8 A.M., at Maidan-i Shuhada"; interview with Akbar Askari, a participant in the event, December 1983.

51. See *Ettilaat*, Shahrivar 20, 1357/1978.

52. Ibid.

53. It refers to the urban areas beyond the boundaries of the municipality provisions, where most informal settlements have been located.

54. *Ettilaat*, Shahrivar 30, 1357/1978.

55. *Ettilaat*, Mehr 5, 1357/1978.

56. *Ettilaat*, Mehr 8, 1357/1978.

57. See the interviews in OPFGI, *Mubarizat-i Daliraneh*.

58. Interview with an eyewitness, February 1993.

59. Ibid.

60. *Ayandegan*, Dey 19, 22, and 27, 1357/1978.

61. *Ayandegan*, Dey 19, 1357/1978.

62. *Ayandegan*, Dey 25, 1357/1978.

63. *Ayandegan*, Dey 20, 1357/January 20, 1979.

64. *Ayandegan*, Dey 10, 1357/1978.

65. *Ayandegan*, ibid.

66. Ibid.

67. *Ayandegan*, Dey 23 and 30, 1357/1978.

68. *Ayandegan*, Dey 30, 1357/1978.

69. *Ayandegan*, Dey 25, 1357/1978.

70. *Ayandegan*, Dey 25, 1357/1978.

71. *Ayandegan*, Dey 24, 1357/1978.

72. The spread of formal education system during the Shah's rule also covered the poor classes. Indeed, by 1980 the ratio of male secondary schools to population in the poor districts of Tehran was not very different from that in the well-off areas (only 20 percent less). But this difference was much higher with respect to the girls secondary schools (60 percent less); see *Census of Tehran 1359[/1980]*, Tehran 1981. In 1980, in Zoorabad squatter community in Karadj, 50 percent of boys attended school and 20 percent of girls; see Institute of Social Studies and Research, *Mutale'e-yi Muqaddamati Darbare-ye Zoorabad, Karadj*, p. 64.

73. This theme was taken up in the 1970s by a number of writers and filmmakers; see, for instance, Gholam Hussein Sa'edi's short story, *Ashghaldouni* (Garbage Place), which in the late 1970s was turned into the movie *Dayere-ye Mina*, directed by Daryoush Mehrjouii .

74. Cited in Banuazizi, "Alounaknishinan," p. 63; and in Kazemi, *Poverty and Revolution in Iran*, pp. 129–130.

75. A great number of speculations exist about the social profile of the Pasdaran and Baseeji groups. However, empirical examination is scarce. Farhad Khosrowkhavar's study seems to support the prevailing view that members of these groups come largely from urban poor families; personal communication, April 1995, Paris; see also his *L'utopie Sacrifiée*.

76. Interviews in OPFGI, *Mubarizat-i Daliraneh*, p. 98.

77. Ibid.

FOUR   The Housing Rebels: The Occupation of Homes and Hotels, 1979–1981

1. These names are all fictitious to preserve the anonymity of the actors.

2. Based upon interviews with Naser, a leading organizer of the operation, December 1994.

3. *Kayhan*, Aban 30, 1362/1983.

4. *Ayandegan*, Bahman 28, 1358/1979.

5. *Kar*, no. 6 (Farvardin 23, 1358/1979): 7.

6. For a detailed description of this incident see Hourcade, "Conseillisme, classes sociales, et espace urbain"; also see Bassri and Hourcade, "L'Expérience conseilliste."

7. *Ettilaat*, "Az Gowdnishini ta Hashiyenishini dar Tehran," Bahman 3, 1372/1993.

8. *Rah-i Kargar*, no. 8 (Aban 1363/1984); no. 13 (Farvardin 1364/1985): 19.

9. Interview with Naser, a leading activist in home takeovers, December 1994.

10. Interview with Naser, ibid.

11. *Ettilaat*, Khordad 9, 1363/1984; also interview with participants in home takeovers in Kermanshah; news from the opposition publications.

12. *Khabar*, no. 5 (16 Esfand 1357), published by the Organization of People Fedaii Guerrillas of Iran.

13. Interview with Reza, a leader of the operation, February 1993.

14. *Middle East Economic Digest* (November 2, 1979): 33.

15. Interview with Fateh, a participant in the raid, February 1993.

16. *Ettilaat*, Dey 24, 1358/1979; also my interviews with one of the participants in the takeovers, October 1993. Karrubi in addition extended some Rls 200 million (U.S.$2.8 million) in loans to the homeless and the small business-holders; see *Ettilaat*, Dey 24, 1358/1979.

17. Interview with an anonymous participant, October 1993.

18. Interview with Fateh, a participant in the operation.

19. Interview with a squatter leader of the Royal Garden Hotel, February

1993.

20. Interview with Fateh, a participant.

21. *Ayandegan*, Khordad 23, 1358/1979.

22. Piran, "Zaghehnishini dar Tehran."

23. *Ayandegan*, Ordibehesht 18, 1358/1979.

24. Ibid.

25. *Pirouzi*, "Gozaresh-i Nafarjam az Mas'ale-ye Maskan," no. 1 (Mehr 1359/1980): 55–58.

26. Interview with a Hotel Royal Garden squatting leader, February 1993; Also interview with Fateh on the occupation of the Hotel Sina.

27. Interview with a Pasdar, in *Ayandegan*, Ordibehesht 18, 1358/1979.

28. Interview with Naser, a leading mobilizer of home takeovers, December 1994.

29. See *Pirouzi*, "Gozaresh-i Nafarjam az Mas'ale-ye Maskan," no. 1 (Mehr 1359/1980): 55–58; See also Bassri and Hourcade, "L'Expérience conseilliste."

30. Interview with Naser, a leading organizer.

31. See Bassri and Hourcade, "L' expérience conseilliste."

32. See Hourcade, "Conseillisme, classes sociales, et espace urbain."

33. See Davis, *Contested Ground*, p. 6.

34. See Bayat, *Workers and Revolution in Iran*.

35. Interview with Fateh an occupation leader of the Hotel Sina in Tehran.

36. Ibid.

37. A shanty dweller, cited in *Ayandegan*, Khordad 23, 1358/1979.

38. *Ayandegan*, Khordad 13, 1358/1979.

39. *Khabar*, no. 5 (Esfand 16, 1357/1978), published by OPFGI; see also *Kar*, no. 72 (Mordad 29, 1359/1980): 7.

40. A shantytown dweller, cited in *Ayandegan*, Khrdad 23, 1358/1979.

41. Cited in *Kar*, Ordibehesht 27, 1358/1979.

42. *Ayandegan*, Ordibehesht 18, 1358/1979.

43. See *Mujahid*, no. 237 (Esfand 2, 1363/1984); see also *Rah-i Kargar*, no. 13 (Farvardin 1364/1985).

44. *Kar*, no 72 (Mordad 28, 1359/1980): 7.

45. See Bassri and Hourcade, "L'Expérience conseilliste," on how the *shura*s were undermined.

46. Ibid.

47. In Portugal the occupation of housing was very organized; it was coordinated not by individual families but by a Neighborhood Commission (NC). The NC had a list of empty apartments and a list of people in need of housing. If a furnished apartment was occupied, the NC would ask the police to be present and take inventories. Any items found would be returned to their owners. The crucial point here is that the occupiers did not want to *own* the homes they took over; rather they aimed to force the owners to rent them out

to needy tenants. Although the owners were forced to sign leases with their tenants, they nevertheless maintained their right to own their apartments. In Iran, however, squatters wanted to *own* the properties they seized, and many even did not consider making any payments for homes they took over. For the Portuguese situation see Hammond, *Building Popular Power*, pp. 126–131; for the British, see Moorhouse, Wilson, and Chamberlain, "Rent Strikes."

48. On the activities of the *Jiahd-i Sazandegui*, Construction Crusade, see Ferdows, "The Reconstruction Crusade and Class Conflict in Iran."

49. Except those that were carefully planned and sanctioned from the top. For instance, some five years later, in August 1985 about 500 students took over a building in Maidan-i Tajrish and converted it into a dorm. The owner of the building had fled the country, leaving it vacant. The students had obtained a prior authorization from the Peace Court (Dadgaah-i Solh), which authorizes such takeovers; see *Ettilaat*, Mordad 28, 1364/1985.

50. Cited in *Ayandegan*, Khordad 13, 1358/1979.

51. See for instance Moorhouse, Wilson, and Chamberlain, "Rent Strikes."

FIVE   Back-Street Politics: Squatters and the State

1. Originally cited in *Kayhan* and quoted in *Kar*, no. 45, Mehr 22, 1371/1992.

2. Joan Nelson, "The Urban Poor," contains a good review of these dichotomies. See also chapter 1 of this book.

3. See *Inqilab-i Islami*, Esfand 22, 1358/1979, p. 6.

4. See Mashadizadeh, *Tahlili az Vizheguiha-ye Barnamehrizi*, pp. 444 and 446.

5. Iranian Center for Urban and Architectural Studies, *Hashiyenishini: Asaar va Peyamadha-ye Aan bar Shahrha*, p. 57.

6. See *Ettilaat-i Syassi-Iqtisadi*, "Tehran, Yek Tasvir-i Aamari," no. 17 (Esfand 1366/1987): 44.

7. Iranian Center for Urban and Architectural Studies, *Hashiyenishini: Aasar va Payamadha-ye Aan bar Shahrha*, report on phase 2, pp. 57–59.

8. A recent survey of two of these urban villages, Akbarabad and Soltanabad, showed that over 70 percent of the inhabitants moved from Greater Tehran. See Iranian Center for Urban and Architectural Studies, *Hashiyenishini dar Iran*, report on phase 4, 2:45–46.

9. For a good profile of Islamshahr see Habibi, "Islamshahr: Yek Majmou'e-ye Zisti." See also various volumes of Iranian Center for Urban and Architectural Studies, *Hashiyenishini dar Iran*.

10. According to the figures available in the comprehensive plan of Islamshahr (1987), some 71 percent of the households stated housing problems to be their main cause of migration to Islamshahr. Of these, over 94 per-

cent came originally from the city of Tehran. See Iranian Center for Urban and Architectural Studies, *Hashiyenishini dar Iran*, report on phase 4, 1:137.

11. *Ettilaat*, "Dar Roust-Shahrha-ye Tehran: Bagherabad," p. 5.

12. Interview with a reporter of *Ettilaat*, Khordad 5 and 7, 1364/1985, p. 5.

13. *Majalle-ye Me'mari va Shahrsazi*, "Editorial," no. 8 (July 1990): 4.

14. Cited in *Hamshahri*, Dey 7, 1371/1992. Urban planners estimate the land area of Tehran to have reached 850 square kilometers by 1990; see *Majalle-ye Me'mari va Shahrsazi*, "Editorial," no. 8 (July 1990): 4.

15. See Iranian Center for Urban and Architectural Studies, *Hashiyenishini dar Iran*, report on phase 5, p. 49.

16. For an impressively detailed survey and mapping of urbanized villages (*aabadis*) on the margin of these cities, see Iranian Center for Urban and Architectural Studies, *Hashiyenishini: Aasar va Payamadha*, report on phase 2.

17. Ahmadian, "Hashiyenishini," pp. 826, 833.

18. Stated by the mayor of Bakhtaran and cited in *Ettilaat*, Bahman 29, 1362/1983.

19. Mayors of Tabriz and Urumiyeh in *Ettilaat*, Farvardin 25, 1363/1984.

20. See *Majalle-ye Me'mari va Shahrsazi*, "A Seminar on Cities and People: Interview with two participants," no. 21 (June 1992): 49–50.

21. See *Middle East Economic Digest* (April 1, 1983): 14.

22. See *Ettilaat*, Esfand 11, 1363/1984.

23. Ibid.

24. At this time the Housing Foundation, a "revolutionary institution" set up after the revolution, had over $88 million in public gifts and $100 million in government aid; see *Ayandegan*, Khordad 13, 1358/1979.

25. *Middle East Economic Digest*, February 11, 1983. In 1979, according to the Minister of Housing, for every 1,000 people there was on average only 117 homes, see *Ayandegan*, Ordibehesht 6, 1358/1079.

26. Kazemi and Wolf, "Urbanization, Migration, and Politics of Protest in Iran," pp. 23–24 of its unpublished version.

27. Indeed for some, informal housing had become a lucrative business. In 1986 huts (of Halabshahr) in Tehran were selling for Rls 150,000–Rls 1,000,000, and the more durable shelters, in the village-like urban quarters, for Rls 1,000,000–Rls 1,500,000. Monthly rents ranged from Rls 8,000 to Rls 25,000. At this time a household in such communities earned on average Rls 50,000 per month (calculated based upon the findings of Parviz Piran, "Zaghehnishini dar Tehran"). A number of the shanty dwellers rented their extra dwellings out to other poor households on daily basis for Rls 300–Rls 500, with the proviso that the latter did not bring children and guests; see Parviz Piran, "Zaghehnishini dar Tehran."

28. For an early analysis of the Construction Crusade see Ferdows, "The Construction Crusade and Class Conflict in Iran."

29. That is, the annual average of Rls 342,630 compared to Rls 777,240 of urban households; see Plan and Budget Organization, 1983, cited in *Ettilaat*, Aban 30, 1363/1984.

30. In a Province of Isfahan survey of fifteen towns, 49.5 percent of respondents pointed to low income as the reason for migration, 35 percent cited water and land, 11 percent better urban services, and 4 percent conflicts with the nomadic chiefs. In Hamadan low income accounted for 77 percent, land 18.4 percent, water 17.1 percent, and poor rural welfare issues 18.4 percent; here, the total comes to more than 100 percent, because some of the reasons mentioned are repeated. See Report of the *Jihad-i Sazandegui* in the Majlis debates, in *Ettilaat*, Aban 30, 1363.

31. For a good analysis of Comprehensive Plans of Tehran and other cities before and after the revolution see Iranian Center for Urban and Architectural Studies, *Hashiyenishini dar Iran*, report on phase 4, vols. 1 and 2.

32. This statement was made in almost all the interviews conducted, especially residents of the Zagheh community behind the ASP building in Tehran.

33. Ministry of Budget and Planning, *Census of Households and Housing, 1365/[1986] (Ostan Tehran)*; *Census of Households and Housing, 1365 (Nationwide)*; Budget and Planning Organization, *Census of Tehran, 1359/[1981]*, Tehran, Statistical Center, 1981.

34. See *Kargaran*, no. 10; *Kargaran*, Mordad 1358/1979.

35. See *Ettilaat*, Tir 6, 1362/1983, p. 5.

36. Ibid.

37. For instance in a poor settlement located on the north side of Ayatollah Kashani Boulevard; see *Ettilaat*, Shahrivar 14, 1363/1984, p. 5.

38. Institute of Social Studies and Research, *Mutale'e-yi Muqaddamati Darbare-ye Zoorabad*, p. 13. The population of the settlement increased to 8,000 by 1991; see *Hamshahri*, Dey 5, 1371/1992, p. 4.

39. Institute of Social Studies and Research, *Mutale'e-yi Muqaddamati Darbare-ye Zoorabad*, p. 104.

40. *Kargaran*, nos. 10 and 11, Mordad 1358/1979.

41. *Ettilaat*, Tir 19 and 21, 1363/1984.

42. *Ettilaat*, Dey 14, 1363/1984; see also letters from the city of Karadj squatter settlers in *Ettilaat*, Dey 14, 1363/1984.

43. *Ettilaat*, Khordad 16, 1363/1984.

44. *Ettilaat*, Bahman 5, 1361/1982.

45. *Ettilaat*, Bahman 16, 1361/1982.

46. Rezaii, "Iran: The Wash-House to All Households," p. 23.

47. Ibid.

48. See *Mujahed*, no. 230, p. 34.

49. See *Rah-i Kargar*, no. 10, 1963/1984.

50. See *Rah-i Kargar*, no. 22, 1364/1985, p. 10; *Rah-i Kargar*, no. 8, Aban 1363/1984.

51. See *Rah-i Kargar*, no. 8, Aban 1363/1984.

52. See *Faryad-i Gowdnishin*, no. 62, p. 3.

53. Interview with residents of the Zagheh community behind the ASP building, Tehran spring 1995.

54. See Piran, "Zaghehnishini dar Tehran."

55. Interviews with Fateh and Reymond, both development volunteers working in the poor neighborhoods of Khak-i Sefid during 1980.

56. See *Ayandegan*, Khordad 1, 1358/1979.

57. See *Faryad-i Gowdnishin*, no. 42, Ordibehesht 24, 1359/1980, pp. 1 and 2.

58. Interview with a resident of Shahrak-i Taleghani, Khak-i Sefid, cited in French from Khosrowkhavar, "Nouvelle banlieue et marginalité," pp. 312–313.

59. For a thorough discussion on this see, Gilbert and Ward, "Community Action by the Urban Poor."

60. For instance, the protests in the Shadshahr (Islamshahr) and Bagh-i Nardeh neighborhoods in the Saveh Road in July 1984, and Shahrak-i Aghanour in May 1985, *Rah-i Kargar*, no. 9, Azar 1363/1984, p. 12; *Rah-i Kargar*, no. 22, Dey 1364/1985, p. 19. The major urban riots of Islamshahr and Akbarabad in mid-April 1995 also began with squatters demanding adequate fresh water. See below.

61. I have witnessed such developments in the course of my life as a rural migrant to Tehran. For some fresh evidence see the report by Piran "Zaghehnishini dar Tehran," *Ettilaat-i Syassi va Iqtisadi*, no. 21, Tir 1367/1988.

62. See *Faryad-i Gowdnishin*, no. 2, Mordad 10, 1358/1979, p. 2.

63. See *Keyhan*, Ordibehesht 1, 1358/1979.

64. See *Inqilab-i Islami*, Tir 8, 1359/1980.

65. Thanks to an anonymous reader who brought this point to my attention.

66. For a detailed report on this see *Faryad-i Gowdnishin*, no. 47, Khordad 28, 1359/1980, pp. 1 and 2.

67. See *Kar*, no. 12, Khordad 3, 1358/1979. In 1980, according to the census of the Organization for Upgrading the South Tehran (*Wahed-i Ijtimaii Sazman-i Omran va Behsazi-ye Jonoub-i Tehran*), the gowds sheltered 10,450 households with 46,210 residents; 85 percent of the heads of households were migrants, while 87 percent of the children had been born in the gowds; for a report on this see *Ettilaat*, Bahman 3, 1372/1993.

68. See also *Ettilaat*, Dey 4, 1373/1994, p. 8.

69. See *Farayad-i Gowdnishin*, no. 1, Tir 3, 1358/1979, p. 1; also no. 17, Aban 23, 1358/1979, p. 4.

70. *Farya-i Gowdnishin*, no. 16, Aban 16, 1358/1979, p. 3.

71. See *Faryad-i Gowdnishin*, no. 63, p. 3.

72. Interviews cited in *Faryad-i Gowdnishin*, no. 65, p. 3.

73. See *Faryad-i Gowdnishin*, no. 47, Farvardin 28, 1359/1979, pp. 1 and 2.

74. *Faryad-i Gowdnishin*, no. 14, Aban 1358/1979, p. 2. The households did not seem to be pleased with this arrangement. A resettled squatter women stated: "Swear to God, this is unfair; we were told 'a revolution has occurred.' We came to believe that our situation would change, that we won't suffer that much. But, the only thing we saw of the revolution was this: one day we heard from the TV: the Shah has gone, and Mr. Khomeini has come; and nothing else," in *Faryad-i Gowdnishin*, no. 14, Aban 1, 1358/1979, p. 2. In addition, overcrowdedness caused tensions among the new residents; *Faryad-i Gowdnishin*, no. 39, p. 1 and 2.

75. See *Faryad-i Gowdnishin*, no. 34, Esfand 22, 1358/1979, p. 1.

76. See Bakhash, *The Reign of the Ayatollahs*, p. 57.

77. See *Faryad-i Gowdnishin*, no. 65, Mehr 30, 1359/1980, p. 1.

78. See Hammond, *Building Popular Power*, chapter 6.

79. See *Ettilaat*, Bahman 27, 1362/1983, p. 15.

80. *Ettilaat*, Esfand 3, 1363/1984.

81. *Ettilaat*, Farvardin 20, 1362/1983.

82. For instance, in the Zageh community behind the ASP building in Tehran; interview with residents, 1995.

83. Reported in *Inqilab-i Islami*, Khordad 4, 1359/May 25, 1980.

84. See Razzaghi, *Iqtisad-i Iran*, p. 569; also *Ettilaat*, Farvardin 23, 1362/1983.

85. *Ettilaat*, Farvardin 23, 1362/1983.

86. *Ettilaat*, Bahman 24, 1362/1983.

87. *Ettilaat*, Bahman 24, 1362/1983.

88. A protagonist described the fate of an Islamic Cooperative: "In this store, we used to sell things without getting any profit. Within the course of only three months, believe me, we made a loss of 3,000 tumans. It was impossible to continue in this way. My original job was to sell machine-made carpets; so I got back to my own job. . . . Unfortunately, Islamic Cooperatives cannot carry on in this situation. [During the revolution] these stores used to do things for the sake of God, expecting no material rewards. But [things cannot go on like this], the cooperatives simply cannot carry on functioning while making losses. Something must be done about this." Cited in *Ayandegan*, Farvardin 26, 1358/1979.

89. Based upon *Reuter News Bulletin*, April 5, 1995. Reports on the death toll varied, ranging from one to fifty; see also *Al-Hayat*, April 6, 1995; *Sharq El-Awsat*, April 5, 1995; *Independent*, April 5, 1995.

90. The impact of such public nagging on the authorities is clear in the memories of Asadullah 'Alam, the Shah's court minister: "I needed to assess constantly the situation, the public opinion and their reflection in society

through various commissions and committees; to find out why people are dissatisfied, and what we can do about it; see 'Alam, *Yaddashtha-ye 'Alam*, p. 49. Similarly, the Islamic regime was sensitive to people's public nagging, as indicated in the words of an official in a meeting of the Council of Supply of Tehran Province with representatives of the Interior Ministry in 1993: "We have various sorts of problems. People complain about everything: high prices, housing, high rents, population density, social decadence, shortage of public amenities in Justice Ministry, office of Attorney General, municipality, and in different offices and so on. On the other hand, the Mujahedin keep instigating and fueling these dissatisfactions. All of these have doubled problems in Tehran. Our task is to make sure uncontrollable incidents will not happen"; cited in *Khavaran* weekly, San Jose, no. 130 (November 5, 1993): 5.

91. Cited in *Jumhuri-ye Islami*, Efand 20, 1360/1981.

92. See *Inqilab-i Islami*, Khordad 20, 1359/1980.

93. For debates on this see *Inqilab-i Islami*, Esfand 22, 1358/1979; Farvardin 18, 1359/1980, p. 2; Farvardin 20, 1359/1980; Khordad 20, 1359/1980; Khordad 31, 1359/1980; *Ettilaat*, Dey 24, 1358/1979; Dey 25, 1358/1979.

94. See *Ettilaat*, Khordad 25, 1359/1980.

95. For an analysis of the law see Kiafar, "Urban Land Policies in Post-Revolutionary Iran."

96. See an interview with the leader of the Housing and Urbanization Commission in the Majlis, *Ettilaat*, Azar 5, 1363/1984.

97. See a report by the Housing Foundation in "Bilan-i Kar-i Bonyad-i Maskan," cited in *Inqilab-i Islami*, Ordibehesht 7, 1359/1980.

98. For information on this see "An Overview of the Activities of the Housing Foundation in the Past Decade," reported in *Ettilaat*, Farvardin 20, 1369/1990, p. 4.

99. See *Ettilaat*, Ordibehesht 13, 1362/1983; and Esfand 8, 1362/1983.

100. See Hoodfar, "Devices and Desires."

101. See Piran, "Zaghehnishini dar Tehran," *Ettilaat-i Syassi-Iqtisadi*, no. 18, p. 35.

102. Stated by Mohsen Habibi, the mayor of Tehran, in *Jihad: A publication of Construction Crusade* 4, no. 62 (Esfand 1362/1983): 15; see also *Ettilaat*, Bahman 29, 1362/1983.

103. Ayatollah Montazeri, cited by the mayor of Tehran, Habibi, *Ettilaat*, Ordibehesht 19, 1363/1984, p. 5.

104. Hojjat El-Islam Damghani, Friday Prayer leader of the city of Ramhormuz, in *Ettilaat*, Esfand 17, 1362/1983.

105. Stated by the mayor of Bakhtaran, cited in *Ettilaat*, Bahman 29, 1362/1983.

106. See *Hamshahri*, Azar 30, 1371/1992, p. 5; and *Majalle-ye Me'mari va Shahrsazi*, no. 8 (Mordad 1369/1990): 15–16. This latter publication rep-

resents the views of city planners and architects in Iran.

107. See for instance Habibi, "Islamshahr," p. 62.

108. For instance see *Ettilaat*, Esfand 3, 1363/1984.

109. As stated by Hojjat Al-Islam Damghani cited in *Ettilaat*, Esfand 17, 1362/1983.

110. Interview with squatters of Aliabad, Khazaneh, in South Tehran, 1995.

111. *Ettilaat*, Azar 20, 1364/1985, p. 15.

112. Minister of Housing, stated in *Ettilaat*, Azar 20, 1364/1985, p. 15.

113. See Schirazi, *The Problem of Land Reform in the Islamic Republic of Iran*, p. 48.

114. Habibi, "Islamshar," p. 72.

115. The figures are for Akbarabad and Soltanabad. See Iranian Center for Urban and Architectural Studies, *Hashiyenishini dar Iran*, report on phase 3, "The Dynamics of Life in the Informal Settlements," p. 75. According to the same survey, about 60 percent of the residents reported to the local *komitehs* to resolve disputes and only 40 percent to the elders.

It should be noted that the composition of security forces changed following the revolution. The local *komitehs* were composed largely of young male vigilantes who unlike the prerevolution urban police were normally recruited from the same localities. Comparatively, the *komites* were regarded as both less bureaucratic and less corrupt.

116. Interview with squatters of Aliabad, Khazaneh, in South Tehran, 1995.

117. Interview with residents of the *Zagheh* community behind the ASP building in Tehran, 1995. They are overwhelmingly from Meshkinshahr, in the Turkish-speaking province of Azarbaijan.

118. See *Ettilaat*, "Zaghehnishini dar Tehran," Bahman 5, 1372/1993; others who stayed in the new apartments continued to occupy their older shacks.

119. See Zahedani, *Hashiyenishini*, p. 72.

120. See Iranian Center for Urban and Architectural Studies, *Hashiyenishini: Aasar va Payamadha*, report on phase 2, p. 70.

121. See *Ettilaat*, Ordibehesht 5 1363/1984; Mordad 1, 1363/1984; and Mordad 8, 1363/1984.

122. *Ettilaat*, Shahrivar 23, 1364/1985.

123. Cited in *Kar*, no. 45 (Mehr 22, 1371): 5.

124. Fall 1993 interview with Fateh, an observer of the incident.

125. Interview with Fateh, fall 1993.

126. *Middle East Economic Digest*, September 14, 1985, p. 8.

127. Interview with residents of a squatter settlement in Tehran, 1995.

128. For detailed descriptions see *Kar*, no. 95 (Bahman 9 1359); and *Rah-i Kargar*, no. 12 (Efand 1363/1984).

129. See *Ettilaat*, Farvardin 25, 1369/1990.

130. See *Hamshahri*, Azar 30, 1371/1992; and Dey 1–2, 1371/1992.

131. See Piran, "Zaghehnishini dar Tehran."

132. For the reports see *New York Times*, August 14, 1991, and June 12, 1991. See also *Abrar*, August 1991.

133. *New York Times*, June 12, 1992.

134. *Middle East Times*, June 2–8, 1992.

135. *The Economist*, June 13, 1992, p. 43.

136. *The Economist*, June 6, 1992, p. 68.

137. Reported in *Buletin-i Kabari-ye Aghazi Nou*, Khordad 24, 1371/1992.

138. See *Jumhuri-ye Islami*, Khordad 12, 1371/1992; *Abrar*, Khordad 12, 1371/1992.

139. *Ettilaat*, Khordad 11, 1371/1992.

140. *Jumhuri-ye Islami*, Khordad 12, 1371/1992.

141. Interview with Fateh, a participant.

142. A government-sponsored report on the growth of informal communities around Tehran stated as early as 1987 that "The developments in recent years show that the governments' strict control of unlawful constructions in Tehran has only led to the transfer of this socioeconomic problem into other areas, just outside the city limits." See Hamsou (Engineering Consultants) *Tarh-i Tawse'eh va 'Umran va Hawze-ye Nufuz-i Islamshahr*, p. 58.

SIX   Workless Revolutionaries: The Movement of the Unemployed

1. Bank Markazi Iran, *Annual Economic Report, 1358/[1980]*, p. 7.

2. See *Paykar*, no. 13 (Mordad 1, 1358/1980): 6.

3. Estimate of Budjet and Plan Organization based on the generalization of a survey of the unemployed in Tehran in 1979; see *Statistical Yearbook, 1361*, p. 102, table 30. The *Tehran Musavvar*, a Tehran weekly, reported on Farvardin 24, 1358/1979, that "according to an official figure, three million workers are out of work, most of them casual and construction laborers"; see *Tehran Musavvar* 1, no. 12 (Farvardin 1358/1979): 12. The Council of Unemployed Diplomehs also came up with a similar figure; see *Pirouzi*, no. 3 (Azar 1359/1980): 31. In 1976 there were some 900,000 unemployed (10.2 percent of the labor force). If the number had reached one million by the advent of the revolution, it follows that some two million people lost their jobs as a result of the revolutionary events. See Farjadi, "Barrasi-ye Bazaar-i Kar, Ishtighal va Bikaari dar Iran," p. 69. However , we know that less than 500,000 jobless had actually registered in the Ministry of labor by 1980. For this and an early discussion of the composition of the unemployed in postrevolution Iran see "Jang, Kar va Bikari," *Pirouzi*, no. 3 (Azar 1359/1980): 30–35.

4. See Plan and Budget Organization, *Barrasi-ye Bikaari dar Tehran, Tabistan 1358.*

5. See Bayat, "Why Don't the Unemployed Rebel?"

6. Interviews with Mustafa, an unemployed workers organizer in the oil city of Abadan, conducted in Los Angeles, May 1986; also see Organization of Peoples Guerrilla Fedaii of Iran (OPGFI), *Gozarishi az Tashkil-i Sandika-ye Kargaran-i Prozheii (Fasli) Abadan.*

7. See *Ayandegan,* Farvardin 25, 1357/1978.

8. See OPGFI, *Gozareshi az Mubarizat-i Kargaran-i Bikaar-Shudeh.*

9. Ibid.

10. Each *tuman* is equivalent of Rls 10; in 1979 the exchange rate was U.S.$1 to Rls 80.

11. See *Paygham-i Imrouz,* Farvardin 11, 1358/1979.

12. See *Paygham-i Imrouz,* Farvardin 11, 1358/1979.

13. See, for instance, *Kargar Beh Pish,* a journal of Paykar Organization, no. 5 (Khordad 8, 1358/1979): 4.

14. See Bazargan, *Masa'el va Mushkilat-i Sal-i Avval-i Inqilab.*

15. OPGFI, *Gozareshi az Karagaran-i Bikaar-Shudeh,* p. 30.

16. See *Tehran Musavvar,* "Bar Bikaaran-i Mutahassen dar Nowrooz Che Gozasht?," Farvardin 10, 1358/1979. See also *Ayandegan,* Farvardin 9, 1358/1979, p. 3; also interviews with Naser, a participant in the operations, December 1994, Germany.

17. A copy of the flyer is in the author's possession.

18. See *Ayndegan,* Esfand 29, 1357/1978.

19. Ibid.

20. See *Tehran Musavvar,* no. 10 (Farvardin 10, 1358/1979): 19.

21. Based upon an interview with Naser, a leading participant in the hunger strike, December 1994. This sense of deception and expectation can be detected in the angry statement of a laid-off worker: "We are now out of work for the last seven months. Is this really the result of our Revolution—that we get left alone without a job and money of our own? Those days at the beginning of the revolution, during our strikes, the managers would threaten us by calling the police. And now, they are doing the same thing, by calling the Pasdars!"; see *Ayandegan,* Khordad 13, 1358/1979, p. 4.

22. *Ayandegan,* Esfand 29, 1357/1978.

23. See *Tehran Musavvar,* no. 10 (Farvardin 10, 1358/1979): 20

24. Interview with Naser, a participant in the hunger strike, December 1994.

25. OPGFI, *Gozareshi az Mubarizat-i Kargaran-i Bikaar-Shudeh.* Also based on my interviews with Qasem, an exiled worker who was active among the unemployed workers of the city of Abadan, and Mehrdad, a left-wing mobilizer.

26. See *Ayandegan,* Khordad 9, 1358/1979.

27. See *Ayandegan*, Farvardin 15, 1358/1979. p. 3.

28. See *Ayandegan*, Farvardin 27, 1358/1979, p. 3.

29. *Kargar Beh Pish*, no. 5 (Khordad 8, 1358/1979): 7.

30. See *Kar*, no. 5 (Farvardin 1358/1979).

31. See *Kar*, no. 7 (Farvardin 30, 1358/1979).

32. See *Kar*, no. 6 (Farvardin 1358/1979).

33. A copy of the resolution is in the author's possession.

34. See *Kar*, no. 9 (Ordibehesht 13, 1359/1980): 8.

35. See *Kar*, no. 7 (Farvardin 30, 1358/1979): 5.

36. Ibid.

37. The leaflet of the Fedaii Organization, dated Esfand 21, 1357/1978, is in the author's possession.

38. *Kar*, no. 9 (Ordibehesht 13, 1358/1979).

39. Interview with Reza, an organizer among the unemployed in the city of Kermanshah (Bakhtaran), February 10, 1993.

40. Ibid.

41. See the statements made by those organizations on May Day 1358. See also Abrahamian, *Khomeinism*, "May Day in the Islamic Republic."

42. For a detailed report on May Day 1979 see *Farhang-i Novin*, no. 4 (Ordibehesht 1358/1979), special issue on May Day.

43. See Bayat, *Workers and Revolution in Iran*, p. 104, table 7.1.

44. See Khalesi, *Tarikhcheh-ye Bast va Bast-nishini*.

45. Khalesi, ibid., sees a continuity, from ancient to contemporary times, in the usage of the concept *bast-nishini* (pp. 59–70). In addition, the term "*tahassun*" has been described literally in the major encyclopedias of both Dehkhoda and Mo'in as a synonym for *bast-nishastan*. While some elements of traditional ideas (such as resort to Royal Court, or *tahassun* in the Ministry of Justice), still persist, the meanings of the term have largely changed over time. In the traditional form, *tahassun* pertained to seeking refuge by individuals and groups in a holy site in an attempt to escape punishment or to voice a protest. It was used as a mechanism of justice in the absence of laws by means of resorting to divine protection. The concept changed slightly at the dawn of modernity. In Iran since the Qajar dynasty (1797–1921), the places of refuge included not only the holy sites but also the royal courts, stables of aristocrats, public telegraph offices, and especially foreign embassies (Khalesi, pp. 19–20). It was in this period that such concepts as political asylum, diplomatic immunity, and the like evolved. In this altered sense, the actors resorted not so much to divine protection as to political authority. Finally, the contemporary connotations of the term are entirely different. Today it is mostly understood as essentially a collective action by a group of people who either pursue publicity for a cause or aim at disruption in order to put pressure on the authorities to meet certain demands. The concept is almost mixed with the modern concept of temporary occupation, where the actors resort neither to God nor to polit-

ical authority, but to public pressure.

46. See Piven and Cloward, *Poor Peoples' Movements*.

47. Interview, conducted in October 1993, with Roham, a reporter on labor issues for the Tehran daily *Paygham-i Imrouz*. The newspaper was published after the revolution 1979 but banned in the summer of that year.

48. July 1993 interview with Merdad, a left-wing activist involved in the unemployed movement.

49. Ibid.

50. December 1994 interview with Naser, a worker activist in the House of Labor, December 1994.

51. OPGFI, *Gozareshi az Tashkil-i Sandika-ye Kargaran-i Bikaar-Shudeh-ye Abadan*.

52. See *Kargar Beh Pish*, no. 5, 1358/1979, p. 11.

53. May 1985 interviews with Mustafa, one of the leaders of SPWA, in Los Angeles.

54. Ibid.

55. Ibid.

56. Ibid.

57. May 1993 interview with Reza, a labor activist.

58. Ibid.

59. Ibid.

60. Ibid.

61. *Ayandegan*, Ordibehesht 4, 1358/1979, p. 3; see also *Tehran Musavvar*, "Gozareshi az Khane-ye Kargar va Sokhanan-i Kargaran-i Bikaar," no. 2 (Khordad 18, 1358/1979): 24–25.

62. The Resolution of the Central Constituent Council of the Unions of the Unemployed Project and Laid-off Workers of Iran. The original text is in the author's possession.

63. See *Middle East Economic Digest*, October 5, 1979, p. 29.

64. Interview with Rohamm, a labor reporter.

65. The point is made clear by considering the statements of many officials immediately after the revolution.

66. An interview with leftist activists involved in the movement confirmed this point.

67. Such as *Kar, Paykar, Khabar-i Kargar, Khabar Nameh, Kargar-i Komonist, Mujahed*.

68. A Marxist-Leninist Organization with Maoist orientation.

69. Interview with Darvishpour, a participant in unemployed workers campaigns in Fall 1993.

70. See Bazargan, *Masa'el va Mushkilat-i Sal-i Avval-i Inqilab*, p. 122.

71. Ibid.

72. See Bank Markazi Iran, *Annual Economic Report*, 1982, p. 8.

73. This was announced by the Labor Ministry, in *Ayandegan*,

Ordibehesht 2, 1358/1979, p. 1. In addition, the Ministry of Roads and Supply announced that it employed some 5,000 skilled and unskilled laborers for road construction; see *Ayandegan*, Khordad 16, 1358/1979, p. 4.

74. For the details, see Bayat, *Workers and Revolution in Iran*.

75. The original flyer issued after the workers began their sit-in is in the author's possession; see also *Kar*, no. 9, Ordibehesht 13, 1358/1979, p. 10.

76. See *Ayandegan*, Mordad 27, 1358/1979, p. 5.

77. See Bank Markazi Iran, *Annual Economic Report*, 1982, p. 50.

78. See *Ayandegan*, Farvardin 21, 1358/1979.

79. See *Ettilaat*, Shahrivar 2, 1364/1985.

80. *Ayandegan*, Tir 17, 1358/1979.

81. Ibid.

82. See Bazergan, *Masa'el va Mushkilat-i Sal-i Avval-i Inqilab*, p. 125.

83. *Ayandegan*, Khordad 9, 1358/1979.

84. *Ayandegan*, Khordad 22, 1358/1979.

85. Ibid.

SEVEN   Street Rebels: The Politics of Street Vending

1. *Jihad*, no. 63, Esfand 1362/1983.

2. Cited in *Ayandegan*, Tir 25, 1358/1979, p. 5.

3. Cited in *Ayandegan*, Ordibehesht, 1358/1979.

4. Plan and Budget Organization, *Barrasi-ye Bikaari dar Tehran, Tabestan 1358*.

5. Plan and Budget Organization, *Census of Tehran, 1359*.

6. See Amirahmadi, *Revolution and Economic Transition*, p. 187.

7. Ibid.

8. De Soto, *The Other Path*. Other studies include Cross, "Organization and Resistance in the Informal Economy." To my knowledge, there are only a few brief studies of street vendors in Iran: Danesh, *Elal va Avamel-i Gostaresh-i Mashaghel-i Kazib*; Plan and Budget Organization, *Barrasi-ye Ijmali-ye Dakkeh-daari dar Irtibat ba Ishtighal va Bikaari*; Fallah and Khameneh, *Barrasi-ye Ejmali-ye Dast-foroushan dar Tehran*. A more serious work is Tom Thompson's "Petty Traders in Iran." Thompson characterizes petty traders by "a subsistence level income," "an underdog status," "an absence of innovation, low level of literacy, and a fragile social network"; see p. 260.

9. For instance, in short stories by Gholam Hussein Saedi (*Dandil*) and Samad Behrangui (*Bist-o-Chahar Saa'at dar Khab va Bidaari*), and in Mehrjoui's film (*Dayer-ye Mina*), vendors portrayed sympathetically still appear as victims and pitiful.

10. The concept "active and passive use" is also discussed in Lis and Soly, "Neighborhood Social Change in the West European Cities."

11. The operations of street vendors are documented in historical works

such as Lapidus, *Muslim Cities in the Later Middle Ages*; Marcus, *The Middle East on the Eve of Modernity*; Abrahamian, *Iran Between Two Revolutions.*

12. See document "E'laan-e Vezarat-e Nazmieh" (Declaration by the Ministry of Order) printed in Willem Floor, "Les premieres règles de police urbane à Tehran," p. 174.

13. A study in 1974 showed that vendors in Tehran paid between Rls 10 and Rls 100 daily in bribes to police officers for their illegal operations; see Fallah and Khameneh, *Barrasi-ye Ejmali-ye Dast-foroushan dar Tehran*, p. 13.

14. The figure is drawn from Bahrmbeygui, *Tehran: An Urban Analysis,* p. 84.

15. See Farjadi, "Barrasi-ye Bazaar-i Kar," p. 76.

16. According to official figures, the total number of urban trading enterprises with one workman was 424,000; of these workmen, 318,000 were petty traders, or *khordeh foroush*; see Goudarzi, "Vizheguiha va Tahavvolat-i Bazaar-i Kar dar Iran," p. 86.

17. See *Mujahed*, no. 137, 1363/1984, p. 13.

18. The Tehran Municipality, cited in *Ettilaat*, Farvardin 6, 1363/1984.

19. Assuming 60 percent married with three children and 40 percent single. The ratio is drawn from a sample survey of street vendors in Shiraz and Tehran; see Sheikhi, "Elal va Payamadha-ye Dast-foroushi (Tehran)," and Sheikhi, *Elal va Avamel-i Dast-foroushi (Shiraz).*

20. See *Ettilaat*, Tir 4, 1363/1984. A Ministry of Planning report in 1985 reached a similar conclusion, stating that "Informal activities—productive or unproductive—will persist in our society in full force." See Danesh, "Elal va Avamel-i Gostaresh-i Mashaghel-i Kazib," p. 32.

21. Their names: Torabi, Sardoubi, Mughaddasi, Islahi, and Oskouii; see Abazari, "Donya-ye Bozorg-i Kitab-foroushan-i Kouchak," pp. 40–41.

22. Abazari, ibid.

23. *Ayandegan*, 12 Tir 1358/1979, p. 5.

24. See Plan and Budget Organization, *Barrasi-ye Ijmali-ye Dakkeh-daari dar Irtibat ba Ishtighal va Bikaari*, p. 13.

25. See *Ettilaat*, Mehr 16 and 17, 1363/1984 for reports on begging and drugs; see especially Khosrowkhavar, "Nouvelle banlieue et marginalité."

26. Interview with a street knife-seller, Tehran, Maidan-i Tajrish, 1995.

27. From a sample of one hundred vendors in the city of Shiraz; see Sheikhi, *Elal va Avamel-i Dast-foroushi dar Shiraz.*

28. Based upon a sample survey of one hundred street vendors in Tehran; see Sheikhi, "Elal va Payamadha-ye Dast-foroushi (dar Tehran)." A survey of *Inqilab-i Islami* carried out ten years earlier put the rural background of the vendors at 60 percent; see *Inqilab-i Islami*, "Gozaresh-i Tahqiqi Darbare-ye Dast-foroushan-i Tehran," Khordad 14 1359/1980.

29. See Sheikhi, "Elal va Payamadha-ye Dast-foroushi (dar Tehran)"; *Inqilab-i Eslami*, "Gozaresh-i Tahqiqi Darbare-ye Dast-foroushan-i Tehran,"

Khordad 14, 1359/1980. A study in 1974 came to similar conclusions concerning the ethnic background of Tehran vendors. It concluded that the "majority of vendors spread throughout the city seem to come from Azarbaijan province, in particular, areas around Ardabil, Ahar, Meshkin Shahr, and so on"; see Fallah and Khameneh, *Barrasi-ye Ejmali-ye Dast-foroushan dar Tehran*, p. 15.

30. Interview with a food vendor, Maidan-i Tajrish, 1995.

31. Statement of vendor in *Ettilaat*, Shahrivar 20, 1363/1984.

32. See *Jihad*, "An Interview with the Mayor of Tehran," *Jihad* 4, no. 62 (Esfand 1362/1983): 16. *Jihad* is the publication of the *Jihad-i Sazandegui*, the Construction Crusade Organization.

33. See *Hamshahri*, "Bazaar-i Sayyed Ismail," Dey 28, 1371/1992, p. 5.

34. In a similar action, a group of 120 vendors, all from a village near Malayer, established their stalls collectively in Maidan-i Fawziyeh, but were removed by the Pasdars. They then moved to another Maidan, Golha, but were harassed by the residents who complained to the police. Eventually evicted from there also, they ended up on a vacant piece of land along Amirabad Avenue; see *Ayandegan*, Tir 16, 1358/1980.

35. See Sheikhi, "Elal va Payamadha-ye Dast-foroushi (dar Tehran," p. 69.

36. See Amirahmadi, *Revolution and Economic Transition*, p. 187.

37. Ibid., p. 188.

38. Athari, "Faqr va Ishtighal dar Iran," p. 76; see also Farjadi, "Barrasi-ye Bazaar-i Kar," p. 69.

39. Interview with the mayor of Tehran, Habibi, in *Jihad*, no. 62, Esfand 1362/1983, p. 14.

40. According to a survey, close to half of the vendors in Tehran cited street trading as an alternative to unemployment; see Sheikhi, "Elal va Payamadha-ye Dast-foroushi (dar Tehran)," p. 68; see also *Ayandegan*, Tir 12, 1358/1979, p. 5, for interviews with the street vendors.

41. In *Ayandegan*, 3 Ordibehesht 1358/1979.

42. Prayer beads.

43. See *Ayandegan*, Khordad 19, 1358/1979.

44. See Sheikhi, "Elal va Payamadha-ye Dast-foroushi (dar Tehran)." A survey of *Inqilab-i Islami* conducted in 1980 estimated that vendors made a daily average earning of Rls 1,500–Rls 3,000, while about 80 percent of them earned Rls 500–Rls 1,000; see *Inqilab-i Islami*, Khordad 14, 1359/1980. Another study provided an estimated income of between Rls 500 and Rls 3,000 a day for 1981; see Plan and Budget Organization, *Barrasi-ye Ijmali-ye Dakkeh-daari dar Irtibat ba Ishtighal va Bikaari*, p. 14.

Sheikhi's survey showed that over half of the vendors were between ten and thirty years of age, some 12 percent below eighteen, and some 20 percent over forty-five.

45. See *Jihad* 4, no. 62 (Esfand 1362/1983): 16. A schoolteacher earned about Rls 1,500 a day at that time.

46. See Sheikhi, "Elal va Payamadha-ye Dast-foroushi (dar Tehran)." A similar survey was conducted by the University of Shiraz for the city of Shiraz in 1985. The general results seem to be very similar to that carried out for Tehran. See Sheikhi, *Elal va Avamel-i Dast-foroushi*. My interviews with vendors support this.

47. Indepth interviews with twenty street vendors in different parts of Tehran, 1995. While in Sheikhi's survey the vast majority of vendors said they disliked their job due to its low status, insecurity, and to the fear of police harassment, about three out of five stated that they would continue working in trade if they had sufficient capital; see p. 69.

48. Cited in Danesh, *Elal va Avamel-i Gostaresh-i Mashaghel-i Kazib*, p. 29.

49. My interviews; see also interviews with street vendors and officials in *Ayandegan*, Tir 12, 1358/1979, p. 5; *Ayandegan*, Tir 25, 1358/1979, p. 5.

50. See *Ayandegan*, Tir 25, 1358/1979, p. 5.

51. Interview with an old cheese vendor, Maidan-i Tajrish, 1995.

52. See *Ettilaat*, Khordad 17, 1362/1983; *Ettilaat*,Tir 4, 1363/1984.

53. In *Ayandegan*, Tir 12, 1358/1979, p. 5.

54. See *Ettilaat*, Mehr 23, 1364/1985.

55. Nateq Nouri, Interior Minister in *Ettilaat*, Dey 18, 1363/1984; *Ettilaat*, Tir 4, 1363/1984.

56. These urban sociologists range from George Simmel to Robert Park, Everett Stonequist, and the rest of the Chicago School such as Louis Wirth.

57. See the very interesting Persian document in Floor, "Les premieres règles de police urbane à Teheran," p. 174.

58. Floor, "The Market Police in Qajar Persia."

59. For a perceptive elaboration of the issue of space as power see Foucault, *Power/Knowledge*. For a more recent discussion, see Davis, *City of Quartz*.

60. This fear of chaos can be sensed in statements by officials, for instance the Minister of Interior, Natiq Nouri, in *Ettilaat*, Dey 18, 1363; see also *Ettilaat*, Tir 4, 1363/1984.

61. Muhammad Malayeri, the head of the CCMAOT in *Ettilaat*, Shahrivar 10, 1364/1985. The left also shared some of these negative representations by terming the phenomenon "hidden unemployment"; *Kar*, Bahman 6, 1360/1981, p. 10.

62. Ayatollah Khameneii, the then leader of Tehran Friday prayer, accused vendors of promoting *fahshaa* and *fisaad* (moral decadence); see also *Ayandegan*, Tir 12, 1358/1979, p. 5.

63. See *Inqilab-i Islami*, Khordad 26, 1359/1980.

64. See *Keyhan*, Azar 14, 1363/1984; *Mujahid*, no. 237, 1363/1984, p. 13.

65. *Ettilaat*, Khordad 17, 1362/1983, p. 15.

66. *Keyhan*, Farvardin 5, 1363/1984.

67. *Ettilaat*, Farvardin 6, 1363/1984.

68. *Ettilaat*, Shahrivar 10, 1364/1985.

69. For the case of Shiraz see *Ettilaat*, Esfand 7, 1362/1983.

70. On one such occasion, in November 1984, Hojjat El-Islam Ramazani in Shiraz warned: "I have given the authorities fifteen days to do away with the obstruction of thoroughfares. If the job is not finished by the deadline, I will ask the *ummat-i hizbullah* to deal directly with them," cited in *Khabar-i Jonoub*, Aban 14, 1363/1984.

71. *Ettilaat*, Farvardin 25, 1363/1984.

72. See *Pasdar-i Islam*, no. 34 (Mehr 1363/1984).

73. Natiq-Nouri, the Interior Minister, warned that "the officials must obey the laws, even if they think they help out the *mustaz'afin*. . . . To be a *hizbullah* means to comply with the laws of the land"; cited in *Ettilaat*, Dey 18, 1363/1984.

74. *Ayandegan*, Esfand 28, 1357/1978.

75. Interview with an anonymous eyewitness, October 1993.

76. See *Kar*, no. 112 (Khordad 29, 1360/1981): 9.

77. Committee Against the Obstruction of Thoroughfares (CAOT) in *Ettilaat*, Farvardin 6, 1363/1984.

78. *Kayhan*, Tir 11, 1363/1984.

79. *Ettilaat*, Ordibehesht 5, 1363/1984.

80. Cited in *Ettilaat*, Esfand 7, 1362/1983.

81. *Ettilaat*, Shahrivar 10, 1364/1985, p. 2. Habibi, the Mayor of Tehran, admitted four months after Ayatollah Khomeini's verdict and ten months after claiming the removal of 90 percent of the vendors, that "Pseudo occupations [*mashaghel-i kazib*] in Tehran must be eliminated only *gradually*"; cited in *Ettilaat*, Dey 18, 1363/1984. Emphasis mine.

82. *Kar* 3, no. 145 (Bahman 6, 1360/1981): 10.

83. See *Kar*, no. 67, Tir 24, 1359/1980, p. 11.

84. See the story in *Rah-i Kargar*, no. 23, 1364/1985, p. 24.

85. See *Ettilaat*, Farvardin 25, 1369/1990.

86. See *Ettilaat*, Shahrivar 10, 1364/1985, p. 2. He justified his actions by referring to the first amendment of Act 55 of the Municipality Law, which prohibits obstruction of public thoroughfares; see *Ettilaat*, Shahrivar 10, 1364/1985, p. 2.

87. Cited in *Ettilaat*, Aban 10, 1363/1984.

88. *Faludeh* is a kind of desert made of starch, sugar, and lemon.

89. See *Kayhan*, Ordibehesht 12, 1362/1983, p. 4.

90. See *Ettilaat*, Tir 4, 1363/1984.

91. Two days later, however, the demolition agents eradicated them in a midnight raid; see *Kar* 2, no. 95 (Bahman 9, 1359/1980). Others, however,

continued to resume operation.

92. Ibid.

93. Ibid.

94. Cited in Danesh, *Elal va Avamel-i Gostaresh-i Mashaghel-i Kazib*, p. 32.

95. See *Ettilaat*, Ordibehesht 2, 1369/1990, p. 5.

96. *Ettilaat*, Esfand 11, 1361/1982.

97. *Ettilaat*, Shahrivar 10, 1364/1985.

98. For instance in Shahr Rey and District 12 of Tehran, 2,130 *basaat*s and stall-holders were removed. Of these, 800 applied to get back to their business through the local mosques. Some 155 were recommended and began their operation in specified locations; *Ettilaat*, Farvardin 6, 1363/1984.

99. See *Ettilaat*, Shahrivar 10, 1364/1985.

100. *Ettilaat*, Esfand 11, 1361/1982; *Ettilaat*, Khordad 17, 1362/1983.

101. As late as October 1985 (Mehr 1364), the city officials in Tehran were still warning the "unlawful" street vendors in Maidan-i Shohada, Beryanak Street, and Sarcheshmeh, all in South Tehran, to evacuate, this time with a new justification. Among the vendors, there are those who, warned the head of COAT, "are escapees from public duty and are engaged in drug-dealing and profiteering"; *Ettilaat*, Mehr 23, 1364/1985.

102. These localities were in Jannat Abad, Pounak, Olympic Village, Shahrak-i Parvaaz, Shahrak-i Azadi, Paykanshahr, and the Bayhaqui parking lot.

103. Officials justified this by suggesting that this was a tradition in Iranian history and was practiced in many developed countries today; see *Hamshahri*, Bahman 26, 1371/1992, p. 9. For reference to the flea markets, see *Hamshahri*, Dey 12, 1371/1992; Bahman 24, 1371/1992; Bahman 26, 1371/1992; Esfand 5, 1371/1992; and Esfand 8, 1371/1992.

104. See *Hamshahri*, Esfand 5, 1371, p. 4.

EIGHT   Grassroots and State Power: The Promise and Perils of
             Quiet Encroachment

1. See Schwedler, "Civil Society and the Study of Middle East Politics."

2. By which I mean people with different ethnic, religious, and class backgrounds, consistently associating with one another according to a set of accepted norms.

3. See Abu-Lughod, "The Romance of Resistance."

4. See Piven and Cloward, *Poor Peoples' Movements*.

5. Foucault, *Knowledge/Power*, p. 98.

6. See for example, Rahnema, "Power and Regenerative Processes in Micro-Spaces" and "Participation," p. 123. Also Escobar, *Encountering Development*.

7. See Friedmann, *Empowerment*, p. 7.

8. For a good critique of planning—its history, rationale, and language, see Escobar, *Encountering Development* and "Planning."

9. A comprehensive report, sponsored by the Ministry of Housing and Urbanization, recommends not only that the informals be formalized but also that the poor should be considered as "citizens" with their share in comprehensive planning. But it falls short of asking for the *participation* of the poor in the planning of their own environments. See Iranian Center for Urban and Architectural Studies, *Hashiyenishini dar Iran*, report on phase 5: "Regarding the Low-Income as Citizens," p. 4.1.

Bibliography

Abazari, Farshideh. "Donya-ye Bozorg-i Kitab-forousha-ye Kouchak" (The wide world of small-scale book vendors). *Tehran Musavvar* (Tir 8, 1358/1979): 40–41.

Abdel Taher, Nadia. *Social Identity and Class in a Cairo Neighborhood. Cairo Papers in Social Science* 9, no. 4 (Winter 1986).

Abrahamian, Ervand. "The Guerrilla Movement in Iran, 1963–1977." *Merip Reports*, no. 86 (March/April 1980).

———. *Iran Between Two Revolutions.* Princeton: Princeton University Press, 1982.

———. *Radical Islam: The Mujahedin of Iran.* London: Tauris, 1989.

———. *Khomeinism.* Berkeley: California University Press, 1993.

Abu-Lughod, Lila. "The Romance of Resistance: Tracing Transformation of Power Through Bedouin Women." *American Ethnologist* 17, no. 1 (February 1990).

Adle, C. B. and Bernard Hourcade, eds., *Tehran: Capitale bicentenaire.* Tehran: Institut Français de Recherche en Iran, 1992.

Ahmadian, M. A. "Hashiyenishini"(Squatter settlement). *Majalle-ye Daneshkade-ye Adabiyat va Ulum-i Insani*, no. 3 (1372/1993): 826–833.

Akbari, Ali Akbar. *Lumpenism*. Tehran: Markaz-i Nashr-i Sepehr, 1973.

'Alam, Asadullah. *Yad-dashtha-ye 'Alam, 1349–1351* ('Alam's memoire, 1970–1972). 2 vols. USA: Swan Overseas Plc., 1993.

Al-Adly, Mona and M. Morsy. "A Study of Street Vendors in Cairo." Unpublished graduate term paper, the American University in Cairo, Spring 1995.

Ale-Ahmad, Jalal. *Plagued by the West (Gharbzadegi)*. Delmor, N.Y.: Caravan, 1982.

Amirahmadi, Houshang. *Revolution and Economic Transition: The Iranian Experience*. Albany: State University of New York Press, 1990.

Amirahmadi, Houshang, and Ali Kiafar. "Tehran: Growth and Contradictions." *Journal of Planning Education and Research* 6, no. 3 (1987).

Amjad, Mohammad. "Rural Migrants, Islam, and Revolution in Iran." *Social Movements, Conflicts, and Change* 16 (1993): 35–51. Eds., L. Kriesberg, M. Dobkowski, and I. Walliaman.

Amraii, Sohbatollah. *Barrasi-ye Moque'iyat-i Ijtimaii-ye Shohada-ye Inqilab-i Islami: Shahrivar 1, 1357-Bahman 30, 1357* (Social background of the martyrs of the Islamic revolution, August 23, 1978–February 19, 1979). Unpublished Master's thesis, University of Tehran, 1982.

Anonymous. ed. *Bahsi Darbare-ye Marja'iyat va Ruhaniyat* (A discussion about marja'iyat and the clergy). Tehran: publisher unknown, n.d.

Arjomand, A. Said. *The Turban for the Crown: The Islamic Revolution in Iran*. Oxford-New York: Oxford University Press, 1988.

Ashraf, Ahmad. *Iran: Imperialism, Class, and Modernization from Above*. Ph.D diss., New School for Social Research, 1971.

———. "The Roots of Emerging Dual Class Structure in Nineteenth-Century Iran." *Iranian Studies* 14, nos. 1–2 (Winter/Spring 1981).

———. "Marateb-i Ijtimaii dar Dowran-i Qajar" (Social status during the Qajar period). *Kitab-i Aagah*, no. 1, Tehran: Intisharat-i Aagah, 1360/1981.

Athari, Kamal. "Faqr va Ishtighal dar Iran" (Poverty and employment in Iran). *Ettilaat-i Syassi-Iqtisadi* 5, nos. 43–44 (1370/1991).

Bahrambeygui, H. *Tehran: An Urban Analysis*. Tehran: Sahab Book Institute, 1977.

Bakhash, Shaul. *The Reign of the Ayatollahs: Iran and the Islamic Revolution*. New york: Basic Books, 1984.

Banani, Amin. *The Modernization of Iran*. Stanford: Stanford University Press, 1961.

Bank Markazi Iran. *Annual Economic Report, 1359*. Tehran: Bank Markari Iran, 1980.

Banuazizi, Ali. "Alounaknishinan-i Khiaban-i Professor Brown" (The shanty dwellers of Professor Brown street). *Alifba* 2, no. 3 (Summer 1362/1983).

Barriga, Miguel. "*Necesidad*: Notes on the Discourse of Urban Politics in the Ajusco Foothills of Mexico City." *American Ethnologist* 23, no. 2 (1996): 291–310

Bassri, Hassan and Bernard Hourcade. "L' Expérience conseilliste." *Peuple Mediterranéans* 29 (October/December 1984).

Bauer, Janet. "Poor Women and Social Consciousness in Revolutionary Iran." In G. Nashat, ed., *Women and Revolution in Iran*, pp. 141–170. Boulder: Westview, 1983.

Bayat, Asef. *Workers and Revolution in Iran*. London: Zed, 1987.

———."Poverty, Urbanization, and Development: The Case of Tehran." Unpublished memo, the American University in Cairo, 1987.

———. "Why Don't the Unemployed Rebel? Or Do They?" Mimeo, The American University in Cairo, 1996.

———. "Cairo's Poor: Dilemmas of Survival and Solidarity," *Middle East Report*, no. 202 (Spring 1997).

Bazargan, Mehdi. *Masa'el va Mushkilat-i Sal-i Avval-i Inqilab* (The problems and difficulties of the first year of the revolution). Tehran: Self-Published, 1362/1983.

———. *Inqilab-i Iran dar Dow Harakat* (The Iranian revolution in two stages). Tehran: Self-Published, 1363/1984.

Behrangui, Samad. *Beest-o-chahar Saa'at dar Khab va Bidaari* (Twenty-four hours in a sleep and awake). Tehran: 1353/1974.

Bienen, H. "Urbanization and Third World Instability." *World Development* 12, no. 7 (1984): 661–691.

Bosworth, Clifford. *The Medieval Islamic Underworld*. Leiden: E. J. Brill, 1976.

Bourdieu, Pierre. "The Social Space and the Genesis of Groups." *Theory and Society* 14, no. 6 (November 1985).

———. "What Makes a Social Class? On the Theoretical and

Practical Existence of Groups." *Berkeley Journal of Sociology* 32 (1987).

Bramwell, B. "Public Space and Local Communities: The Example of Birmingham, 1840–1880." In G. Kearns and C. Whithers, eds., *Urbanizing Britain: Essays on Class and Communities in the Nineteenth Century*, pp. 31–54. Cambridge: Cambridge University Press, 1991.

Bromley, Ray and Gerry, Chris. eds., *Casual Work and Poverty in Third World Cities*. Chichester, N.Y.: John Wiley, 1979.

Brown, Kenneth, et al., eds. *Middle Eastern Cities in Comparative Perspective*. London: Ithaca Press, 1986.

Brown, Kenneth, et al. *Etat, ville et mouvements sociale au Maghreb et au Moyen-Orient/Urban Crises and Social Movements in the Middle East*. Paris: Editions L'Harmattan, 1989.

Burt, C. "Popular Struggles in Peru." Paper presented at Conference on Inequality and New Forms of Popular Representation in Latin America, Columbia University. New York, March 3–5, 1994.

Castells, Manuel. "Is There an Urban Sociology?" In C. Pickvance, ed., *Urban Sociology*. London: Tavistock Press, 1976.

———. "Squatters and the State in Latin America." In J. Gugler, ed., *Urbanization of the Third World*. Oxford: Oxford University Press, 1982.

———. *Cities and the Grassroots*. Berkeley: University of California Press, 1983.

Central Intelligence Agency. *The World Fact Book, 1992*. USA: CIA, 1992.

Colburn, F.D., ed. *Everyday Forms of Peasant Resistance*. New York: Sharpe, 1989.

Connel, J. "Tehran: Urbanization and Development." Discussion paper. Institute of Development Studies, University of Sussex: 1973.

Cornelius, Wayne. "Urbanization and Political Demand-Making: Political Participation Among the Migrant Poor in Latin American Cities. *American Political Science Review* 68 (1974): 1125–1146.

———. *Politics and the Migrant Poor in Mexico City*. Stanford: Stanford University Press, 1975.

Crompton, Rosemary. *Class and Stratification: An Introduction to Current Debate*. Oxford: Oxford University Press, 1993.

Cross, John. "Organization and Resistance in the Informal Economy: Historical Parallels in the 'Formalization' of Street Vendors in Mexico City." Unpublished memo, the American University in Cairo, 1995.

Danesh, Abul-Hassan. *Rural Exodus and Squatter Settlements in the Third World: Case of Iran*. Lanham, Md.: University Press of America, 1987.

————. *Elal va Avamel-i Gostaresh-i Mashaghel-i Kazib dar Shahrya-ye Bozorg* (The causes of the expansion of parasitic occupations in large cities). Tehran: Planning and Budget Organization, 1363/ 1984.

Davis, John. E. *Contested Ground: Collective Action and the Urban Neighborhood*. Ithaca: Cornell University Press, 1991.

Davis, Mike. *City of Quartz*. London: Verso, 1990.

Daunton, M. J. "Public Place and Private Space: The Victorian City and the Working-Class Household." In D. Fraser and A. Sutcliffe, eds., *The Pursuit of Urban History*, pp. 212–233. London: Edward Arnold, 1993.

Denoeux, Guilain. *Urban Unrest in the Middle East*. Albany: State University of New York Press, 1993.

De Soto, Hernando. *The Other Path: The Invisible Revolution in the Third World*. New York: Harper and Row, 1989.

Draper, Hal. *Karl Marx's Theory of Revolution: The Politics of Social Classes*. Vol. 2. New York: Monthly Review Press, 1978.

Durkheim, Emil. *The Division of Labor in Society*. New York: Free Press, 1971.

Eckstein, Susan. *The Poverty of Revolution: The State and the Urban Poor in Mexico*. Princeton: Princeton University Press, 1977.

Escobar, Arturo. "Imagining a Post-Development Era? Critical Thought, Development and Social Movements." *Social Text* 31/32 (1992).

————. "Planning." In W. Sasch, ed., *The Development Dictionary*. London: Zed, 1995

————. *Encountering Development: The Making and Unmaking of the Third World*. Princeton: Princeton University Press, 1995.

Ettilaat. "Isti'fa-ye Ra'is-e Bonyad-i Maskan va Mushkel-i Maskan" (The resignation of the director of the Housing Foundation, and the problem of housing) (Esfand 11, 1363/1984).

————. "Dar Rousta-Shahrha-ye Tehran: Bagherabad" (In the urban villages of Tehran) (Kardad 5 and 6, 1364/1985).

————. "Bilan-i Fa'aliyatha-ye Bonyad-i Maskan dar Dah Sal-i

Gozashteh" (An overview of the activities of the Housing Foundation in the past ten years) (Farvardin 20, 1369/1990): 4.

―――. "Barrasi-ye Tajrube-ye Bazsazi-ye Manatiq-i Zaghehnishin-i Tehran" (An overview of the experience of the reconstruction of Tehran shanty-settlements) (Bahman 3 and 5, 1372/1994).

Ettilaat-i Syassi-Iqtisadi. "Tehran: Yek Tasvir-i Amari" (Tehran: A statistical view) no. 17 (Esfand 1366/1989): 43–45.

Fallah, Jamal and Ali Khameneh. *Barrasi-ye Ijmali-ye Dast-foroushan dar Tehran* (A brief study of street vendors in Tehran). Tehran: Tehran University, Department of Urban Planning: 1353/1974.

Fanon, Frantz. *The Wretched of the Earth.* London: Penguin, 1967.

Farjadi, Gholamali. "Barrasi-ye Bazaar-i Kar, Ishtighal va Bikaari dar Iran" (A survey of the labor market, employment, and unemployment in Iran). *Barnameh va Tawse'eh* 2, no. 3 (Fall 1992).

Ferdows, Emad. "The Reconstruction Crusade and Class Conflict in Iran." *MERIP Reports* 13, no. 113 (March-April 1983).

Firoozi, Frydoon. "Tehran: A Demographic and Economic Analysis." *Middle Eastern Studies* 10 (January 1974): 60–76.

Floor, Willem. "The Market Police in Qajar Persia." *Die Welt Islams* 13 (1971).

―――. "Political Role of Lutis in Iran." In M. Bonine and N. Keddie, eds., *Modern Iran: The Dialectics of Continuity and Change.* Albany: State University of New York Press, 1981.

―――. "Les premières règles de police urbane à Teheran." In C. Adle and B. Hourcade, eds., *Teheran: Capitale bicentenaire.* Tehran: Institut Français de Recherche en Iran, 1992.

Foucault, Michèle. *Power/Knowledge.* New York: Pantheon, 1972.

Frank, Andre Gunder and Martha Fuentes. "Nine Theses on New Social Movements." *Newsletter of International Labour Studies* 34 (July 1987).

Freud, Sigmund. *Civilization and Its Discontents.* New York: Norton, 1961.

Friberg, M. and B. Hettne. "Local Mobilization and World System Politics." *International Social Science Journal* 40, nos. 1–4 (1988).

Friedmann, John. "The Dialectic of Reason." *International Journal of Urban and Regional Research* 13, no. 2 (1989): 217–244.

―――. "The Latin American *barrio* Movement as a Social

Movement: Contribution to a Debate." *International Journal of Urban and Regional Research* 13, no. 3 (1989): 501–510.

———. *Empowerment: The Politics of Alternative Development.* Cambridge: Blackwell, 1992.

Garreton, M. A. "Popular Mobilization and Military Regime in Chile: The Complexities of Invisible Transition." In S. Eckstein, ed., *Power and Popular Protest: Latin American Social Movements,* Berkeley: University of California Press, 1989.

Ghannam, Farha. "Relocation and the Creation of 'Modern' Subjects: Urban Planning and Identity Formation in Cairo, Egypt." Unpublished paper, 1992.

———. "Relocation, Gender, and the Production of Urban Space in Cairo." *Middle East Report,* no. 202, (Spring 1997).

Geisse, G. and F. Sabatini. "Latin American Cities and Their Poor." In M. Dogan and J. Kasarda, eds., *The Metropolis Era,* vol. 1 (*A World of Giant Cities*), Newbury Park: Cal.: Sage, 1988.

Gilbert, Alan and Joseph Gugler. *Cities, Poverty, and Development.* Oxford: Oxford University Press, 1982.

Gilbert, Alan and Peter Ward. "Community Action by the Urban Poor: Democratic Involvement, Community Self-Help, or a Means of Social Control." *World Development* 12, no. 8 (1984).

Goudarzi, Mohsen. "Vizheguiha va Tahavvolat-i Bazaar-i Kar dar Iran, 1355–1365" (The characteristics of and developments in Iranian labor market, 1976–86). *Ettilaat-i Syassi-Iqtisadi* 5, nos. 43–44 (1370/ 1991).

Gramsci, Antonio. *Prison Notebooks.* New York: International Publishers, 1971.

Habibi, Mohsen. "Islamshahr: Yek Majmou'e-ye Zisti-ye Kamel va ya Yek Majmou'e-ye Zisti-ye Tarkibi?" (Islamshahr: A complete community or a composite one?). *Goft-o-gou* 1 (Tir 1372/1973).

Hammond, John. *Building Popular Power: Workers' and Neighborhood Movements in the Portuguese Revolution.* New York: Monthly Review Press, 1988.

Hamshahri. "Bazaar-i Sayyed Ismail" (The Sayyed Ismail market). (Dey 1371/1992): 5.

Hamsou (Engineering Consultants). *Tarh-i Tawse'eh va Umran, va Hawze-ye Nufuz-i Islamshahr* (Islamshahr, a development plan). Tehran: Ministry of Housing and Urbanization, 1987, vol. 6.

Hinton, James. "Militant Housewives: The British Housewives'

League (BHL) and the Attlee Government." *History Workshop Journal* 38 (Fall 1994).

Hobsbawm, Eric. *Primitive Rebels: Studies in Archaic Forms of Social Movements in the Nineteenth and Twentieth Centuries.* New York/London: Norton, 1959.

———. "Cities and Insurrections." In E. Hobsbawm, *Revolutionaries.* London: Quartet, 1982.

Hoodfar, Homa. "Devices and Desires: Population Policy and Gender Roles in the Islamic Republic." *Middle East Report* 24, no. 190 (1994).

Hooglund, Eric. *Land and Revolution in Iran.* Austin: Texas University Press, 1982.

Hopkins, Nicholas, ed. *Informal Sector in Egypt. Cairo Papers in Social Science* 14, no. 4 (1992).

Hourcade, Bernard. "Conseillisme, classes sociales et espace urbain: Les squatters du sud de Teheran, 1978–1981." In K. Brown et al., eds., *Urban Crises and Social Movements in the Middle East.* Paris: Editions L' Harmattan, 1989.

Hourcade, Bernard and Farhad Khosrowkhavar. "L'Habitat révolutionaire: Teheran, 1977–81." *herodote* 31 (October/December 1993): 62–83.

Huntington, Samuel. *Political Order in Changing Society.* Ithaca: Yale University Press, 1968.

Huntington, Samuel and Joan Nelson. *No Easy Choice: Political Participation in Developing Countries.* Cambridge: Harvard University Press, 1976.

Husseinzadeh Dalir, Karim. *Tarh-i Tahqiqi-ye Hashiyenishinan-i Tabriz* (A Research plan of Tabriz squatters). Tabriz: Tabriz University, Institute of Urban Studies, 1361/1982.

Inqilab-i Islami. "Gozareshi Tahqigi Darbare-ye Dast-foroushan-i Tehran" (An investigative report on Tehran street vendors) (Khordad 14, 1359/1980).

———. "Bilan-i Kar-i Bonyad-i Maskan" (A balance sheet of the Housing Foundation) (Ordibehesht 7, 1359/1980).

Institute of Social Studies and Research. *Mutale'e-yi Muqaddamati Darbare-ye Zoorabad (Islamabad) Karadj: Mowredi az Hashiyenishini* (An introductory investigation about Zoorabad (Islamabad) Karadj: A case of squatter settlement). Tehran: Tehran University, 1360/1981.

Iranian Center for Urban and Architectural Studies. *Hashiyenishini: Aasar va Payamadha-ye Aan bar Shahrha* (Squatter settlement: Its effect and implications on the cities). Report on phase 2. Tehran: Ministry of Housing and Urbanization, , 1373/1994.

──────. *Hashiyenishini dar Iran: Elal va Rah-i Halha* (Squatter Settlement in Iran: The causes and solutions). Report on phase 3: "The dynamics of life in informal settlements." Tehran: Ministry of Housing and Urbanization, 1374/1995.

──────. *Hashiyenishini dar Iran: Elal va Rah-i Halha*. Report on phase 4: "Housing, informal settlements, and spatial development planning," 2 vols. Tehran: Ministry of Housing and Urbanization, 1374/1995.

──────. *Hashiyenishini Dar Iran: Elal va Rah-i Halha*. Report on phase 5; "Recognizing the low-income as citizens." Tehran: Ministry of Housing and Urbanization, 1374/1995.

Jihad. "Musahebeh ba Shahrdar. (An interview with the mayor of Tehran) 4, no. 62 (Esfand 1362): 16.

El-Kadi, Galilah. "Le Caire: La ville spontanée sous controle." *Monde Arabe* 1, special issue (1994).

Karpat, Kemal. *The Gecekondu: Rural Migration and Urbanization.* Cambridge: Cambridge University Press, 1976.

Katouzian, Homa. *The Political Economy of Modern Iran, 1926–1979.* London: Macmillan, 1981.

Kazemi, Farhad. *Poverty and Revolution in Iran.* New York: New York University Press, 1980.

──────. "Urban Migrants and the Revolution." *Iranian Studies* 13, nos. 1–4 (1980).

──────. and Wolf, R. "Urbanization, Migration, and Politics of Protest in Iran." In M. Bonine ed., *Middle East Cities in Crisis.* Miami: University Press of Florida, forthcoming.

Kazerouni, M. R. and Qal'egolabi, H. "Tasvir-i Aamari-ye Hashiyenishinan" (A statistical exposition of the squatters, Iran). *Kitab-i Jum'eh* 12 (1979).

Khalesi, Abbas. *Tarikhche-ye Bast va Bastnishini* (A short history of Bastnishini). Tehran: publisher unknown, 1987.

Khomeini, Ruhollah. *Sahife-ye Nour* (Collected works of Ayatollah Khomeini). 19 vols. Tehran: Ministry of National Guidance, 1982.

Khosrowkhavar, Farhad. "Nouvelle banlieue et marginalité: La cité Taleghani à Khak-e Sefid." In C. Adle and B. Hourcade, eds., *Teheran:*

Capitale bicentenaire. Tehran: Institut Français de Recherche en Iran, 1992.

————. *L'Utopie Sacrifiêe*, Paris: Press FNSP, 1993.

Kiafar, Ali. "Urban Land Policies in Postrevolutionary Iran." In C. Bina and H. Zangeneh, eds., *Modern Capitalism and Islamic Ideology in Iran*. New York: St. Martin's, 1992.

Lajevardi, Habib. *Labor Unions and Autocracy in Iran*. Syracuse: Syracuse University Press, 1985.

Lapidus, Ira. *Muslim Cities in the Later Middle Ages*. Cambridge: Cambridge University Press, 1984.

Leacock, E. ed. *The Culture of Poverty: A Critique*. New York: Simon and Schuster, 1971.

Leeds, A. and E. Leeds. "Accounting for Behavioral Differences: Three Political Systems and the Responses of Squatters in Brazil, Peru, and Chile." In J. Walton and L. Magotti, eds., *The City in Comparative Perspective*. London/New York: John Willey, 1976.

Leiva, F. I. and James Petras. "Chile: New Urban Movements and Transition to Democracy." *Monthly Review* (July/August 1987).

Lessinger, Johanna. "Nobody Here to Yell at Me: Political Activism Among Petty Retail Traders in an Indian City." In S. Peattaer, ed., *Markets and Marketing: Monograph in Economic Anthropology* 4 (Boston, 1985).

Lewis, Oscar. *Children of Sanchez*. London: Penguin, 1961.

————. "The Culture of Poverty." In O. Lewis, *Anthropological Esssays*. New York: Random House, 1970.

Majalle-ye Me'mari va Shahrsazi. "Editorial." no. 8 (1369/1990).

————. "A Seminar on Cities and People: Interview with two Participants." No. 21 (Khordad 1371): 49–50.

Lis, Catharina and H. Soly. "Neighborhood Social Change in West European Cities: Sixteenth to Nineteenth Centuries." *International Review of Social History* 38, no. 1 (April 1993).

Marcus, Abraham. *The Middle East on the Eve of Modernity: Aleppo in the Eighteenth Century*. New York: Columbia University Press, 1989.

Mashadizadeh, Naser. *Tahlili az Vizheguiha-ye Barnamehrizi-ye Shahri dar Iran* (An analysis of the specificities of urban planning in Iran). Tehran: University of Ilm va San'at, 1373/1995.

McGee, T. G. "The Poverty Syndrome: Making Out in the Southeast Asian City." In R. Bromley and C. Gerry, eds., *Casual Work and Poverty in Third World Cities.* Chichester, U.K./New York: Wiley, 1979.

Melucci, Alberto. "The New Social Movements: A Theoretical Approach." *Social Science Information* 19, no. 2 (1980): 199–226.

Milani, Mohsen. *The Making of the Islamic Revolution in Iran.* Boulder: Westview, 1988.

Ministry of Planning and Budget. *Census of Households and Housing, 1365 (Ostan-i Tehran).* Tehran: Statistical Center, 1986.

———. *Census of Households and Housing, 1365 (Nationwide).* Tehran: Statistical Center, 1986.

Mirsepassi-Ashtiani, Ali. "The Crisis of Secularism and Political Islam in Iran." *Social Text* 12, no. 3 (Spring 1994), pp 51–84.

Mitchell, Timothy. *Colonizing Egypt.* Cambridge: Cambridge University Press, 1988.

———. "Everyday Metaphors of Power." *Theory and Society* 19 (1990): 545–577.

Moaddel, Mansoor. *Class, State, and Ideology in the Iranian Revolution.* New York: Columbia University Press, 1993.

Moore, Barrington. *Injustice: The Social Bases of Obedience and Revolt.* White Plains, N.Y.: Sharpe, 1978.

Moorhouse, Bert, M. Wilson, and C. Chamberlain. "Rent Strikes: Direct Action and the Working Class." *Socialist Register, 1972* (1972).

Morrison, M. and P. Gutkind, eds., *Housing Urban Poor in Africa.* Syracuse: Maxwell School of Citizenship and Public Affairs, 1982.

Mottahedeh, Roy. *The Mantle of the Prophet: Religion and Politics in Iran.* New York: Pantheon, 1985.

Nelson, Joan. *Access to Power: Politics and the Urban Poor in Developing Nations.* Princeton: Princeton University Press, 1979.

———. "The Urban Poor: Disruption or Political Integration in Third World Cities." *World Politics* 22 (April 1970): 393–414.

Oldham, Linda, Haguer El Hadidi, and Hussein Tamaa. *Informal Communities in Cairo: The Basis of a Typology. Cairo Papers in Social Science* 10, no. 4 (Winter 1987).

Oncu, Ayse. "Street Poltics." In A. Oncu, C. Keyder, and S. Ibrahim, eds., *Developmentalism and Beyond: Society and Politics in Egypt and Turkey.* Cairo: The American University in Cairo Press, 1994.

Organization of the Peoples Fedaii Guerrillas of Iran (OPFGI). *Mubarizat-i Dalirane-ye Mardum-i Kharej az Mahdudeh* (Courageous struggles of the people of the squatter settlements). Tehran: OPFGI, 1357/1978.

————. *Gozareshi az Mubarizat-i Kargaran-i Bikaar-shudeh (Rah va Sakhtiman, Ta'sissat, va Karkhanijat* (A report about the struggles of the laid-off workers (in construction, power, and factories)). Tehran: OPFGI, 1358/1979.

————. *Gozareshi az Tashkil-i Sandika-ye Kargaran-i Prozhe'ii (Fasli) Abadan* (A report about the formation of seasonal workers' union in Abadan). Tehran: OPFGI, 1358/1979.

Palma, Diego. "Comments on John Friedmann's 'The Dialectic of Reason.' " *International Journal of Urban and Regional Research* 13, no. 3 (1989).

Park, Robert. "Human Migration and the Marginal Man." *American Journal of Sociology* 33, no. 6 (1928): 881–893.

Parsa, Misagh. *The Social Origins of the Iranian Revolution.* New Brunswick, N.J.: Rutgers University Press, 1989.

Perlman, Janice. "Rio's Favelas and the Myth of Marginality." *Politics and Society* 5 (1975): 131–160.

————. *The Myth of Marginality.* Berkeley: University of California Press, 1976.

Piran, Parviz. "Zaghehnishini dar Tehran" (Shanty-dwelling in Tehran). *Ettilaat-i Syassi-Iqtisadi* 17–22 (1366/1987).

Pirouzi. "Jang, Kar, Bikaari" (The war, work, and unemployment), no. 3 (Azar 1359/1980): 30–35.

Piven, Frances and Cloward, Richard. *Poor Peoples' Movements: Why They Succeed, How They Fail.* New York: Vintage, 1979.

Plan and Budget Organization. *Barrasi-ye Bikaari dar Tehran: Tabistan 1358* (An overview of unemployment in Tehran: Summer 1979). Tehran: Statistical Center, 1358/1979.

————. *Tehran 59: Aamarguiri-ye Tehran, 1359* (The Tehran of 1980: A Statistical profile). Tehran: Statistical Center, 1360/1981.

————. *Barrsi-ye Ijmali-ye Dakkeh-daari dar Irtibat ba Ishtighal va Bikaari* (A brief overview of street vending in the light of the unemployment problem). Tehran: Tehran Planning Organization, 1360/1981.

————. *Statistical Yearbook, 1361.* Tehran: Statistical Center, 1982.

Portes, Alejandro and Walton, John. *Urban Latin America: The Political Conditions from Above and Below.* Austin: Tezas University Press, 1976.

Portes, Alejandro, Manuel Castells, and L. Benton. eds. *The Informal Economy: Studies in Advanced and Less-Developed Countries*. Baltimore: Johns Hopkins University Press, 1989.

Power, J. *World of Hunger: A Strategy for Survival*. London: Temple South, 1976.

Rahnama, Ali and and Nomani, Farhad. *Secular Miracle: Religion, Politics and Economic Policy in Iran*. London: Zed, 1990.

Rahnema, Majid. "Power and Regenerative Processes in Microspaces." *International Social Science Journal* 117 (August 1988): 361–375.

———. "Participation." In W. Sachs, ed., *The Development Dictionary*. London: Zed, 1995.

Razzaqui, Ebrahim. *Iqtisad-i Iran* (The Iranian economy). Tehran: Nashr-i Ney, 1367/1988.

Rezaii, Behjat. "Iran: The Wash-house to All Households." *Spare Rib* 115 (February 1982): 23.

Roberts, Bryan. "Comments on John Friedmann's 'The Dialectic of Reason.'" *International Journal of Urban and Regional Research* 13, no. 3 (1989).

Sa'edi, Gholam Hussein. *Dandil: Stories from Iranian Life*. New York: Random House, 1981.

Saidnia, Ahmad. "Sakhtar-i Tehran" (The structure of Tehran). In Y. Kiani, ed., *Shahrya-ye Iran* (The Iranian cities). Tehran: Chapkhane-ye Sahab, 1370/1991.

Al-Sayyad, N. "Informal Housing in a Comparative Perspective: On Squatting, Culture, and Development in a Latin American and Middle Eastern Culture." *Review of Urban and Regional Development Studies* 5, no. 1 (1993): 3–18.

Schuurman, Frans and van Naerssen, Ton. *Urban Social Movements in the Third World*. London: Croom Helm, 1989.

Schirazi, Asgar. *The Problem of Land Reform in the Islamic Republic of Iran*. Berlin: Free University of Berlin, 1987.

Schwedler, Jillian. "Civil Society and the Study of Middle East Politics." In J. Schwedler, ed., *Toward Civil Society in the Middle East? A Primer*. Boulder, Colo./London: Lynne Rienner, 1995.

Scott, James. "Everyday Forms of Resistance." *Journal of Peasant Studies* 13, no. 2 (1986).

———. *Weapons of the Weak: Everday Forms of Peasant Resistance*. New Haven/London: Yale University Press, 1985.

————. *Domination and the Arts of Resistance: Hidden Transcripts*. New Haven/London: Yale University Press, 1990.

Sethuraman, S. V., ed. *The Urban Informal Sector in Developing Countries*. Geneva: ILO, 1981.

Shahri, Ja'far. *Tehran-i Qadim* (The old Tehran). 5 vols. Tehran: Amir Kabir, 1368/1989.

Shariati, Ali. *Jahatguri-ye Tabaqati-ye Islam*. Tehran: Dafter-i Tadvin va Tanzim-i Asar-i Ali Shariati, 1359/1980.

Sheikhi, Muhammad. "Elal va Payamadha-ye Dast-foroushi (Tehran)" (The causes and implications of street vending, Tehran). *Ettilaat-i Syassi-Iqtisadi* 35 (Farvardin-Ordibehesht 1369/1990).

————. *Elal va Avamel-i Dast-foroushi dar Shiraz)* (Factors behind the street vending in Shiraz). Shiraz: Shiraz University, 1364/1985.

Shorter, Frederic. *Cairo's Leap Forward: People, Households, and Dwelling Space*. Cairo Papers in Social Science 12, no. 1 (Spring 1989).

Simmel, Georg. "The Stranger." In Kurt Wolff, ed., *The Sociology of George Simmel*. New York: Free Press, 1950.

Singerman, Diane. *Avenue of Participation: Family, Politics, and Networks in Urban Quarters of Cairo*. Princeton: Princeton University Press, 1995.

Smelser, Neil. *Theory of Collective Behavior*. New York: Free Press, 1971.

Soliman, Ahmad. "Government and Squatters in Alexandria: Their Roles and Involvements." *Open House International* 10, no. 3 (1985): 43–49.

————. "Informal Land Aquisition and the Urban Poor in Alexandria." *Third World Planning Review* 9, no. 1 (1987): 21–39.

————. "Housing Consolidation and the Urban Poor: The Case of Hagar El Nawateyah, Alexandria." *Environment and Urbanization* 4, no. 2 (1992): 184–195.

Spodek, Howard. "The Self-Employed Women's Association (SEWA) in India: Feminist, Gandhian Power in Development." *Economic Development and Cultural Change* 43, no. 1 (October 1994).

Stiefel, M. and Wolfe, M. *A Voice for the Excluded: Popular Participation in Development, Utopia or Necessity?* London: Zed, 1994.

Stokes, S. "Politics and Latin America's Urban Poor: Reflections from a Lima Shanty Town." *Latin American Research Review* 26, no. 2 (1991).

Stonequist, Everett. "The Problem of the Marginal Man," *American Journal of Sociology* 41, no. 1 (1935): 1–12.

Tadros, Helmi, Mohamed Feteeha, and Allen Hibbard,. *Squatter Markets in Cairo. Cairo Papers in Social Science* 13, no. 1 (Spring 1990).

Taliqani, Mahmoud. *Mutali'at-i Jame'e Shinasi-ye Shahr-i Tehran* (Sociological Studies of Tehran). Vol. 3, "Housing." Tehran: Institute of Cultural Studies, 1369/1990.

Tarrow, Sidney. *Power in Movement: Social Movements, Collective Action, and Politics.* Cambridge: Cambridge University Press, 1994.

Tawfiq, Inaz. "Discourse Analysis of Informal Housing in Egypt." Graduate term paper. The American University in Cairo, Department of Sociology, 1995.

Tehran Musavvar. "Gozareshi az Khane-ye Kargar va Sokhanan-i Kargaran-i Bikaar" (A report from the House of Labor and what the unemployed workers said) 37, no. 2 (Khordad 18, 1358/1979): 24–25.

———. "Bar Bikaaran-i Mutahassen dar Nowrooz Che Gozasht?" (What went on to the unemployed during the sit-in on the new year's day?) 10 (Farvardin 10, 1358/1979).

Thompson, Edward. "The Moral Economy of the English Crowd in the Eighteenth Century." *Past and Present* 50 (February 1971).

———. *Customs in Common.* London: Merlin, 1991.

Thompson, Tom. "Petty Traders in Iran." In M. Bonine and N. Keddie, eds., *Modern Iran: The Dialectics of Continuity and Change.* Albany: State University of New York Press, 1981.

Tilly, Charles. *From Mobilization to Revolution.* Reading, Mass.: Addison-Wesley, 1978.

Touraine, Alain. *The Voice and the Eye: An Analysis of Social Movements.* Cambridge: Cambridge University Press, 1977.

———. "Comments on John Friedmann's 'Dialectic of Reason.' " *International Journal of Urban and Regional Research* 13, no. 3 (1989).

Vandemoortele, Jan. "The African Employment Crisis of the 1980s." in C. Grey-Johnson, ed., *The Employment Crisis in Africa: Issues in Human Resources Development Policy.* Harare: African Association for Public Administration and Management, 1990.

Velez-Ibanez, Carlos. *Rituals of Marginality: Politics, Process, and*

Culture Change in Urban Central Mexico, 1969–1974. Berkeley: University of California Press, 1983.

Vielle, Paul. *Jaygah-i Kargaran-i Tehran* (The status of workers in Tehran). Tehran: University of Tehran, 1359/1980.

Wignaraja, Ponna. ed. *New Social Movements in the South: Empowering the People.* London: Zed, 1993.

Wirth, Lewis. "Urbanism as a Way of Life." *American Journal of Sociology* 44 (1938): 1–24.

World Bank. *World Development Report, 1995.* Oxford: Oxford University Press, 1995.

Worsley, Peter. *The Three Worlds.* London: Weidenfeld and Nicholson, 1984.

Zahidani, Said. *Hashiyenishini* (Squatter settlement). Shiraz: Shiraz University, 1369/1990.

Glossary

aab-anbaar.	Underground water reservoir.
'ard.	Honor (Arabic).
OPFG.	Organization of People Fedaii Guerrillas.
abirourizi.	Scandal, disgrace.
abirou.	Honor.
akhund.	Low-ranking clergyman.
alounaknishinan.	Hut settlers.
amaleh.	Construction worker.
anjuman.	Association.
avaam-zadegui.	Populism, following ordinary people.
awqaf.	Endowments.
badbakhtha.	Destitute.
basaati.	Stall-holding.
basij.	Mobilization, refers to voluntary militia.
bazresan.	Observers.
bast-nishini.	Sit-in.
ba-taqwa.	Pious.
bikaar-shudeh.	Laid off.
bimari-ye ijtimaii.	Social disease.
bimari-ye mosre'.	Afflicting disease.
bisaz-o-befroush.	Land developer.
Bonyad-i Mustaz'afin.	The Foundation of the Oppressed.

chare-ii neest.	"There is no other way out".
charkh-daari.	Push-cart vending.
dadgah-i zedd-i munkarat.	Anti-vice court.
dakkeh-daari.	Kiosk-holding.
darugheh.	Traditional nineteenth-century market police.
dast-foroushi.	Street vending.
dihaati.	Of rural origin.
diplomeh.	High school graduate.
doost va doshman.	Friends and foes.
fadiha.	Scandal (Arabic).
fahshaa.	Prostitution.
faludeh.	A kind of desert.
faqir.	Poor.
faqir va bichareha.	Poor and wretched.
farrash.	One who spreads the carpets or cushions; janitor.
fisaad.	Corruption.
fishaari.	Street fountain.
fitwa.	Religious verdict.
gowd.	A south Tehran squatter district.
gowdnishin.	Settler of the gowd.
hammali.	Portering, being a porter.
haqq-i bikaari.	Unemployment benefit.
haram.	Religiously proscribed.
harim.	Sacred.
hashiyeh.	Margin.
hashiyenishini.	Literally, living on the margin; squatter settlement.
huwzeh.	Islamic seminary.
hey'at.	Occasional religious sermons, often ethnically based.
hikayat.	Tales.
hizbullahi.	Member of progovernment informal groups set up after the revolution in Iran.
imamzadeh.	Saint.
inqilab.	Revolution.
Inqilab-i Islami.	Islamic Revolution.
insan-i hashiye-ii.	Marginal man.
ishghal.	Occupation.
istiz'af.	Being oppressed.
Jihad-i Sanzandegui.	Construction Crusade.
jonoubi.	Southerner.
jouy.	Creek; refers to street ditch.

kaanun.	Center.
Khane-ye Kargar.	House of Labor.
kharej-i mahdudeh.	Outside municipal boundaries.
Khatt-i Sevvum.	The Third Line (referring to Maoist groups).
khushnishin.	Nonagricultural rural settler.
komiteh.	Committee (refers to postrevolutionary urban security force).
koucheh.	Alleyway.
koukhnishinan.	Poor urban shantytown dwellers.
laat.	Street bully.
mahallat.	Neighborhoods.
mahalle.	Neighborhood.
maidan.	A square.
manatiq al-ashwa'yya.	Informal settlements (in Egypt).
mardum-i dar sahneh.	Literally, people on the stage; refers to the street mobilization of the people loyal to the Islamic government.
mashaghel-i kazib.	Fake occupations.
mashaghel-i angali.	Parasitic occupations.
Muharram.	Arabic month, during which Imam Hussein, grandson of the Prophet, was killed.
mujahed.	Warrior; here refers to members of the Mujahedin-i Khalq organization.
Mujahedin-i Khalq.	An oppositional radical Islamic organization in Iran.
munafiq.	Literally "hypocrite"; used by the Islamic government in Iran to refer to the Mujahedin-i Khalq.
munkarat.	Evil doings.
mustaz'afin.	Downtrodden.
na'mal eih?.	"What should we do?" (Egyptian).
nahadha-ye inqilabi.	Revolutionary institutions.
pasban.	Low-ranked policeman.
Pasdaran.	Revolutionary guards.
pedar-i taajdaar.	The crowned father (referring to the Shah).
qachaqui.	Underground, illegal.
rowze-khani.	Islamic preaching.
sadd-i ma'bar.	Obstruction.
sandika.	Syndicate.
sar-i koucheh.	Intersection of alleyway and street.
sar-qufli.	Key money.
sepahi-ye danesh.	Literacy corps.
shahrdari.	Municipality.

sharbat.	Sweet drinks.
shura.	Council.
shura-ye muassess.	Steering committee.
Shuraha-ye Mahallat.	Neighborhood Councils.
ta'ziyeh.	Passion play.
tabaqeh-ye seiiha.	Third-class people (referring to the poor).
tahassun.	Sit-in, seeking sanctuary.
tasbih.	Prayer beads.
tawghouti.	Refers to the culture and people associated with the Shah's regime.
tuman.	Iranian money, equivalent to Rls 10.
ulama.	Learned men; scholar-theologian.
umma.	Masses (Arabic).
uzgal.	Tacky, shoddy, squalid, sleazy.
vaam-i bikaari.	Unemployment loan.
wahdat-i kalameh.	Unity, unity of purpose.
zagheh.	Hut.
zaghehnishini.	Hut dwelling.

Index

Page numbers in *italics* indicate illustrations.

CPSIA information can be obtained
at www.ICGtesting.com
Printed in the USA
LVOW10s1934190118
563177LV00009B/56/P

9 780231 108591